Real-Resumes for Construction Jobs...
including real resumes used to change careers
and transfer skills to other industries

Anne McKinney, Editor

PREP PUBLISHING

FAYETTEVILLE, NC

PREP Publishing
1110½ Hay Street
Fayetteville, NC 28305
(910) 483-6611

Copyright © 2002 by Anne McKinney

Library of Congress Cataloging-in-Publication Data

Real-resumes for construction jobs : including real resumes used to change careers and transfer skills to other industries / Anne McKinney, editor.
      p. cm. -- (Real-resumes series)
   ISBN 1-885288-27-1 (trade pbk.)
   1. Résumés (Employment) 2. Construction workers. I. McKinney, Anne, 1948-
II. Series.

   HF5383 .R39583 2002
   650.14'2--dc21
                                                      2002020598
                                                            CIP

Printed in the United States of America

By PREP Publishing

Business and Career Series:

RESUMES AND COVER LETTERS THAT HAVE WORKED

RESUMES AND COVER LETTERS THAT HAVE WORKED FOR MILITARY PROFESSIONALS

GOVERNMENT JOB APPLICATIONS AND FEDERAL RESUMES

COVER LETTERS THAT BLOW DOORS OPEN

LETTERS FOR SPECIAL SITUATIONS

RESUMES AND COVER LETTERS FOR MANAGERS

REAL-RESUMES FOR COMPUTER JOBS

REAL-RESUMES FOR MEDICAL JOBS

REAL-RESUMES FOR FINANCIAL JOBS

REAL-RESUMES FOR TEACHERS

REAL-RESUMES FOR STUDENTS

REAL-RESUMES FOR CAREER CHANGERS

REAL-RESUMES FOR SALES

REAL ESSAYS FOR COLLEGE & GRADUATE SCHOOL

REAL-RESUMES FOR AVIATION & TRAVEL JOBS

REAL-RESUMES FOR POLICE, LAW ENFORCEMENT & SECURITY JOBS

REAL-RESUMES FOR SOCIAL WORK & COUNSELING JOBS

REAL-RESUMES FOR CONSTRUCTION JOBS

REAL-RESUMES FOR MANUFACTURING JOBS

Judeo-Christian Ethics Series:

SECOND TIME AROUND

BACK IN TIME

WHAT THE BIBLE SAYS ABOUT...Words that can lead to success and happiness

A GENTLE BREEZE FROM GOSSAMER WINGS

BIBLE STORIES FROM THE OLD TESTAMENT

Fiction:

KIJABE...An African Historical Saga

Table of Contents

A WORD FROM THE EDITOR:
ABOUT THE REAL-RESUMES SERIES

Welcome to the Real-Resumes Series. The Real-Resumes Series is a series of books which have been developed based on the experiences of real job hunters and which target specialized fields or types of resumes. As the editor of the series, I have carefully selected resumes and cover letters (with names and other key data disguised, of course) which have been used successfully in real job hunts. That's what we mean by "Real-Resumes." What you see in this book are *real* resumes and cover letters which helped real people get ahead in their careers.

The Real-Resumes Series is based on the work of the country's oldest resume-preparation company known as PREP Resumes. If you would like a free information packet describing the company's resume preparation services, call 910-483-6611 or write to PREP at 1110½ Hay Street, Fayetteville, NC 28305. If you have a job hunting experience you would like to share with our staff at the Real-Resumes Series, please contact us at preppub@aol.com or visit our website at http://www.prep-pub.com.

The resumes and cover letters in this book are designed to be of most value to people already in a job hunt or contemplating a career change. If we could give you one word of advice about your career, here's what we would say: Manage your career and don't stumble from job to job in an incoherent pattern. Try to find work that interests you, and then identify prosperous industries which need work performed of the type you want to do. Learn early in your working life that a great resume and cover letter can blow doors open for you and help you maximize your salary.

This book is dedicated to those seeking jobs in the construction field. We hope the superior samples will help you manage your current job campaign and your career so that you will find work aligned to your career interests.

Real-Resumes for Construction Jobs...
including real resumes used to change careers
and transfer skills to other industries

Anne McKinney, Editor

As the editor of this book, I would like to give you some tips on how to make the best use of the information you will find here. Because you are considering a career change, you already understand the concept of managing your career for maximum enjoyment and self-fulfillment. The purpose of this book is to provide expert tools and advice so that you *can* manage your career. Inside these pages you will find resumes and cover letters that will help you find not just a job but the type of work you want to do.

**Introduction:
The Art of
Changing
Jobs...
and Finding
New Careers**

Overview of the Book

Every resume and cover letter in this book actually worked. And most of the resumes and cover letters have common features: most are one-page, most are in the chronological format, and most resumes are accompanied by a companion cover letter. In this section you will find helpful advice about job hunting. Step One begins with a discussion of why employers prefer the one-page, chronological resume. In Step Two you are introduced to the direct approach and to the proper format for a cover letter. In Step Three you learn the 14 main reasons why job hunters are not offered the jobs they want, and you learn the six key areas employers focus on when they interview you. Step Four gives nuts-and-bolts advice on how to handle the interview, send a follow-up letter after an interview, and negotiate your salary.

The cover letter plays such a critical role in a career change. You will learn from the experts how to format your cover letters and you will see suggested language to use in particular career-change situations. It has been said that "A picture is worth a thousand words" and, for that reason, you will see numerous examples of effective cover letters used by real individuals to change fields, functions, and industries.

The most important part of the book is the Real-Resumes section. Some of the individuals whose resumes and cover letters you see spent a lengthy career in an industry they loved. Then there are resumes and cover letters of people who wanted a change but who probably wanted to remain in their industry. Many of you will be especially interested by the resumes and cover letters of individuals who knew they definitely wanted a career change but had no idea what they wanted to do next. Other resumes and cover letters show individuals who knew they wanted to change fields and had a pretty good idea of what they wanted to do next.

Whatever your field, and whatever your circumstances, you'll find resumes and cover letters that will "show you the ropes" in terms of successfully changing jobs and switching careers.

Before you proceed further, think about why you picked up this book.
* Are you dissatisfied with the type of work you are now doing?
* Would you like to change careers, change companies, or change industries?
* Are you satisfied with your industry but not with your niche or function within it?
* Do you want to transfer your skills to a new product or service?
* Even if you have excelled in your field, have you "had enough"? Would you like the stimulation of a new challenge?
* Are you aware of the importance of a great cover letter but unsure of how to write one?
* Are you preparing to launch a second career after retirement?
* Have you been downsized, or do you anticipate becoming a victim of downsizing?
* Do you need expert advice on how to plan and implement a job campaign that will open the maximum number of doors?
* Do you want to make sure you handle an interview to your maximum advantage?

- Would you like to master the techniques of negotiating salary and benefits?
- Do you want to learn the secrets and shortcuts of professional resume writers?

Using the Direct Approach

As you consider the possibility of a job hunt or career change, you need to be aware that most people end up having at least three distinctly different careers in their working lifetimes, and often those careers are different from each other. Yet people usually stumble through each job campaign, unsure of what they should be doing. Whether you find yourself voluntarily or unexpectedly in a job hunt, the direct approach is the job hunting strategy most likely to yield a full-time permanent job. The direct approach is an active, take-the-initiative style of job hunting in which you choose your next employer rather than relying on responding to ads, using employment agencies, or depending on other methods of finding jobs. You will learn how to use the direct approach in this book, and you will see that an effective cover letter is a critical ingredient in using the direct approach.

The "direct approach" is the style of job hunting most likely to yield the maximum number of job interviews.

Lack of Industry Experience Not a Major Barrier to Entering New Field

"Lack of experience" is often the last reason people are not offered jobs, according to the companies who do the hiring. If you are changing careers, you will be glad to learn that experienced professionals often are selling "potential" rather than experience in a job hunt. Companies look for personal qualities that they know tend to be present in their most effective professionals, such as communication skills, initiative, persistence, organizational and time management skills, and creativity. Frequently companies are trying to discover "personality type," "talent," "ability," "aptitude," and "potential" rather than seeking actual hands-on experience, so your resume should be designed to aggressively present your accomplishments. Attitude, enthusiasm, personality, and a track record of achievements in any type of work are the primary "indicators of success" which employers are seeking, and you will see numerous examples in this book of resumes written in an all-purpose fashion so that the professional can approach various industries and companies.

Using references in a skillful fashion in your job hunt will inspire confidence in prospective employers and help you "close the sale" after interviews.

The Art of Using References in a Job Hunt

You probably already know that you need to provide references during a job hunt, but you may not be sure of how and when to use references for maximum advantage. You can use references very creatively during a job hunt to call attention to your strengths and make yourself "stand out." Your references will rarely get you a job, no matter how impressive the names, but the way you use references can boost the employer's confidence in you and lead to a job offer in the least time.

You should ask from three to five people, including people who have supervised you, if you can use them as a reference during your job hunt. You may not be able to ask your current boss since your job hunt is probably confidential.

A common question in resume preparation is: "Do I need to put my references on my resume?" No, you don't. Even if you create a references page at the same time you prepare your resume, you don't need to mail, e-mail, or fax your references page with the resume and cover letter. Usually the potential employer is not interested in references until he meets you, so the earliest you need to have references ready is at the first interview. Obviously there are exceptions to this standard rule of thumb; sometimes an ad will ask you to send references with your first response. Wait until the employer requests references before providing them.

An excellent attention-getting technique is to take to the first interview not just a page of references (giving names, addresses, and telephone numbers) but an actual letter of reference written by someone who knows you well and who preferably has supervised or employed you. A professional way to close the first interview is to thank the interviewer, shake his or her hand, and then say you'd like to give him or her a copy of a letter of reference from a previous employer. Hopefully you already made a good impression during the interview, but you'll "close the sale" in a dynamic fashion if you leave a letter praising you and your accomplishments. For that reason, it's a good idea to ask supervisors during your final weeks in a job if they will provide you with a written letter of recommendation which you can use in future job hunts. Most employers will oblige, and you will have a letter that has a useful "shelf life" of many years. Such a letter often gives the prospective employer enough confidence in his opinion of you that he may forego checking out other references and decide to offer you the job on the spot or in the next few days.

With regard to references, it's best to provide the names and addresses of people who have supervised you or observed you in a work situation.

Whom should you ask to serve as references? References should be people who have known or supervised you in a professional, academic, or work situation. References with big titles, like school superintendent or congressman, are fine, but remind busy people when you get to the interview stage that they may be contacted soon. Make sure the busy official recognizes your name and has instant positive recall of you! If you're asked to provide references on a formal company application, you can simply transcribe names from your references list. In summary, follow this rule in using references: If you've got them, flaunt them! If you've obtained well-written letters of reference, make sure you find a polite way to push those references under the nose of the interviewer so he or she can hear someone other than you describing your strengths. Your references probably won't ever get you a job, but glowing letters of reference can give you credibility and visibility that can make you stand out among candidates with similar credentials and potential!

The approach taken by this book is to (1) help you master the proven best techniques of conducting a job hunt and (2) show you how to stand out in a job hunt through your resume, cover letter, interviewing skills, as well as the way in which you present your references and follow up on interviews. Now, the best way to "get in the mood" for writing your own resume and cover letter is to select samples from the Table of Contents that interest you and then read them. A great resume is a "photograph," usually on one page, of an individual. If you wish to seek professional advice in preparing your resume, you may contact one of the professional writers at Professional Resume & Employment Publishing (PREP) for a brief free consultation by calling 1-910-483-6611.

Part One: Some Advice About Your Job Hunt

What if you don't know what you want to do?

Your job hunt will be more comfortable if you can figure out what type of work you want to do. But you are not alone if you have no idea what you want to do next! You may have knowledge and skills in certain areas but want to get into another type of work. What *The Wall Street Journal* has discovered in its research on careers is that most of us end up having at least three distinctly different careers in our working lives; it seems that, even if we really like a particular kind of activity, twenty years of doing it is enough for most of us and we want to move on to something else!

Figure out what interests you and you will hold the key to a successful job hunt and working career. (And be prepared for your interests to change over time!)

That's why we strongly believe that you need to spend some time figuring out *what interests you* rather than taking an inventory of the skills you have. You may have skills that you simply don't want to use, but if you can build your career on the things that interest you, you will be more likely to be happy and satisfied in your job. Realize, too, that interests can change over time; the activities that interest you now may not be the ones that interested you years ago. For example, some professionals may decide that they've had enough of retail sales and want a job selling another product or service, even though they have earned a reputation for being an excellent retail manager. We strongly believe that interests rather than skills should be the determining factor in deciding what types of jobs you want to apply for and what directions you explore in your job hunt. Obviously one cannot be a lawyer without a law degree or a secretary without secretarial skills; but a professional can embark on a next career as a financial consultant, property manager, plant manager, production supervisor, retail manager, or other occupation if he/she has a strong interest in that type of work and can provide a resume that clearly demonstrates past excellent performance in *any* field and *potential* to excel in another field. As you will see later in this book, "lack of exact experience" is the last reason why people are turned down for the jobs they apply for.

How can you have a resume prepared if you don't know what you want to do?

You may be wondering how you can have a resume prepared if you don't know what you want to do next. The approach to resume writing which PREP, the country's oldest resume-preparation company, has used successfully for many years is to develop an "all-purpose" resume that translates your skills, experience, and accomplishments into language employers can understand. What most people need in a job hunt is a versatile resume that will allow them to apply for numerous types of jobs. For example, you may want to apply for a job in pharmaceutical sales but you may also want to have a resume that will be versatile enough for you to apply for jobs in the construction, financial services, or automotive industries.

"Lack of exact experience" is the last reason people are turned down for the jobs for which they apply.

Based on more than 20 years of serving job hunters, we at PREP have found that your best approach to job hunting is **an all-purpose resume** and **specific cover letters tailored to specific fields** rather than using the approach of trying to create different resumes for every job. If you are remaining in your field, you may not even need more than one "all-purpose" cover letter, although the cover letter rather than the resume is the place to communicate your interest in a narrow or specific field. An all-purpose resume and cover letter that translate your experience and accomplishments into plain English are the tools that will maximize the number of doors which open for you while permitting you to "fish" in the widest range of job areas.

Your resume will provide the script for your job interview.
When you get down to it, your resume has a simple job to do: Its purpose is to blow as many doors open as possible and to make as many people as possible want to meet you. So a well-written resume that really "sells" you is a key that will create opportunities for you in a job hunt.

This statistic explains why: The typical newspaper advertisement for a job opening receives more than 245 replies. And normally only 10 or 12 will be invited to an interview.

But here's another purpose of the resume: it provides the "script" the employer uses when he interviews you. If your resume has been written in such a way that your strengths and achievements are revealed, that's what you'll end up talking about at the job interview. Since the resume will govern what you get asked about at your interviews, you can't overestimate the importance of making sure your resume makes you look and sound as good as you are.

So what is a "good" resume?
Very literally, your resume should motivate the person reading it to dial the phone number or e-mail the screen name you have put on the resume. When you are relocating, you should put a local phone number on your resume if your physical address is several states away; employers are more likely to dial a local telephone number than a long-distance number when they're looking for potential employees.

If you have a resume already, look at it objectively. Is it a limp, colorless "laundry list" of your job titles and duties? Or does it "paint a picture" of your skills, abilities, and accomplishments in a way that would make someone want to meet you? Can people understand what you're saying? If you are attempting to change fields or industries, can potential employers see that your skills and knowledge are transferable to other environments? For example, have you described accomplishments which reveal your problem-solving abilities or communication skills?

How long should your resume be?
One page, maybe two. Usually only people in the academic community have a resume (which they usually call a *curriculum vitae*) longer than one or two pages. Remember that your resume is almost always accompanied by a cover letter, and a potential employer does not want to read more than two or three pages about a total stranger in order to decide if he wants to meet that person! Besides, don't forget that the more you tell someone about yourself, the more opportunity you are providing for the employer to screen you out at the "first-cut" stage. A resume should be concise and exciting and designed to make the reader want to meet you in person!

Should resumes be functional or chronological?
Employers almost always prefer a chronological resume; in other words, an employer will find a resume easier to read if it is immediately apparent what your current or most recent job is, what you did before that, and so forth, in reverse chronological order. A resume that goes back in detail for the last ten years of employment will generally satisfy the employer's curiosity about your background. Employment more than ten years old can be shown even more briefly in an "Other Experience" section at the end of your "Experience" section. Remember that your intention is not to tell everything you've done but to "hit the high points" and especially impress the employer with what you learned, contributed, or accomplished in each job you describe.

Your resume is the "script" for your job interviews. Make sure you put on your resume what you want to talk about or be asked about at the job interview.

The one-page resume in chronological format is the format preferred by most employers.

Once you get your resume, what do you do with it?
You will be using your resume to answer ads, as a tool to use in talking with friends and relatives about your job search, and, most importantly, in using the "direct approach" described in this book.

When you mail your resume, always send a "cover letter."
A "cover letter," sometimes called a "resume letter" or "letter of interest," is a letter that accompanies and introduces your resume. Your cover letter is a way of personalizing the resume by sending it to the specific person you think you might want to work for at each company. Your cover letter should contain a few highlights from your resume— just enough to make someone want to meet you. Cover letters should always be typed or word processed on a computer—never handwritten.

Never mail or fax your resume without a cover letter.

1. Learn the art of answering ads.
There is an "art," part of which can be learned, in using your "bestselling" resume to reply to advertisements.

Sometimes an exciting job lurks behind a boring ad that someone dictated in a hurry, so reply to any ad that interests you. Don't worry that you aren't "25 years old with an MBA" like the ad asks for. Employers will always make compromises in their requirements if they think you're the "best fit" overall.

What about ads that ask for "salary requirements?"
What if the ad you're answering asks for "salary requirements?" The first rule is to avoid committing yourself in writing at that point to a specific salary. You don't want to "lock yourself in."

There are two ways to handle the ad that asks for "salary requirements."
First, you can ignore that part of the ad and accompany your resume with a cover letter that focuses on "selling" you, your abilities, and even some of your philosophy about work or your field. You may include a sentence in your cover letter like this: "I can provide excellent personal and professional references at your request, and I would be delighted to share the private details of my salary history with you in person."

What if the ad asks for your "salary requirements?"

Second, if you feel you must give some kind of number, just state a range in your cover letter that includes your medical, dental, other benefits, and expected bonuses. You might state, for example, "My current compensation, including benefits and bonuses, is in the range of $30,000-$40,000."

Analyze the ad and "tailor" yourself to it.
When you're replying to ads, a finely tailored cover letter is an important tool in getting your resume noticed and read. On the next page is a cover letter which has been "tailored to fit" a specific ad. Notice the "art" used by PREP writers of analyzing the ad's main requirements and then writing the letter so that the person's background, work habits, and interests seem "tailor-made" to the company's needs. Use this cover letter as a model when you prepare your own reply to ads.

Date

Mr. Arthur Wise
National Real Estate, Inc.
9439 Goshen Lane
Dallas, TX 22105

Dear Mr. Wise:

I would appreciate an opportunity to show you in person, soon, that I am the energetic, dynamic individual you are looking for as your Sales Manager for National Real Estate, Inc.

Here are just three reasons why I believe I am the effective young professional you seek:

- *I am a proven salesperson* with a demonstrated ability to "prospect" and produce sales. In my current job as a sales representative, I contact more than 150 business professionals per week and won my company's annual award for outstanding sales performance.

- *I enjoy traveling and am eager to assist in the growth of your business.* I am fortunate to have the natural energy, industry, and enthusiasm required to put in the long hours necessary for effective sales performance.

- *I understand the real estate business and my lifestyle is suited to the long hours and weekend work.* Single and available to meet customers at their convenience, I have completed Real Estate School in Dallas and hold a license in Texas.

I am fortunate to have the natural energy, industry, and enthusiasm required to put in the long hours necessary for effective sales performance. You will find me, I am certain, a friendly, good-natured person whom you would be proud to call part of your "team." I would enjoy the opportunity to share my proven sales techniques and extensive knowledge with other junior sales professionals in a management and development position.

I hope you will call or write me soon to suggest a convenient time when we might meet to discuss your needs further and how I might serve them.

Yours sincerely,

Your Name

Employers are trying to identify the individual who wants the job they are filling. Don't be afraid to express your enthusiasm in the cover letter!

2. Talk to friends and relatives.

Don't be shy about telling your friends and relatives the kind of job you're looking for. Looking for the job you want involves using your network of contacts, so tell people what you're looking for. They may be able to make introductions and help set up interviews.

About 25% of all interviews are set up through "who you know," so don't ignore this approach.

3. Finally, and most importantly, use the "direct approach."

The "direct approach" is a strategy in which you choose your next employer.

More than 50% of all job interviews are set up by the "direct approach." That means you actually mail, e-mail, or fax a resume and a cover letter to a company you think might be interesting to work for.

To whom do you write?

In general, you should write directly to the *exact name* of the person who would be hiring you: say, the vice-president of marketing or data processing. If you're in doubt about to whom to address the letter, address it to the president by name and he or she will make sure it gets forwarded to the right person within the company who has hiring authority in your area.

How do you find the names of potential employers?

You're not alone if you feel that the biggest problem in your job search is finding the right names at the companies you want to contact. But you can usually figure out the names of companies you want to approach by deciding first if your job hunt is primarily geography-driven or industry-driven.

In a **geography-driven job hunt,** you could select a list of, say, 50 companies you want to contact **by location** from the lists that the U.S. Chambers of Commerce publish yearly of their "major area employers." There are hundreds of local Chambers of Commerce across America, and most of them will have an 800 number which you can find through 1-800-555-1212. If you and your family think Atlanta, Dallas, Ft. Lauderdale, and Virginia Beach might be nice places to live, for example, you could contact the Chamber of Commerce in those cities and ask how you can obtain a copy of their list of major employers. Your nearest library will have the book which lists the addresses of all chambers.

In an **industry-driven job hunt,** and if you are willing to relocate, you will be identifying the companies which you find most attractive in the industry in which you want to work. When you select a list of companies to contact **by industry,** you can find the right person to write and the address of firms by industrial category in *Standard and Poor's, Moody's,* and other excellent books in public libraries. Many Web sites also provide contact information.

Many people feel it's a good investment to actually call the company to either find out or double-check the name of the person to whom they want to send a resume and cover letter. It's important to do as much as you feasibly can to assure that the letter gets to the right person in the company.

On-line research will be the best way for many people to locate organizations to which they wish to send their resume. It is outside the scope of this book to teach Internet research skills, but librarians are often useful in this area.

What's the correct way to follow up on a resume you send?

There is a polite way to be aggressively interested in a company during your job hunt. It is ideal to end the cover letter accompanying your resume by saying, "I hope you'll welcome my call next week when I try to arrange a brief meeting at your convenience to discuss your current and future needs and how I might serve them." Keep it low key, and just ask for a "brief meeting," not an interview. Employers want people who show a determined interest in working with them, so don't be shy about following up on the resume and cover letter you've mailed.

It pays to be aware of the 14 most common pitfalls for job hunters.

STEP THREE: Preparing for Interviews

But a resume and cover letter by themselves can't get you the job you want. You need to "prep" yourself before the interview. Step Three in your job campaign is "Preparing for Interviews." First, let's look at interviewing from the hiring organization's point of view.

What are the biggest "turnoffs" for potential employers?

One of the ways to help yourself perform well at an interview is to look at the main reasons why organizations *don't* hire the people they interview, according to those who do the interviewing.

Notice that "lack of appropriate background" (or lack of experience) is the *last* reason for not being offered the job.

The 14 Most Common Reasons Job Hunters Are Not Offered Jobs (according to the companies who do the interviewing and hiring):

1. Low level of accomplishment
2. Poor attitude, lack of self-confidence
3. Lack of goals/objectives
4. Lack of enthusiasm
5. Lack of interest in the company's business
6. Inability to sell or express yourself
7. Unrealistic salary demands
8. Poor appearance
9. Lack of maturity, no leadership potential
10. Lack of extracurricular activities
11. Lack of preparation for the interview, no knowledge about company
12. Objecting to travel
13. Excessive interest in security and benefits
14. Inappropriate background

Department of Labor studies have proven that smart, "prepared" job hunters can increase their beginning salary while getting a job in *half* the time it normally takes. (4½ months is the average national length of a job search.) Here, from PREP, are some questions that can prepare you to find a job faster.

Are you in the "right" frame of mind?

It seems unfair that we have to look for a job just when we're lowest in morale. Don't worry *too* much if you're nervous before interviews. You're supposed to be a little nervous, especially if the job means a lot to you. But the best way to kill unnecessary fears about job hunting is through 1) making sure you have a great resume and 2) preparing yourself for the interview. Here are three main areas you need to think about before each interview.

Do you know what the company does?

Don't walk into an interview giving the impression that, "If this is Tuesday, this must be General Motors."

Research the company before you go to interviews.

Find out before the interview what the company's main product or service is. Where is the company heading? Is it in a "growth" or declining industry? (Answers to these questions may influence whether or not you want to work there!)

Information about what the company does is in annual reports, in newspaper and magazine articles, and on the Internet. If you're not yet skilled at Internet research, just visit your nearest library and ask the reference librarian to guide you to printed materials on the company.

Do you know what you want to do for the company?

Before the interview, try to decide how you see yourself fitting into the company. Remember, "lack of exact background" the company wants is usually the last reason people are not offered jobs.

Understand before you go to each interview that the burden will be on you to "sell" the interviewer on why you're the best person for the job and the company.

How will you answer the critical interview questions?

Put yourself in the interviewer's position and think about the questions you're most likely to be asked. Here are some of the most commonly asked interview questions:

Anticipate the questions you will be asked at the interview, and prepare your responses in advance.

Q: "What are your greatest strengths?"

A: Don't say you've never thought about it! Go into an interview knowing the three main impressions you want to leave about yourself, such as "I'm hard-working, loyal, and an imaginative cost-cutter."

Q: "What are your greatest weaknesses?"

A: Don't confess that you're lazy or have trouble meeting deadlines! Confessing that you tend to be a "workaholic" or "tend to be a perfectionist and sometimes get frustrated when others don't share my high standards" will make your prospective employer see a "weakness" that he likes. Name a weakness that your interviewer will perceive as a strength.

Q: "What are your long-range goals?"

A: If you're interviewing with Microsoft, don't say you want to work for IBM in five years! Say your long-range goal is to be *with* the company, contributing to its goals and success.

Q: "What motivates you to do your best work?"

A: Don't get dollar signs in your eyes here! "A challenge" is not a bad answer, but it's a little cliched. Saying something like "troubleshooting" or "solving a tough problem" is more interesting and specific. Give an example if you can.

Q: "What do you know about this organization?"

A: Don't say you never heard of it until they asked you to the interview! Name an interesting, positive thing you learned about the company recently from your research. Remember, company executives can sometimes feel rather "maternal" about the company they serve. Don't get onto a negative area of the company if you can think of positive facts you can bring up. Of course, if you learned in your research that the company's sales seem to be taking a nose-dive, or that the company president is being prosecuted for taking bribes, you might politely ask your interviewer to tell you something that could help you better understand what you've been reading. Those are the kinds of company facts that can help you determine whether or not you want to work there.

Go to an interview prepared to tell the company why it should hire you.

Q: "Why should I hire you?"

A: "I'm unemployed and available" is the wrong answer here! Get back to your strengths and say that you believe the organization could benefit by a loyal, hard-working cost-cutter like yourself.

In conclusion, you should decide in advance, before you go to the interview, how you will answer each of these commonly asked questions. Have some practice interviews with a friend to role-play and build your confidence.

STEP FOUR: Handling the Interview and Negotiating Salary

Now you're ready for Step Four: actually handling the interview successfully and effectively. Remember, the purpose of an interview is to get a job offer.

A smile at an interview makes the employer perceive of you as intelligent!

Eight "do's" for the interview

According to leading U.S. companies, there are eight key areas in interviewing success. You can fail at an interview if you mishandle just one area.

1. **Do wear appropriate clothes.**
You can never go wrong by wearing a suit to an interview.

2. **Do be well groomed.**
Don't overlook the obvious things like having clean hair, clothes, and fingernails for the interview.

3. **Do give a firm handshake.**
You'll have to shake hands twice in most interviews: first, before you sit down, and second, when you leave the interview. Limp handshakes turn most people off.

4. **Do smile and show a sense of humor.**
Interviewers are looking for people who would be nice to work with, so don't be so somber that you don't smile. In fact, research shows that people who smile at interviews are perceived as more intelligent. So, smile!

5. **Do be enthusiastic.**
Employers say they are "turned off" by lifeless, unenthusiastic job hunters who show no special interest in that company. The best way to show some enthusiasm for the employer's operation is to find out about the business beforehand.

6. Do show you are flexible and adaptable.

An employer is looking for someone who can contribute to his organization in a flexible, adaptable way. No matter what skills and training you have, employers know every new employee must go through initiation and training on the company's turf. Certainly show pride in your past accomplishments in a specific, factual way ("I saved my last employer $50.00 a week by a new cost-cutting measure I developed"). But don't come across as though there's nothing about the job you couldn't easily handle.

7. Do ask intelligent questions about the employer's business.

An employer is hiring someone because of certain business needs. Show interest in those needs. Asking questions to get a better idea of the employer's needs will help you "stand out" from other candidates interviewing for the job.

8. Do "take charge" when the interviewer "falls down" on the job.

Go into every interview knowing the three or four points about yourself you want the interviewer to remember. And be prepared to take an active part in leading the discussion if the interviewer's "canned approach" does not permit you to display your "strong suit." You can't always depend on the interviewer's asking you the "right" questions so you can stress your strengths and accomplishments.

Employers are seeking people with good attitudes whom they can train and coach to do things their way.

An important "don't": Don't ask questions about salary or benefits at the first interview.
Employers don't take warmly to people who look at their organization as just a place to satisfy salary and benefit needs. Don't risk making a negative impression by appearing greedy or self-serving. The place to discuss salary and benefits is normally at the second interview, and the employer will bring it up. Then you can ask questions without appearing excessively interested in what the organization can do for you.

Now...negotiating your salary
Even if an ad requests that you communicate your "salary requirement" or "salary history," you should avoid providing those numbers in your initial cover letter. You can usually say something like this: "I would be delighted to discuss the private details of my salary history with you in person."

Once you're at the interview, you must avoid even appearing *interested* in salary before you are offered the job. Make sure you've "sold" yourself before talking salary. First show you're the "best fit" for the employer and then you'll be in a stronger position from which to negotiate salary. **Never** bring up the subject of salary yourself. Employers say there's no way you can avoid looking greedy if you bring up the issue of salary and benefits before the company has identified you as its "best fit."

Don't appear excessively interested in salary and benefits at the interview.

Interviewers sometimes throw out a salary figure at the first interview to see if you'll accept it. You may not want to commit yourself if you think you will be able to negotiate a better deal later on. Get back to finding out more about the job. This lets the interviewer know you're interested primarily in the job and not the salary.

When the organization brings up salary, it may say something like this: "Well, Mary, we think you'd make a good candidate for this job. What kind of salary are we talking about?" You may not want to name a number here, either. Give the ball back to the interviewer. Act as though you hadn't given the subject of salary much thought and respond something like this: "Ah, Mr. Jones, I wonder if you'd be kind enough to tell me what salary you had in mind when you advertised the job?" Or ... "What is the range you have in mind?"

Don't worry, if the interviewer names a figure that you think is too low, you can say so without turning down the job or locking yourself into a rigid position. The point here is to negotiate for yourself as well as you can. You might reply to a number named by the interviewer that you think is low by saying something like this: "Well, Mr. Lee, the job interests me very much, and I think I'd certainly enjoy working with you. But, frankly, I was thinking of something a little higher than that." That leaves the ball in your interviewer's court again, and you haven't turned down the job either, in case it turns out that the interviewer can't increase the offer and you still want the job.

Last, send a follow-up letter.
Mail, e-mail, or fax a letter right after the interview telling your interviewer you enjoyed the meeting and are certain (if you are) that you are the "best fit" for the job. The people interviewing you will probably have an attitude described as either "professionally loyal" to their companies, or "maternal and proprietary" if the interviewer also owns the company. In either case, they are looking for people who want to work for *that* company in particular. The follow-up letter you send might be just the deciding factor in your favor if the employer is trying to choose between you and someone else. You will see an example of a follow-up letter on page 16.

A cover letter is an essential part of a job hunt or career change.
Many people are aware of the importance of having a great resume, but most people in a job hunt don't realize just how important a cover letter can be. The purpose of the cover letter, sometimes called a **"letter of interest,"** is to introduce your resume to prospective employers. The cover letter is often the critical ingredient in a job hunt because the cover letter allows you to say a lot of things that just don't "fit" on the resume. For example, you can emphasize your commitment to a new field and stress your related talents. The cover letter also gives you a chance to stress outstanding character and personal values. On the next two pages you will see examples of very effective cover letters.

Special help for those in career change
We want to emphasize again that, especially in a career change, the cover letter is very important and can help you "build a bridge" to a new career. A creative and appealing cover letter can begin the process of encouraging the potential employer to imagine you in an industry other than the one in which you have worked.

As a special help to those in career change, there are resumes and cover letters included in this book which show valuable techniques and tips you should use when changing fields or industries. The resumes and cover letters of career changers are identified in the table of contents as "Career Change" and you will see the "Career Change" label on cover letters in Part Two where the individuals are changing careers.

Salary negotiation can be tricky.

A follow-up letter can help the employer choose between you and another qualified candidate.

A cover letter is an essential part of a career change.

Please do not attempt to implement a career change without a cover letter such as the ones you see in Part Two and in Part Three of this book. A cover letter is the first impression of you, and you can influence the way an employer views you by the language and style of your letter.

Date

Exact Name of Person
Exact Title
Exact Name of Company
Address
City, State, Zip

**Addressing the Cover
Letter:** Get the exact
name of the person to
whom you are writing. This
makes your approach
personal.

Dear Exact Name of Person (or Dear Sir or Madam if answering a blind ad):

I would appreciate an opportunity to talk with you soon about how I could contribute to your organization through my education, experience, and knowledge.

Second Paragraph: You
have a chance to talk
about whatever you feel is
your most distinguishing
feature.

As you will see from my enclosed resume, I received my B.S. in Electrical Engineering, Manufacturing concentration, from Arizona State University. In order to complete this rigorous degree program, I was required to pass graduate-level courses in Digital Signal Processing, Project Management for Engineers, and Switching Theory. Since earning my degree, I have supplemented my education with additional courses in AUTOCAD V.15, C Programming, and Java.

Third Paragraph: You
bring up your next most
distinguishing qualities and
try to
sell yourself.

I earned rapid advancement with Concord, Inc., a division of Varsity Corporation located in Santa Fe, NM, and was working at the Varsity Corporation's Automotive Division in Santa Fe. Originally hired as a Production Technician, I rapidly advanced to a shift supervisor's job before my selection as a Quality Technician. I had completed the screening and interviewing process and was offered a position as an Engineering Intern when I was laid off due to serious business declines. I was, however, offered a job as an Assembly Technician at a company site in another state. Because of personal reasons, however, I do not wish to relocate at this time.

Fourth Paragraph: Here
you have another
opportunity to reveal
qualities or achievements
which will impress your
future employer.

Among my strongest skills are my ability to anticipate problems, analyze situations, and develop the solutions which will result in increasing productivity and profitability. In earlier jobs in shipping and receiving operations, as well as in technical jobs with Varsity, I have initiated changes which have resulted in reduced man-hours and lowered costs.

Final Paragraph: He asks
the employer to contact
him. Make sure your
reader knows what the
"next step" is.

If you can use a positive, results-oriented professional with diversified technical skills related to manufacturing operations, I hope you will contact me soon to arrange a time when we might meet to discuss your needs. I can assure you in advance that I have an excellent reputation and can provide outstanding references.

Sincerely,

**Alternate Final
Paragraph:** It's more
aggressive (but not too
aggressive) to let the
employer know that you
will be calling him or her.
Don't be afraid to be
persistent. Employers are
looking for people who
know what they want to
do.

Gary Andrew Laredo

Date

Exact Name of Person
Exact Title
Exact Name of Company
Address
City, State, Zip

Dear Exact Name of Person (or Dear Sir or Madam if answering a blind ad):

I would appreciate an opportunity to talk with you soon about how I could contribute to your organization through my strong communication and organizational skills as well as my highly motivated nature and "can-do" attitude.

Most recently I excelled in manufacturing jobs, first at Jones Manufacturing and then at Crosby Manufacturing. At Crosby, I was credited with making contributions which allowed the company to achieve its goal of "zero defects" in on-time shipping, and I was a member of a department which qualified for ISO 9000 certification on the company's first attempt.

While I was highly regarded by my employer and can provide excellent references at the appropriate time, recent downturns in business forced the company to reduce its workforce, displacing myself and many of my co-workers. I have taken the opportunity to strengthen my administrative and financial skills with a Bank Teller training course from Carson City Community College. I am confident that my outgoing personality and excellent work habits would be well suited to any environment that requires strict attention to detail.

In a previous position, I worked in a clerical/secretarial capacity for Classic Hair Coifs in Carson City. I essentially performed the functions of an office manager or administrative assistant, scheduling appointments, ordering supplies, operating a multi-line phone system, and handling all correspondence.

If your organization could benefit from a motivated, detail-oriented young professional with exceptional organizational, customer service, and communication skills, I hope you will contact me to suggest a time when we could meet to discuss your needs. I assure you in advance that I have an excellent reputation and could quickly become a strong asset to your company.

Sincerely,

Karen Marie Steardon

CC: Mr. Michael Reardon

Semi-blocked Letter

Date
Three blank spaces

Address

Salutation
One blank space

Body

One blank space

Signature

cc: Indicates you are sending a copy of the letter to someone

Date

Exact Name of Person
Title or Position
Name of Company
Address (number and street)
Address (city, state, and zip)

Dear Exact Name:

Follow-up Letter

A great follow-up letter
can motivate the employer
to make the job offer, and
the salary offer may be
influenced by the style and
tone of your follow-up
letter, too!

I am writing to express my appreciation for the time you spent with me on 9 December, and I want to let you know that I am sincerely interested in the position of Controller which you described.

I feel confident that I could skillfully interact with your 60-person work force in order to obtain the information we need to assure expert controllership of your manufacturing company, and I would cheerfully travel as your needs require. I want you to know, too, that I would not consider relocating to Salt Lake City to be a hardship! It is certainly one of the most beautiful areas I have ever seen.

As you described to me what you are looking for in a controller, I had a sense of "déjà vu" because my current boss was in a similar position when I went to work for him. He needed someone to come in and be his "right arm" and take on an increasing amount of his management responsibilities so that he could be freed up to do other things. I have played a key role in the growth and profitability of his multi-unit business, and he has come to depend on my sound financial and business advice as much as my day-to-day management skills.

It would be a pleasure to work for a successful individual such as yourself, and I feel I could contribute significantly to your business not only through my accounting and business background but also through my strong qualities of loyalty, reliability, and trustworthiness. I am confident that I could learn Quick Books rapidly, and I would welcome being trained to do things your way. I send best wishes for the holidays, and I look forward to hearing from you again soon.

Yours sincerely,

Jacob Evangelisto

In this section, you will find resumes and cover letters of construction professionals—and of people who want to work in the construction field. How do construction professionals differ from other job hunters? Why should there be a book dedicated to people seeking jobs in the construction field? Based on more than 20 years of experience in working with job hunters, this editor is convinced that resumes and cover letters which "speak the lingo" of the field you wish to enter will communicate more effectively than language which is not industry-specific. This book is designed to help people (1) who are seeking to prepare their own resumes and (2) who wish to use as models "real" resumes of individuals who have successfully launched careers in the construction field or advanced in the field. You will see a wide range of experience levels reflected in the resumes in this book. Some of the resumes and cover letters were used by individuals seeking to enter the field; others were used successfully by senior professionals to advance in the field.

Newcomers to an industry sometimes have advantages over more experienced professionals. In a job hunt, junior professionals can have an advantage over their more experienced counterparts. Prospective employers often view the less experienced workers as "more trainable" and "more coachable" than their seniors. This means that the mature professional who has already excelled in a first career can, with credibility, "change careers" and transfer skills to other industries.

Construction professionals fare best in a job hunt when they utilize industry terminology which vividly communicates to others what they have been doing.

Newcomers to the field may have disadvantages compared to their seniors. Almost by definition, the inexperienced construction professional—the young person who has recently earned a college degree, or the individual who has recently received certifications respected by the industry—is less tested and less experienced than senior managers, so the resume and cover letter of the inexperienced professional may often have to "sell" his or her potential to do something he or she has never done before. Lack of experience in the field she wants to enter can be a stumbling block to the junior manager, but remember that many employers believe that someone who has excelled in anything—academics, for example—can excel in many other fields.

Some advice to inexperienced professionals...
If senior professionals could give junior professionals a piece of advice about careers, here's what they would say: Manage your career and don't stumble from job to job in an incoherent pattern. Try to find work that interests you, and then identify prosperous industries which need work performed of the type you want to do. Learn early in your working life that a great resume and cover letter can blow doors open for you and help you maximize your salary.

Special help for career changers...
For those changing careers, you will find useful the resumes and cover letters marked "Career Change" on the following pages. You can also consult the Table of Contents for page numbers of resumes and cover letters showing career changers.

Exact Name of Person
Exact Title
Exact Name of Company
Address
City, State, Zip

ACCOUNTANT   Dear Exact Name of Person (or Dear Sir or Madam if answering a blind ad):

With the enclosed resume, I would like to make you aware of my versatile background with an emphasis on accounting and office management as well as of my reputation as an innovative, customer-service-oriented professional.

As you will see from my resume, I offer a diverse background in construction, manufacturing, and service environments and have always earned respect for my ability to adapt to change, pressure, and deadlines. Having studied Business and Accounting in college, I am building a track record of effectiveness in dealing with people ranging from office and accounting clerks, to temporary workers, to management professionals, to accounts and corporate financial officers. With a knack for quickly learning and mastering advances in computer technology, I am proficient in creating databases and in using automated systems for accounting, data processing, and purchasing activities.

In my present job as Staff Accountant and Office Manager for Ready Mixed Concrete, I have been credited with developing creative ideas for streamlining procedures. In addition to preparing payroll for 106 employees at five plants, I process and manage a wide range of tax and accounting activities including overseeing Worker's Compensation, OSHA compliance reporting, and health insurance plan support. Among my accomplishments has been reducing the time needed to process payroll from three days to one and taking the financial report process which had been six months behind to a point where it is now consistently completed on time.

In earlier jobs in accounts payable and payroll processing, I was recruited by one construction company to handle their accounts payable for multimillion-dollar projects and process payroll for more than 200 employees. For a large temporary services firm with eight branches, I worked in the corporate office processing weekly payroll for approximately 3,000 people. Earlier I earned promotion from Accounts Receivable and Collections Specialist to Department Secretary with Tom's Food, Inc., a manufacturer of snack foods with plants throughout the country.

If you can use an experienced and mature professional who has long been recognized as a reliable and honest individual with high personal standards, I hope you will contact me soon to suggest a time when we might meet to discuss your needs. I can assure you in advance that I can provide outstanding references.

Sincerely,

Catherine Dabbs

CATHERINE DABBS

1110½ Hay Street, Fayetteville, NC 28305   •   preppub@aol.com   •   (910) 483-6611

OBJECTIVE	To offer a background of accomplishments and reputation as a results-oriented professional with strong knowledge of accounting and office management to an organization that can use an enthusiastic, energetic professional with experience in collections and customer service.
EDUCATION	Studied **Business and Accounting,** Columbus College, Columbus, GA.
COMPUTERS & SPECIAL SKILLS	Knowledgeable of Microsoft Access and database creation; utilize automated systems while handling purchasing, accounting, and data processing activities. Proficient with software programs including the following:

QuickBooks Pro   PeachTree Accounting
Word   Excel
MS Front Page, Excel, Outlook, and Works

Broad experience in office operations and customer service; use standard office machines.

EXPERIENCE	**STAFF ACCOUNTANT** and **OFFICE MANAGER.** Metro Products & Construction Company dba Ready Mixed Concrete, Columbus, GA (2001-present). Excelling in handling diverse responsibilities, have been credited with making changes which have significantly improved operating procedures while supervising three people including accounting clerks and office staff for a business with five separate plant locations.

- Streamlined operations in the accounting department and have implemented changes which have reduced the time needed to complete support activities; for instance, payroll processing which had taken three days is now completed in one.
- Improved the process for producing monthly and yearly financial reports for the CPAs and owners – a function which had been six months behind is now consistently on time.
- Applied knowledge in database creation to establish a new system for tracking equipment purchases and status of computers, printers, vehicles, and other equipment.
- Prepare payroll for up to 106 employees in the company's five plants.
- Manage Worker's Compensation claims and yearly audits, preparation of forms for OSHA, and monthly approval of employee health insurance; prepare daily bank deposits; post payroll and accounts payable check numbers; issue and then post manual checks; prepare the petty cash sheet; process state and federal tax payments.
- Verify data between the general ledger, accounts payable, and accounts receivable.

ACCOUNTS PAYABLE AND PAYROLL TECHNICIAN. Metric Constructors, Columbus, GA (1999-01). Was recruited by this commercial construction company to handle accounts payable for multimillion-dollar projects and to process payroll for 200 employees.
- Assisted in purchasing support for large projects; prepared weekly and monthly reports for Project Managers and Supervisors.

PAYROLL TECHNICIAN. Mega Force, Columbus, GA (1999). Processed weekly payroll for approximately 3,000 people at the corporate office of a company with eight branches.
- Polished data entry skills inputting daily employee information and job orders.

Advanced with Tom's Food, Inc., Columbus, GA while earning a reputation as a detail-oriented, positive, and enthusiastic professional:
ACCOUNTS RECEIVABLE AND COLLECTIONS SPECIALIST. (1991-98). Dealt with more than 1,100 accounts which included distributors and grocery store chains.
- Researched past due accounts and made weekly and monthly reports.

PERSONAL	Creative individual who thrives under the challenge of deadlines. Notary Public.

Date

Exact Name of Person
Title or Position
Name of Company
Address (number and street)
Address (city, state, and zip)

APARTMENT COMPLEX MANAGER

Dear Exact Name of Person: (or Dear Sir or Madam if answering a blind ad)

With the enclosed resume, I would like to indicate my interest in your organization and my desire to explore employment opportunities. I am in the process of relocating permanently to the Ashland area, where my family lives.

As you will see from my enclosed resume, I offer extensive experience in all aspects of apartment rentals management. In my current job, on my own initiative I directed the set-up of 35 corporate apartments and personally marketed the concept to area businesses. This concept has been so successful that the owners of the complex have decided to double the number of corporate rentals by next year.

I hope you will welcome my call soon to arrange a brief meeting at your convenience to discuss your current and future needs and how I might serve them. Thank you in advance for your time.

Sincerely yours,

Annette Chase

ANNETTE CHASE

1110½ Hay Street, Fayetteville, NC 28305 • preppub@aol.com • (910) 483-6611

OBJECTIVE	To benefit an organization that can use an articulate, motivated professional with exceptional communication, organizational, and negotiation skills who offers experience in accounts payable, accounts receivable, and office management.
EXPERIENCE	**APARTMENT COMPLEX MANAGER.** Grant's Village, Portland, OR (1998-present). Supervise all aspects of the operation of this exclusive 200-unit apartment complex, including overseeing leasing and maintenance as well as coordinating the fitness center and landscaping efforts.

- Process accounts payable, making disbursements for corporate utility bills; maintenance and other upkeep; advertising and promotions; and other expenses.
- Manage accounts receivable, taking in monthly lease payments from existing residents and security deposits from new residents, as well as other payments.
- Develop and maintain excellent relationships with local vendors, setting up new accounts and preserving connections with existing suppliers.
- Supervise one office employee and a three-person maintenance crew.
- Direct the rental and set-up of 35 corporate apartments.
- Inspect units being vacated and schedule cleaning and maintenance to ensure apartments are prepared for incoming residents.

Excelled in the following track record of advancement to increasing responsibilities with UDC of Oregon (1995-98).
MARKETING ASSOCIATE. The Village at Smithfield, Portland, OR (1996-98). Was promoted by UDC to a job equivalent to Assistant Manager with this 356-unit complex; credited with decreasing the number of delinquent accounts through my collections skill and knowledge in handling cases through Small Claims Court.

- Performed accounts payable and receivable, processing bills from vendors and utility companies for property and receiving lease payments and security deposits from residents.
- Processed lease applications and familiarized new residents with our lease and policies; conducted move-in and move-out inspections.
- Supervised and trained one employee; processed weekly reports promptly.
- Oversaw two corporate accounts.

LEASING MANAGER/ASSISTANT MANAGER. Morganton & Associates, Portland, OR (1995-96). Began with the company as a floating leasing agent and was assigned for two months to the 253-unit Cumberland Trace Apartments complex and then to The Village at Cliffdale before being promoted to Assistant Manager of the 280-unit Morganton Place Apartments.

- Collected accounts receivable and disbursed accounts payable for the property.
- Leased apartments and processed applications; handled lease signings; conducted move-in and move-out inspections; processed weekly reports; wrote a monthly newsletter.

AFFILIATION	Received NALP designation, Portland County Apartment Association.
COMPUTERS	Experienced with Rent Roll and Prentice Hall property management programs.
PERSONAL	Excellent references upon request. Known for my strong work ethic. Am single (never married). Have family in the Ashland area, which I consider home.

Exact Name of Person
Title or Position
Name of Company
Address (no., street)
Address (city, state, zip)

APPRENTICE ELECTRICIAN

Dear Exact Name of Person (or Dear Sir or Madam if answering a blind ad):

I would appreciate an opportunity to talk with you soon about how I could contribute to your organization through my excellent technical electronics skills as well as through my reputation as a knowledgeable and effective troubleshooter.

As you will see from my enclosed resume, through training and experience I have earned a reputation for my technical expertise related to electronics troubleshooting, repair, and maintenance. My experience covers several areas in the electronics field such as television, residential security alarms, and telephone switching operations.

My TV and security system experience has been gained since leaving the U.S. Army. While serving my country in the military, I earned advancement to supervisory roles and was often called on to diagnose difficult problems. After the war in the Middle East, I was placed in charge of seeing to the details of reestablishing communication services for my unit at Ft. Hood, TX, a major military facility.

I hope you will welcome my call soon to arrange a brief meeting at your convenience to discuss your current and future needs and how I might serve them. Thank you in advance for your time.

Sincerely yours,

Norman S. Watt

Alternate last paragraph:
I hope you will call or write me soon to suggest a time convenient for us to meet and discuss your current and future needs and how I might serve them. Thank you in advance for your time.

NORMAN S. WATT

1110½ Hay Street, Fayetteville, NC 28305 • preppub@aol.com • (910) 483-6611

OBJECTIVE   To offer excellent technical electronics skills and troubleshooting abilities to an organization that can use a hard worker with a reputation for initiative, ambition, and drive to succeed.

TRAINING   Excelled in U.S. Army-sponsored technical and leadership development courses including:
  Mobile Subscriber Equipment (MSE) and maintenance supervisor's courses
  Professional leadership development school
  Principles of electronics and solid state equipment
  SB3614A communication equipment/NET equipment
Completed four semester hours of solid state electronics and three semester hours of electric circuits, Central Texas College, Germany.

SPECIAL SKILLS   Use standard and specialized test equipment; offer expertise in the following areas:

troubleshooting relays	electronic schematics	oscilloscopes
computer-aided troubleshooting	electronic board repairs	multimeters

  troubleshooting and repair of DC power supplies
  diagnosing defective automatic telephone switchboards
  current-voltage relationships in component soldering
  transistor and operational amperes and solid-state logic
  performing diagnostic tests on basic AC and DC circuits
  subscriber dial-tone multiple-frequency, dial pulse, and hand-cranked systems

EXPERIENCE   **APPRENTICE ELECTRICIAN.** Wong Electrical Contractors, Ft. Bragg, NC (2002-present). Completed inside wiring jobs including installing switches, lights, and outlets for new housing for thousands of soldiers at the largest U.S. military base in the world.

MASTER CONTROL OPERATOR. Channel 89 TV, Anytown, NC (2001). Gained experience in activities ranging from airing TV programs according to prepared program logs, to conducting minor maintenance on tapes and recorders, to following procedures for powering up the station's transmitter, to assisting the chief engineer.

SECURITY SYSTEM INSTALLER. Matthews Security, Anytown, SC (1997-00). Became familiar with several types of security alarm products while installing them in private residences: inspected the home to determine how and where to install the particular system, completed the installation, programmed the system, and tested for errors.
- Became skilled in all phases of installation including pulling wires under foundations or through attics, wiring equipment, setting up control panel wiring, hard wiring up to 18 separate zones, troubleshooting, and repairing system failures.

Received training and polished my skills in the electronics field, U.S. Army:
TELEPHONE MAINTENANCE SHOP SUPERVISOR. Ft. Hood, TX (1990-96). Supervised five specialists; directed scheduling and the preparation of forms and records.

TELEPHONE MAINTENANCE SPECIALIST. Germany (1987-89). Earned a reputation as a talented troubleshooter and was often called on to solve unique problems found in a wide range of equipment; performed diagnostic tests on basic AC and DC circuits in order to diagnose defective automatic telephone switchboard operations.

PERSONAL   Strong moral character. Offer a positive attitude and dedication to excellence.

CAREER CHANGE

DAVID BERKLEY

1110½ Hay Street, Fayetteville, NC 28305

preppub@aol.com • (910) 483-6611

CAD OPERATOR

OBJECTIVE

To contribute to an organization through my extensive background in mechanical drafting and experience with AutoCAD systems.

EXPERIENCE

RETAIL SALES REPRESENTATIVE. New York City (1999-present). Working outside my field in retail sales and customer service.

CAD OPERATOR. H.L. Yoh, New York City (1998-99). For a contract firm with a project for General Electric in Mebane, NY, worked on AutoCAD-13 while updating drawings for the "Critical to Quality" project and also converted manual drawings to AutoCAD-13 drawings. Completed "AN" changes to current CAD files according to engineering mark-ups.

RETAIL STORE MANAGER. Motzno's Department Store, Woodland, NY (1996-98). As co-manager of a family-owned business, assisted with duties including ordering, managing clerks, handling banking transactions, and performing building maintenance.

ELECTRICAL DRAFTSMAN. Center-Line Design, Castle Hayne, NY (1997). Assigned to a project at Occidental Chemical for this contract firm, prepared drawings for new electrical projects such as plant lighting, alarm systems, and motor controls to electrical code specifications. Updated existing plant drawings from previous projects.

MECHANICAL DRAFTSMAN. Manpower Technical, Castle Hane, NY (1996). Assigned to a project at Tipper-Tie in Apex, NY, used AutoCAD-12 to prepare new drawings of food processing machinery for a plant engineering department. Revised older manual drawings to incorporate geometric tolerancing.

CAD OPERATOR. Memorex-Telex, Woodland, NY (1993-96). Worked extensively with AutoCAD-11 and 12 while preparing new electrical, mechanical, and P.C. board assembly and fabrication drawings.
- Completed engineering changes to existing drawings and worked on Daisy computer systems to update schematics and component locators.

CAD OPERATOR and **DRAFTSMAN.** Manpower Technical, Woodland, NY (1985-93). Worked in temporary assignments on a variety of projects for various corporations to include the following:
- CAD OPERATOR – Exide Electronics, Woodland, NY: prepared new electrical schematic drawings and changed existing ones as well as machined parts drawings and custom-built power supply layouts for a manufacturer of uninterruptable power supply systems.
- DESIGN DRAFTSMAN – Firestone Tire, Wilson, NY: prepared

sketches of new conveyers while also maintaining responsibility for all detail drawings and calculations. Designed equipment layouts which resulted in more efficient use of available space.

- MECHANICAL AND ELECTRICAL DRAFTSMAN – International Paper, Wilson, NY: worked closely with both mechanical and electrical groups while preparing detail and assembly drawings of soft drink packaging machinery at a research and development facility.

- MECHANICAL DRAFTSMAN – Memorex-Telex, Wilson, NY: prepared drawings of complex molded and fabricated computer parts as well as creating artwork for machine labels.

- MECHANICAL DRAFTSMAN – Tipper-Tie, Apex, NY: worked on two projects two years apart which included the following duties and accomplishments:
  Prepared detail and assembly drawings for meat processing equipment
  Attended two short courses in geometric tolerancing
  Created detail and assembly drawings of food packaging machinery
  Incorporated geometric tolerancing to critical dimensions

- MECHANICAL AND ELECTRICAL DRAFTSMAN – CRS Sirrine, Research Triangle Park, NY: worked closely with engineering personnel while preparing both mechanical and electrical drawings for a U.S. Navy electrical power substation; also assisted in preparing drawings for a pulp wood conveyer system.

- MECHANICAL DRAFTSMAN – Baker-Perkins, Wilson, NY: worked on two projects two years apart which included the following duties and accomplishments:
  Prepared detail and assembly drawings for the cereal production industry
  Made complex drawings of electrical, mechanical, and hydraulic assemblies
  Worked with the design group to draw new masters of commercial ovens
  Redrew ovens, conveyers, loaders, unloaders, and other equipment

- DRAFTSMAN and CADAM OPERATOR – IBM, Wilson, NY: worked on four different projects for this major corporation:
  created new masters and completed engineering changes to drafting standards
  worked as a CADAM Operator and quality standards inspector
  coordinated incoming work for the engineering department
  became familiar with IBM drafting standards and CADAM system
  completed isometric drawings and installation instructions

- DRAFTSMAN – Becton-Dickinson, Research Triangle Park, NY: prepared detail and assembly drawings of a new laser body fluid analysis machine for the engineering department's research and development section.

- DESIGN DRAFTSMAN – Black and Decker, Wilson, NY: drew complex and detailed drawings of housing for electrical hand tools with the responsibility for seeing that moving parts fit together and allowed space for internal moving parts.

- CIVIL DRAFTSMAN – Novo Biochemical, Wilson, NY: located and drew maps of electrical conduit lines and pipe lines for a waste treatment system.

- ELECTRICAL DRAFTSMAN – Burroughs-Wellcome Co., Greenville, NY: as the draftsman for a facilities engineering department, updated drawings and performed field inspections of plant electrical equipment as well as wiring and fusing applications for minimum code requirements. Designed a duct system for the packaging line.

- MECHANICAL DRAFTSMAN – Corning Glass, Wilson, NY: worked for the research and development department preparing detail drawings for new machines along with assembly drawings, schematics, and bills of materials.

- MECHANICAL DESIGN DRAFTSMAN – E.I. Dupont, Wilson, NY: as a facilities draftsman, completed piping and equipment layout drawings and engineering changes to existing drawings. Prepared drawings of security and TV monitoring equipment.

PERSONAL   Am available for travel or relocation according to employer needs.

Date

Exact Name of Person
Exact Title
Exact Name of Company
Address
City, State, Zip

CARPENTER   Dear Exact Name of Person (or Dear Sir or Madam if answering a blind ad):

With the enclosed resume, I would like to make you aware of my interest in exploring employment opportunities with your organization and introduce you to my construction industry background. I am single, hold a current passport, and am available for relocation worldwide as your needs require.

As you will see from my resume, I am currently excelling as a Carpenter with a leading construction firm in South Carolina. I am experienced in working at every stage of the construction process, and I am known for my intense commitment to safety and quality control. Although I am held in the highest regard by my current employer, I am selectively exploring employment opportunities with firms which operate worldwide. I can provide outstanding references at the appropriate time.

In prior experience, I served my country with distinction in the U.S. Army, where I began my career as a Carpenter after earning a Certificate of Completion of Apprenticeship as a Carpenter from the state of California. The U.S. Army identified my management potential and I was quickly placed in supervisory positions. I subsequently excelled as an Instructor and Training Chief, and I was then selected to receive specialized training related to the nuclear, biological, and chemical (NBC) field. After NBC training, I was handpicked for positions in which I handled the responsibility of managing NBC resources, training employees in NBC matters, and managing chemical defense programs. In one position as a Senior NBC Operations Advisor, I served as the "subject matter expert" on NBC training for Special Operations soldiers at Ft. Bragg. On my own initiative, I revised and implemented the most detailed inspection checklist for NBC programs ever used in that organization, and I revised inventory control programs in order to better track equipment. I won numerous medals and other awards, including the Bronze Star, which recognized my technical expertise as well as my management skills.

While serving in the U.S. Army, I gained a reputation as an outstanding manager and mentor. I truly enjoyed helping other soldiers develop their skills to their fullest potential, and I mentored one individual who became Soldier of the Year.

If my background and skills interest you, I hope you will contact me to suggest a time when we could meet in person to discuss your needs. Thank you.

Yours sincerely,

Bryce Cunningham

BRYCE CUNNINGHAM

1110½ Hay Street, Fayetteville, NC 28305 • preppub@aol.com • (910) 483-6611

OBJECTIVE

I am single and available for worldwide relocation on an extended basis in order to apply my extensive construction background and engineering knowledge for the benefit of a company involved in global construction activities.

EXPERIENCE

CARPENTER. Williams Construction, Charleston, SC (2000-present). Expertly apply my skills as a carpenter in every phase of construction, including the framing and finishing stages of construction. Build decks and fireplace mantles and other fixtures.

STEEL ERECTOR. Cahill & Sons, Charleston, SC (1993-99). Worked as a steel erector for a Virginia company which had a contract to help build a new multimillion-dollar facility.

U.S. Army experience: Served my country with distinction and was promoted to managerial positions while gaining expert knowledge related to nuclear, biological, and chemical (NBC) matters:
OPERATIONS MANAGER. Ft. Campbell, KY (1992-93). As a proud member of the Special Forces, conducted land navigation training, managed counter-drug missions, and provided guidance in NBC matters.
- On a formal performance evaluation, was described as "proactive and dedicated to safety in a high-risk training environment."

SENIOR NBC OPERATIONS ADVISOR. Ft. Bragg, NC (1991-92). Was the trusted advisor to a senior Special Forces executive on NBC matters and was the "subject matter expert" for all NBC training for Special Operations soldiers.
- Prepared detailed written documents pertaining to NBC training. Revised and implemented the most detailed inspection checklist for NBC/Language programs ever seen. Recommended and implemented significant modifications to the NBC and Language programs.
- Revised the chemical defense equipment status report to better track all group chemical equipment. Flawlessly accounted for hundreds of thousands of dollars in assets.
- On a formal performance evaluation, was commended for "flawlessly coordinating Special Forces operations for several major projects."

OPERATIONS MANAGER ("First Sergeant"). Ft. Bragg, NC (1988-91). In the Army's only Special Operations support organization, was in charge of directing aviation re-fueling and warehouse support. Was praised on a formal evaluation for "unparalleled knowledge and ability in supply related procedures and knowledge."

Highlights of other military experience:
Began my military career as a **CARPENTER.** Exhibited skill while laying out job sites per blueprints and diagrams, and performed detailed carpentry work. Was promoted rapidly to **SENIOR CARPENTER & ASSISTANT SECTION CHIEF,** which placed in the position of training and managing trades personnel. Cross-trained in electrical and plumbing work.

EDUCATION

Completed more than two years of college-level training which included the following courses:
Received **Certificate of Completion of Apprenticeship as a Carpenter,** California Apprenticeship Council.
Graduated from the U.S. Army **Chemical School** and **Chemical Staff Specialist School.**

PERSONAL

Can provide excellent personal and professional references.

Date

Exact Name of Person
Title or Position
Name of Company
Address (no., street)
Address (city, state, zip)

Dear Exact Name of Person (or Dear Sir or Madam if answering a blind ad):

I would appreciate an opportunity to talk with you soon about how I could contribute to your organization through my strong interest in the field of geotechnical engineering, quality control and inspection, and materials testing as well as through my experience, education, and communication skills.

You will see by my enclosed resume that while earning my B.S. in Mathematics, I gained practical experience in summer and part-time positions which included Concrete Technician and Engineering Technician. I am certified by the state of Virginia as a Concrete Technician and was promoted to Quality Control Inspector after only six months with a pre-cast company in Virginia.

I feel that I offer well-developed communication skills partially as a result of my eight years of service in the U.S. Army where I was heavily involved in training and supervision of teams of up to nine well-trained people. I also refined my ability to communicate effectively during a period where I tutored students in mathematics at a college learning center where most of my students needed assistance in pre-calculus or calculus.

My computer skills include familiarity with DOS and UNIX operating systems with some experience in programming in Pascal. I enjoy technical challenges and learning new theories and mechanics.

I hope you will welcome my call soon to arrange a brief meeting at your convenience to discuss your current and future needs and how I might serve them. Thank you in advance for your time.

Sincerely yours,

Arthur M. Fall

Alternate last paragraph:
I hope you will call or write me soon to suggest a time convenient for us to meet and discuss your current and future needs and how I might serve them. Thank you in advance for your time.

ARTHUR M. FALL

1110½ Hay Street, Fayetteville, NC 28305 • preppub@aol.com • (910) 483-6611

OBJECTIVE

To offer my strong analytical and mathematical abilities to an organization that can use a technically oriented young professional with a reputation as a team player known for outstanding communication, problem-solving, and planning abilities.

EDUCATION

Bachelor of Science degree in Mathematics, Mary Washington College, Fredericksburg, VA, degree requirements completed 2002.
- Was inducted into Pi Mu Epsilon National Mathematics Honor Society as a math major with a 3.5 GPA.
- Earned departmental honors in mathematics in recognition of my high GPA and completion of a semester of directed study with a presentation made to department faculty.
- Active member of the Mathematical Association of America (MAA).

LICENSE

Was licensed as a Concrete Technician by the Virginia Department of Transportation.

TECHNICAL KNOWLEDGE

Familiar with Windows and UNIX operating systems and use computer software such as Excel, Lotus 1-2-3, Word, and WordPerfect; limited experience with programming.

EXPERIENCE

Gained practical experience and refined my time management skills while juggling the demands of attending college full time and working to help finance my education:

CARPENTER'S HELPER. Maxton Construction, Washington, DC (2001-present). Earned a reputation as a dependable and trustworthy employee while learning commercial carpentry working on ceilings and dry walls.

QUALITY ASSURANCE CLERK. Roadway Package System, Hartwood, VA (1999-00). Polished customer service skills while involved in activities including redirecting packages which had been improperly routed, processing damaged parcels, maintaining various types of records and documentation, and responding to customer complaints and problems.

MATHEMATICS TUTOR. Germanna Community College, Locust Grove, VA (1998-00). Applied my well-developed communication skills and mathematical abilities while helping students who were experiencing difficulties in subjects such as precalculus and calculus.

ENGINEERING TECHNICIAN. Geotechnical Materials Testing, Inc. (GMTI), Stafford, VA (1998). Further enhanced my knowledge of concrete testing and learned soil testing techniques while preparing reports prior to collecting samples.

QUALITY CONTROL INSPECTOR/CONCRETE TECHNICIAN. Rotonda Pre-Cast, Fredericksburg, VA (1997-98). Promoted to Quality Control Inspector after six months, was involved in testing concrete and aggregates as well as in preparing and filing reports.

TRAINING SUPERVISOR and **TEAM LEADER.** U.S. Army, Ft. Bragg, NC, and Germany (1990-96). Advanced to supervisory roles as the leader of teams with as many as nine members: oversaw training and performance of subordinates while ensuring the proper maintenance and security of equipment.
- Earned recognition for accomplishments including graduating with honors from **two** professional development training programs.

PERSONAL

Working knowledge of the German language. Enjoy reading scientific/technical books on subjects such as quantum mechanics. Like technical challenges and learning new theories.

Date

Exact Name of Person
Title or Position
Name of Company
Address (number and street)
Address (city, state, and zip)

CHIEF EXECUTIVE OFFICER, HOME IMPROVEMENTS COMPANY

Dear Exact Name of Person: (or Sir or Madam if answering a blind ad)

With the enclosed resume, I would like to make you aware of my interest in joining your management team in some capacity in which you could utilize my proven skills in increasing profit, cutting costs, restructuring operations for greater efficiency, and improving market share.

I have excelled in management positions with the General Electric Corporation and then with Baylor Industries, a $7 billion company which acquired General Electric's $1.1 billion electrical control and motor business. In one job as a Plant Manager, I transformed an unprofitable plant into a profitable one and then grew sales from $52 to $82 million. In another position as a Plant Manager, I increased sales 25% annually, from $83 million to $148 million, while managing 800 employees, eight assembly sites, and $4.5 million in annual capital investments. In earlier jobs as a Product Line Manager with General Electric, I introduced new product lines and modified the way the company did business through its sales channels, customer base structure, investment strategy, pricing structure, and other areas.

I was recruited for my most recent position, which involved directing the operations of a home improvements company with two manufacturing plants and a distribution warehouse. Through my leadership, we boosted revenue from $48 million to $64 million and the company was acquired by Capel Industries. Although I have played a key role in its divestiture, I have decided not to remain with the company.

If your company can utilize a strong and insightful leader, I would enjoy the opportunity to talk with you in person about your needs and how I might serve them. I offer a reputation as a visionary thinker, aggressive cost cutter, creative strategist, and resourceful opportunity finder. I believe a company must continuously analyze the ways it does business in order to assure maximum efficiency. For example, as a Plant Manager, I profitably outsourced shipping, logistics, mail, document management, and network maintenance functions previously performed internally, and we made highly profitable quality and productivity improvements. I have a strong customer orientation which was derived from my earliest jobs in technical sales and product line management.

If my executive abilities interest you, please contact me. I can provide outstanding references, and I am willing to relocate anywhere in the U.S.

Sincerely,

Milo Germano

MILO GERMANO

1110½ Hay Street, Fayetteville, NC 28305 • preppub@aol.com • (910) 483-6611

OBJECTIVE	To contribute to the profitability of an organization that can use a resourceful executive who has introduced new product lines, restructured operations for greater productivity, and managed internal change to cut costs, improve quality, and increase market share.
EXPERIENCE	**CHIEF EXECUTIVE OFFICER.** Tyson Home Improvements, Winston, SC (2000-present). Was recruited by this home improvement products company with two manufacturing plants and a distribution warehouse; **boosted revenues from $48 million in 2000 to $64 million in 2002.**

- In large measure due to the results achieved through my leadership, the company became an acquisition target and was acquired by Capel, Inc. in 2000; assisted in the transition of the company to new management and was offered a top management role, but I have decided not to remain with Capel, Inc.
- Cut costs by $1 million in 2000; reduced management head count 30%; shrank inventories while simultaneously improving customer satisfaction; established controls to avoid the chronic inventory shortages which had plagued the company.
- Introduced JIT and Kanban while promoting a union-free, multiracial environment.

Excelled in this "track record" of promotion within the General Electric Corporation, and then within Baylor Industries, a $7 billion company which acquired General Electric's $1.1 billion electrical control and distribution business:

PLANT MANAGER. Baylor Industries, Sheraton, GA (1994-00). Directed the plant during its period of greatest growth; **sales increased by 25% annually, from $83 million in 1994 to $148 million in 2000.** Managed 800 employees, eight sites assembling electrical motor control products, $4.5 million in annual capital investments, and an expense budget of $85 million.

- Introduced two new major product lines representing $115 million in sales.
- Implemented multiple marketing expert systems which reduced cycle times 50% while improving total quality; also introduced JIT II.
- Planned and implemented the consolidation of businesses from five locations to one without the loss of any major customers.
- Profitably invested $6 million in quality and productivity improvements which included advanced robotics, computer, phone, and other productivity equipment.
- Profitably outsourced shipping, logistics, mail, document management, and network maintenance functions previously performed internally.
- Reduced inventory by $2 million (25%) through Kanban, cycle-time improvements, fewer suppliers, and product rationalization; gained ISO 9002 certification.

PLANT MANAGER. General Electric Corporation, Dawson, GA (1988-94). Transformed an unprofitable business into a profitable one in my first year of managing this troubled plant; then **grew sales from $52 million to $82 million** over six years while growing market share by 19% and increasing price realization to become #2 in the market.

PRODUCT LINE MANAGER. General Electric Corporation, Philadelphia, PA (1981-88). Introduced product lines representing $40 million in investment and developed strategies including product migration and rationalization to increase market share.

- Changed customer base from OEM to dealer, which increased operating profit 20%; also shifted the sales channel from corporate direct to independent manufacturer's representatives, which reduced selling expenses by $500,000.
- In previous jobs with General Electric, excelled in **technical sales** and **customer service.**

EDUCATION	**B.S. in Industrial Engineering**, Virginia Tech, Blacksburg, VA. Postgraduate courses in management, marketing, finance, and accounting at George Washington University, University of Dallas, University of Virginia, and Michigan State.

Date

Exact Name of Person
Title or Position
Name of Company
Address (no., street)
Address (city, state, zip)

CONSTRUCTION FOREMAN

Dear Exact Name of Person (or Dear Sir or Madam if answering a blind ad):

Can you use a resourceful young professional with extensive operations and project management experience along with a "track record" of outstanding results in safety, cost reduction, and other areas?

As you will see from my resume, I am currently excelling as a project manager/ foreman for a multimillion-dollar company operating all over the east coast. My results in 1995 have been impressive; I have greatly exceeded my targeted 20% profit margin by actually performing 32% above profit while finishing all jobs within or ahead of schedule and with no accidents.

In both my current job and in a previous job as Manager of Operations with a major fire prevention company working under contract to GE, IBM, and other industrial giants, I have acquired expert knowledge of OSHA, EPA, and other regulations. I have been trained and certified by OSHA in soil testing and I have worked closely with OSHA officials regarding HAZMAT, MSDS, and other areas.

I am particularly proud of the contributions I have made to my employers in the areas of cost reduction. On numerous occasions I have discovered ways to free up working capital by decreasing inventory carrying costs, automating manual functions, and monitoring everyday activities to find new ways to streamline operations and decrease both overhead and variable costs.

You would find me in person to be a congenial individual who prides myself on my ability to get along well with people at all levels. I can provide excellent references from all previous employers, including from my current company.

I hope you will write or call me soon to suggest a time when we might meet to discuss your current and future goals and how I might help you achieve them. Thank you in advance for your time.

Sincerely yours,

Jake M. North

Alternate last paragraph:
I hope you will welcome my call soon to arrange a brief meeting at your convenience to discuss your current and future needs and how I might serve them. Thank you in advance for your time.

JAKE M. NORTH

1110½ Hay Street, Fayetteville, NC 28305　　•　　preppub@aol.com　　•　　(910) 483-6611

OBJECTIVE　　To benefit an organization that can use a skilled operations manager who offers extensive knowledge of OSHA requirements, indepth experience in project management and cost/inventory control, as well as expertise in recruiting, training, and managing personnel.

EDUCATION　　**B.S. degree in Business Administration**, Temple University, Ambler, PA, 1995.
- Concentrated in courses in Finance, Management, and Human Resources.

CERTIFICATION　　Trained and certified by OSHA in soil testing; have worked closely with OSHA and am very familiar with OSHA, EPA, and other safety guidelines.

EXPERIENCE　　**FOREMAN/PROJECT MANAGER.** Framingham Construction, Framingham, TX (2001-present). Am being groomed for further promotion by this multimillion-dollar company which operates in states from GA, across to FL, and into VA; manage projects which involve laying utility lines, erecting overhead lines, and installing transformer boxes in commercial and industrial projects such as factories, shopping malls, and large-scale housing developments.
- Am considered one of the company's most knowledgeable managers on OSHA.
- Work with representatives of all the building trades while essentially operating as a profit center; in the past year, exceeded my goal of producing a 20% profit margin by actually performing 32% above profit.
- Operate backhoe and boom truck; read blueprints; perform all terminating in hot boxes.
- Finished all jobs on time or early while establishing a perfect safety record of no accidents on the projects I managed.

ASSISTANT OF OPERATIONS. Joseph & Feiss, Utica, NY (1999-01). Made impressive contributions to this company which moved its manufacturing facilities to lower-cost Mexico.
- For this company which manufactures expensive men's suits, worked side-by-side with the Operations Manager; personally discovered an overordering bias and made changes which reduced excess inventory by $150,000 per year.
- For more than 500 employees, established production schedules, assured optimum use of production capacity, and coordinated raw materials and labor.
- Developed a computer program which significantly improved inventory control.

MANAGER OF OPERATIONS. Caution Equipment, Waterville, NY (1995-99). Shortly after college graduation, excelled in a position which was created for me by this fast-growing company; rapidly automated all office communication and thereby greatly improved overall decision making and the working relationships among sales, personnel, transportation, administrative, and other personnel.
- Played a key role in obtaining the first million-dollar sale for this fire prevention company working under contract to IBM, GE, and major wire manufacturers.
- Prudently reduced a $1 million excess inventory to a safe $300,000 level.
- On my own initiative, established excellent working relationships with OSHA and authored company policy/procedures related to HAZMAT, MSDS, and other areas; assured that company vehicles met DOT standards for carrying Halon.
- Monitored policies and procedures in all company areas, from personnel training to safety management, in order to identify new ways to improve efficiency and lower costs.
- Directed inventory and warehouse stock control, warehousing, sales order entry, customer service, traffic and shipping, and other areas.

PERSONAL　　Strong negotiator; skills in assets management, budget planning, cost control, problem solving.

Date

Exact Name of Person
Exact Title
Exact Name of Company
Address
City, State, Zip

CONSTRUCTION FOREMAN

Dear Exact Name of Person (or Dear Sir or Madam if answering a blind ad):

With the enclosed resume, I would like to make you aware of my interest in exploring employment opportunities with your organization and introduce you to my skills as a foreman.

Since high school I have worked as a Foreman for a Nebraska-based company, HCI, which handles projects all over the U.S. Within the company, I have primarily worked as a foreman on projects which involve the creation of Gray's stores in existing malls. Responsible for demolition through completion, I have become skilled at finding resourceful ways to stay on schedule despite encountering numerous problems due to faulty specifications on blueprints and in site surveys. **"Keeping on schedule in my specialty!"** I am accustomed to working on a bonus system in which I have to maintain labor hours within a budget, and **I have always been under budget and have always received a bonus on every project.**

I am proud of my safety record. **I have never had an injury on any of my sites.** I grew up in a construction family since my father owned a construction company, so I was trained in various construction crafts at an early age. While on site, I have a hands-on style and always wear my pouch, working alongside the tradesmen. I have become skilled at resolving disputes among the various building craftsmen, and I have trained many other foremen for my employer.

If you can use a dedicated, safety-conscious young foreman to enhance your bottom-line results, I hope you will contact me to suggest a time when we might discuss your needs. I can provide excellent references at the appropriate time, but I would appreciate your not contacting my current employer until after we talk. Thank you in advance for your time.

Yours sincerely,

Hayden Jeffries

HAYDEN JEFFRIES

1110½ Hay Street, Fayetteville, NC 28305　　•　　preppub@aol.com　　•　　(910) 483-6611

OBJECTIVE　　I want to benefit an organization that can use an experienced young construction foreman who offers an excellent track record of results based on my ability to control costs, coordinate with others, and bring projects in on time and within budget.

EDUCATION　　Graduated from Axtell High School, Axtell, NE, 1998.

EXPERIENCE　　**1999-present: Since graduation from high school, have worked for one company, and can provide outstanding personal and professional references at the appropriate time:**
CONSTRUCTION FOREMAN. XYZ, a Nebraska company doing business all over the U.S. Work on projects on which I am the foreman on 5,200-square-foot projects in retail malls where my company is in charge of layout, frame, and the finished package. Worked on six-week projects in locations including Chattanooga, TN; Kennesaw, GA; Lincoln, NE; Salt Lake City, UT; Provo, UT; Lubbock, TX; and other cities. In each city, I supervise up to 40 people on a job and up to 12 people on any one day.
- Am in charge of the construction of Gray's stores, which merchandise upscale clothing, at locations in existing malls; am responsible for demolition through completion of the project.
- Recruit and hire tradespeople, as needed; on the job sites, manage all tradespeople and craftsmen including blocklayers, drywallers, framers, carpenters, masons and concrete workers, plumbers, heating and electrical technicians, pipefitters, and others.
- Train new foremen on matters related to scheduling, layout, dispute resolution, materials ordering, as well as contracting and subcontracting.
- Wear my pouch at all times while on the job and have a hands-on management style of working alongside the technical tradesmen; am skilled and cross-trained in numerous technical construction areas.
- Frequently resolve problems due to faulty specifications on blueprints and in site surveys; coordinate with inspectors and mechanical engineers as well as the corporate office.
- Have become skilled in identifying errors in load calculations and in figuring out resourceful methods of staying on schedule despite design problems which cause delays. **"Keeping on schedule is my specialty."**
- Learned to resolve conflicts among tradespeople when they have to be in the same area at the same time.
- Am accustomed to working on a bonus system in which I have to maintain labor hours within a budget; **have always been under budget and always received a bonus on every project.**
- Am highly safety conscious: **have never had an injury on a work site.**

Other experience: Grew up in a construction family since my dad owned a construction company; was trained in various trades when I was a youth, and have an in-depth understanding of the "nuts and bolts" of the construction business.

PERSONAL　　My strengths are my scheduling ability and my quality control skills.

Exact Name of Person
Title or Position
Name of Company
Address (no., street)
Address (city, state, zip)

CONSTRUCTION
FOREMAN

Dear Exact Name of Person: (or Dear Sir or Madam if answering a blind ad)

Can you use a resourceful professional with extensive operations and project management experience along with a "track record" of outstanding results in safety, cost reduction, and other areas?

As you will see from my resume, I am currently excelling as a project manager and foreman for a multimillion-dollar company operating all over the east coast. My results have been impressive; I have greatly exceeded my targeted 20% profit margin by actually performing 32% above profit while finishing all jobs within or ahead of schedule and with no accidents.

As Manager of Operations with a major fire prevention company working under contract to GE, IBM, and other industrial giants, I have acquired expert knowledge of OSHA, EPA, and other regulations. I have been certified by OSHA in soil testing and have worked with OSHA officials regarding HAZMAT and MSDS.

I am particularly proud of the contributions I have made in the areas of cost reduction. On numerous occasions I have discovered ways to free up working capital by decreasing inventory carrying costs, automating manual functions, and monitoring everyday activities to find new ways to streamline operations and decrease both overhead and variable costs.

You would find me in person to be a congenial individual who prides myself on my ability to get along well with people at all levels. I can provide excellent references from all previous employers, including from my current company.

I hope you will write or call me soon to suggest a time when we might meet to discuss your current and future goals and how I might help you achieve them. Thank you in advance for your time.

Sincerely yours,

Napoleon Radosevich

NAPOLEON RADOSEVICH

1110½ Hay Street, Fayetteville, NC 28305 • preppub@aol.com • (910) 483-6611

OBJECTIVE   To benefit an organization that can use a skilled operations manager who offers extensive knowledge of OSHA requirements, in-depth experience in project management and cost/inventory control, as well as expertise in recruiting, training, and managing personnel.

EXPERIENCE   **CONSTRUCTION FOREMAN.** B&K Construction, Roanoke, VA (1994-present). Am being groomed for further promotion by this multimillion-dollar company which operates in states from WA, across to CA, and into Canada; manage projects which involve laying utility lines, erecting overhead lines, and installing transformer boxes in commercial/industrial projects such as factories, shopping malls, and large-scale housing developments.
- Am considered one of the company's most knowledgeable managers on OSHA.
- Work with representatives of all the building trades while essentially operating as a profit center; in the past year, exceeded my goal of producing a 20% profit margin by actually performing 32% above profit.
- Finished all jobs on time or early while establishing a perfect safety record of no accidents.

ASSISTANT OPERATIONS MANAGER. Brooks Brothers, Utica, NY (1991-93). Made impressive contributions to this company which, upon the ratification of NAFTA in 1993, immediately moved its manufacturing facilities to lower-cost Mexico.
- For this company which manufactures expensive men's suits, worked side-by-side with the Operations Manager; personally discovered an over- ordering bias and made changes which reduced excess inventory by $150,000 per year.
- For more than 500 employees, established production schedules, assured optimum use of production capacity, and coordinated raw materials and labor.
- Played a key role in developing a computer program which improved inventory control.

MANAGER OF OPERATIONS. Caution Equipment, Waterville, NY (1988-91). Shortly after college graduation, excelled in a position which was created for me by this fast-growing company; rapidly automated all office communication and thereby greatly improved overall decision making and the working relationships among sales, personnel, transportation, administrative, and other personnel.
- Played a key role in obtaining the first million-dollar sale for this fire prevention company working under contract to IBM, GE, and major wire manufacturers.
- Prudently reduced a $1 million excess inventory to a safe $300,000 level.
- On my own initiative, established excellent working relationships with OSHA and authored company policy/procedures related to HAZMAT, MSDS, and other areas; assured that company vehicles met DOT standards for carrying Halon.
- Monitored policies and procedures in all company areas, from personnel training to safety management, in order to identify new ways to improve efficiency and lower costs.
- Directed inventory and warehouse stock control, warehousing, and traffic and shipping.

MANAGER OF PERSONNEL. Tele-Tector of Montgomery County, Plymouth Meeting, PA (1983-88). Left this 40-person security alarm company where I worked while in high school and college when the owner sold it to Wells Fargo; after beginning in an entry-level job, advanced to handle the development and management of personnel policies and programs

EDUCATION   **B.S. degree in Business Administration**, Temple University, Ambler, PA, 1987.
- Concentrated in courses in Finance, Management, and Human Resources.

CERTIFICATION   Have been trained and certified by OSHA in soil testing; have worked closely with OSHA and am very familiar with OSHA, EPA, and other safety guidelines.

PERSONAL   Offer an ability to use computers to solve management problems. Excellent references.

Exact Name of Person
Title or Position
Name of Company
Address (no., street)
Address (city, state, zip)

**CONSTRUCTION
MANAGER**

Dear Exact Name of Person (or Dear Sir or Madam if answering a blind ad):

With the enclosed resume, I would like to initiate the process of exploring employment opportunities in your organization.

As you will see from my resume, I am an experienced construction manager with extensive experience in hospital environments and health care facilities. I have managed multimillion-dollar contracts while supervising craftsmen in all construction trades. I am especially respected for my ability to bring projects in on time and within budget.

In recent projects, I have supervised the construction of new patient towers, directed construction of new health care facilities, and managed renovation of existing facilities with minimum disruption of medical center operations.

You would find me in person to be a congenial individual who prides myself on my ability to get along well with people at all levels. I can provide excellent references from all previous employers, including from my current company.

I hope you will write or call me soon to suggest a time when we might meet to discuss your current and future goals and how I might help you achieve them. Thank you in advance for your time.

Sincerely yours,

Dennis R. Plant

DENNIS R. PLANT

1110½ Hay Street, Fayetteville, NC 28305 • preppub@aol.com • (910) 483-6611

OBJECTIVE

To offer a background of 18 years experience in construction including six in construction management and eight in health care facility construction projects with proven strengths in inspiring the confidence and trust of others and effective negotiating skills.

TRAINING

Completed training leading to certification in the following areas:

OSHA Construction Safety and Health

Contracting for Professional Services

Mechanical Blueprinting

ITT Cable Repair

EXPERIENCE

CONSTRUCTION MANAGER. Folsom Medical Center, Folsom, SC (2000-present). Completed construction and renovation projects while taking care of operational aspects including preparing cost estimates, preparing and monitoring schedules for in-house projects, and overseeing quality control to ensure the highest quality workmanship.

- Enhanced my knowledge of JCAHO (Joint Commission on Accreditation for Health-Care Organizations), DFS (Division of Facility Services), and Interim Life Safety.
- Evaluated and approved/disapproved design changes; recommended cost reductions.
- Resolved complex contract issues in close cooperation with architects and engineers.

Completed projects for Crayford, Inc. (1996-2000) at the Folsom Medical Center, Folsom, SC:
SITE MANAGER. (1999-00). Oversaw the $19 million project to construct a 187,000-sq. ft. four-story Patient Services Tower (with full mechanical basement) which housed eight operating rooms, intensive care units, fifteen LDR, three delivery rooms, a coffee shop, pharmacy, and additional support services.

- Coordinated daily field activities of individual prime contractors while also reviewing contractor quotes and monthly billings.
- Handled the resolution of design and coordination conflicts, monitored contract compliance, and provided quality control oversight.
- Participated in project scheduling, job progress meetings, and monitored safety.

SITE MANAGER. (1998-99). Managed a contract to build a $5.5 million two-floor 31,000-sq. ft. vertical expansion of an existing six-floor patient tower complete with an 8,000-sq. ft. penthouse mechanical room; the project also included adding two elevators and renovating four existing elevators to serve the two new floors.

SITE MANAGER. (1997). Directed the construction of a $3.2 million, 15,000-sq. ft. Central Energy Plant which housed boilers, chillers, cooling towers, pumps, emergency generators, and other major mechanical and electrical equipment capable of servicing the existing South Patient Tower and future Patient Service Tower.

PROJECT SUPERINTENDENT. (1996). Provided managerial support in areas including the following: documentation, review and awarding of subcontracts, supervision of an adequate work force, scheduling, quality control, inspection, monitoring safety compliance, and ensuring contract compliance.

- Completed the following projects in various states: 27,000-sq. ft. expansion and 3,700-sq. ft. Linear Accelerator addition to a medical office building; 4,200-sq. ft. cat scan and ophthalmology addition.

Highlights of earlier experience: As a Project Superintendent for XYZ Construction Company in Dallas, TX. Completed numerous commercial construction projects with individual job costs between $250,000 and $1.5 million.

Date

Exact Name of Person
Title or Position
Name of Company
Address (no., street)
Address (city, state, zip)

**CONSTRUCTION
MANAGER**   Dear Exact Name:

I would appreciate an opportunity to talk with you soon about how I could contribute to The Mayo Clinic. I am responding to your ad for a Construction Manager with this *confidential* resume and cover letter to express my interest in receiving your consideration for this position.

As you will see from my enclosed resume, I offer approximately 18 years of progressively increasing responsibility in construction management with the specialized knowledge in a hospital environment that you require.

I would like to point out that I am experienced in working within JCAHO (Joint Commission on Accreditation of Healthcare Organizations), DFS (Division of Facility Services), and Interim Life Safety guidelines through my extensive background in construction management in a hospital environment.

Known for my dedication to high quality and compliance with safety standards, I have always been effective in supervising projects and seeing that work is completed on schedule.

I hope you will welcome my call soon to arrange a brief meeting at your convenience to discuss the current and future needs of The Mayo Clinic and how I might serve them. Thank you in advance for your time. I can provide outstanding references.

Sincerely yours,

Christopher Oxendine

CHRISTOPHER OXENDINE

1110½ Hay Street, Fayetteville, NC 28305 • preppub@aol.com • (910) 483-6611

OBJECTIVE

To offer a background of 18 years experience in construction including six in construction management and eight in healthcare facility construction projects with proven strengths in inspiring the confidence and trust of others and effective negotiating skills.

TRAINING

Currently enrolled in an AUTO CAD V-12 class, Wake County Technical Community College.
- Completed training leading to certification in the following areas:
  OSHA Construction Safety and Health
  Mechanical Blueprinting
  Institute of Government Contracting for Professional Services: ITT Cable Repair

EXPERIENCE

CONSTRUCTION MANAGER. Duke University Hospital, Durham, NC (2000-present). Completed construction and renovation projects while taking care of operational aspects including preparing cost estimates, preparing and monitoring schedules for in-house projects, and overseeing quality control to ensure the highest quality workmanship; manage dozens of skilled tradesmen.
- Further enhanced my knowledge of JCAHO (Joint Commission on Accreditation for Healthcare Organizations), DFS (Division of Facility Services), and Interim Life Safety.
- Evaluated and approved design changes; made recommendations that reduced costs.
- Applied communication skills as liaison among administration, staff, and architects as well as while working closely with staff members to coordinate in-house projects.

Completed numerous projects for Bechtel Corporation, San Francisco, CA (1990-2000):
SUPERINTENDENT. (1998-00). Oversaw the $19 million project to construct a 187,000-sq. ft. four-story Patient Services Tower (with full mechanical basement) which housed eight operating rooms, intensive care units, fifteen LDRs, three delivery rooms, a coffee shop, pharmacy, and additional support services.
- Coordinated field activities of contractors while reviewing contractor quotes and billings.
- Handled the resolution of design and coordination conflicts, monitored contract compliance, and provided quality control oversight.
- Maintained contact with architects and engineers; completed project documentation.
- Prepared and maintained correspondence with the owner, architect, and contractors.
- Participated in project scheduling, job progress meetings, and monitored safety.

SUPERINTENDENT. (1995-97). Managed a contract to build a $5.5 million two-floor 31,000-sq. ft. vertical expansion of an existing six-floor patient tower complete with an 8,000-sq. ft. penthouse mechanical room; the project also included adding two elevators and renovating four existing elevators to serve the two new floors.

SUPERINTENDENT. (1990-94). Directed the construction of a $3.2 million, 15,000-sq. ft. Central Energy Plant which housed boilers, chillers, cooling towers, pumps, emergency generators, and other major mechanical and electrical equipment capable of servicing the existing South Patient Tower and future Patient Service Tower.

PROJECT FOREMAN. Lawrence Kaplan and Associates, Madison, WI (1988-90). Provided managerial support in areas including the following: documentation, review and awarding of subcontracts, supervision of an adequate work force, scheduling, quality control, inspection, monitoring safety compliance, and ensuring contract compliance.
- Completed these projects: 27,000-sq. ft. expansion and 3,700-sq. ft. Linear Accelerator addition to a medical office building; 4,200-sq. ft. cat scan and ophthalmology addition.

PERSONAL

Offer computer experience with Word and the Windows operating system.

Date

Exact Name of Person
Title or Position
Name of Company
Address (no., street)
Address (city, state, zip)

CONSTRUCTION PROJECT COORDINATOR

Dear Exact Name of Person (or Dear Sir or Madam if answering a blind ad):

I would appreciate an opportunity to talk with you soon about my desire to contribute to your organization through my background and experience related to construction quality control and project management.

As you will see by my resume, I am presently working as a Project Coordinator on one of the world's largest American military bases. After excelling as a Quality Control Manager, I advanced to this job which involves representing a management company throughout the processes of contract negotiations, planning and coordinating arrangements for all phases of construction projects, and seeing them through to satisfactory completion. A versatile and adaptable professional, I offer hands-on experience with construction, waste water treatment, beautification, and other types of projects.

I offer a solid background in the construction industry dating from my six years in the U.S. Navy where I refined my supervisory and managerial expertise, as well as my technical skills in computer operations and heavy equipment handling. My reputation for sound judgment, a strong work ethic, and well-developed one-on-one communication skills has been earned while advancing to manage crews of up to 25 employees in multifaceted projects.

In almost every position I have been involved in enforcing and teaching safety which has resulted in fewer and less serious accidents. My communication skills have also been applied while instructing heavy construction operation and tile-setting techniques.

I hope you will welcome my call soon to arrange a brief meeting at your convenience to discuss your current and future needs and how I might serve them. Thank you in advance for your time.

Sincerely yours,

Richard A. Martinez

Alternate last paragraph:
I hope you will call or write me soon to suggest a time convenient for us to meet and discuss your current and future needs and how I might serve them. Thank you in advance for your time.

RICHARD A. MARTINEZ

1110½ Hay Street, Fayetteville, NC 28305 • preppub@aol.com • (910) 483-6611

OBJECTIVE

I want to offer my broad base of experience related to the construction industry to an organization that can benefit from my knowledge of project management and quality control as well as from my superior communication, motivational, and technical skills.

EDUCATION

B.S., Construction Management, East Carolina University, Greenville, NC, 1998. Excelled in specialized training including a 40-hour OSHA (Occupational Safety and Health Administration) safety course and other programs on power-activated tools, computer applications unique to the construction industry, and construction management.

EXPERIENCE

Excelled in these two jobs with Wilson Management Services, Inc., Ft. Bragg, NC:
PROJECT COORDINATOR. (2000-present). Representing the company as liaison with government project managers, am in charge of preparing proposals and negotiating arrangements and then overseeing projects through to completion.
- Maintained productive working relationships with military representatives and quickly gained their respect for my professional knowledge.
- Located proper subcontractors for each phase of the job and coordinated operations.

QUALITY CONTROL MANAGER. (1998-00). Advanced from this position which involved ensuring the safety and quality of all phases of construction projects; saw that work was done according to specifications and coordinated the submission of shop drawings.
- Demonstrated my ability to manage multifaceted projects to completion.

QUALITY CONTROL SUPERVISOR, WASTE WATER PROJECT. Cherry Point Construction, Cherry Point, NC (1997-98). Coordinated with Navy personnel as the representative for quality control and safety on a waste water treatment project; became very familiar with OSHA safety requirements.

BEAUTIFICATION PROJECTS SUPERVISOR. Thomas Farm, Greenville, NC (1995-97). Developed the strategy for various beautification projects on a 275-acre estate and supervised work crews engaged in different aspects of operations.
- Planned and coordinated the installation of an "environmentally friendly" drainage system for an underground sprinkler system.

CARPENTER. Holiday Construction, Cherry Point, NC (1993-95). Supervised an eight-person crew building military housing units.

CONSTRUCTION OPERATIONS SUPERVISOR. U.S. Navy, Port Hueneme, CA (1988-93). Planned, developed, and carried out construction projects including such aspects as manpower utilization, cost estimates, and personnel supervision.
- Provided guidance on safety aspects of job performance.
- Supervised a 12-person rock crushing operation and a builder's shop.
- Became licensed to operate a variety of heavy equipment:

water trucks — up to 2,000 gals.	front-end loaders	trucks — up to 10-ton
dump trucks — 20-ton dumps	rock crushers	bulldozers

COMPUTERS

Offer a solid background in most engineering and construction-oriented software.

PERSONAL

Described as an industrious professional with superior technical skills and work ethic.

Grant Construction Company
P.O. Box 9471
Charlotte, NC 28299-9471

CONSTRUCTION
SUPERINTENDENT

Dear Sir or Madam:

I would appreciate an opportunity to talk with you soon about how I could contribute to your organization through my extensive expertise as a construction superintendent on both residential and commercial jobs.

As you will see from my resume, I have been involved in construction activities ranging from building custom staircases, to building bank vaults and churches, to building decks and sun rooms. I am comfortable supervising workers on both residential and commercial construction jobs, and I have earned a reputation as a skilled supervisor of construction workers from every trade.

The owner of an extensive inventory of tools related to nearly every kind of construction job, I am knowledgeable of all the building codes and I have always developed an excellent working relationship with building inspectors.

You would find me in person to be an honest and reliable person whom you could count on to always get the job done, no matter what.

I hope you will call or write me soon to suggest a time when we might meet to discuss your current and future needs and how I might serve them. Thank you in advance for your time.

Sincerely yours,

Andy C. Axion

ANDY C. AXION

1110½ Hay Street, Fayetteville, NC 28305   •   preppub@aol.com   •   (910) 483-6611

OBJECTIVE

To contribute to an organization through my experience in supervising construction projects, my thorough knowledge of all building codes, as well as my versatile expertise in numerous kinds of custom building and remodeling activities.

TECHNICAL SKILLS

Offer "hands-on" experience in remodeling offices/houses and in building the following:
New houses ranging in price from $75,000 to $225,000.
Metal buildings ranging from 2,000 square feet to 16,000 square feet

Custom staircases	Cabinets of all types	A 25,000-sq.-ft freezer
A bank vault	A new church	Warehouses
A 10,000-sq.-ft loading dock	Numerous decks and sun rooms	

TOOLS

Have my own extensive inventory of tools for nearly every type of construction job.

EXPERIENCE

CONSTRUCTION SUPERINTENDENT. Self-employed, Dunn, NC (2000-present). Have established an excellent reputation as an honest and reliable construction superintendent while building houses in the $75,000 to 225,000 price range and handling a wide variety of repair and remodeling and maintenance jobs on existing residential and commercial construction.
- Built specialty items including a 25,000-sq. ft. freezer in five-degrees-below-zero weather.
- Operated all types of construction equipment ranging from a crane to a backhoe.
- Became skilled in jobs that required specialty concrete pouring: while building a bank vault, poured a concrete 12" floor, walls, and roof.
- Have become an expert in building custom staircases.
- Am known for my ability to get along well with subcontractors, and have learned how to motivate and manage them in such a way that the job is accomplished in the most cost-effective and quality-conscious way.
- Have supervised as many as 12 subcontractors working simultaneously on a job.

CONSTRUCTION FOREMAN. XYZ Builders, Charlotte, NC (1995-00). Was the foreman for a company which specialized in remodeling jobs.
- Was frequently involved in supervising the building of new construction; built three main banks.
- Built a church from start to finish; was commended for the artistic baptistry I constructed.
- Supervised between 8 to 15 people.

WELDER. Steel Works, Inc., Marquette, MI (1990-95). Worked frequently in weather that was 13 degrees below zero; often performed welding while working 200 feet up in the air on a swing scaffold.

SECURITY POLICEMAN. U.S. Air Force, Wichita, KS, and Shaw AFB, SC (1985-89). As a military policeman, improved my communication and public relations skills while performing investigations, patrolling roads, and upholding the law generally.

EDUCATION

Graduated from high school in Michigan in industrial arts; studied accounting for two years at a technical college; completed extensive studies on my own initiative in building.

PERSONAL

Construction skills include framing, footings, painting, roofing, wiring, and plumbing.

Date

Exact Name of Person
Exact Title
Exact Name of Company
Address
City, State, Zip

**CONSTRUCTION
SUPERINTENDENT**

Dear Exact Name of Person (or Dear Sir or Madam if answering a blind ad):

With the enclosed resume, I would like to make you aware of my interest in exploring employment opportunities with your organization and introduce you to my skills as a construction superintendent.

As you will see from my resume, I have recently excelled as superintendent of two projects for K.L. Smith Construction. In April 2002, I took over the management of a construction project for a new Kroger grocery store in Tennessee which was six weeks behind schedule. After taking over, I assured that we met all schedule dates, and the store opened as originally expected. I was credited with rescuing the project and preventing my employer from being replaced by a competing firm. In a subsequent project, I took over the management of a Food Lion renovation which was behind schedule and over budget, and I have managed its on-time completion and restored the customer's confidence in my employer.

In previous experience, I have worked as a Field Superintendent on a restaurant, as Assistant Superintendent on a shopping center, and as a Journeyman Carpenter on a historic renovation project. I am skilled at managing every type of trade professional, and I am considered a highly professional carpenter in my own right. I have become skilled at finding resourceful ways to keep a project on time and within budget, and I am known for my emphasis on safety at all times.

If you can use a dedicated, safety-conscious construction superintendent to enhance your bottom-line results, I hope you will contact me to suggest a time when we might discuss your needs. I can provide excellent references, but I would appreciate your not contacting my current employer until after we talk. I am mobile and will relocate according to your needs. Thank you in advance for your time.

Yours sincerely,

Nicklaus Dover

NICKLAUS DOVER

1110½ Hay Street, Fayetteville, NC 28305　•　preppub@aol.com　•　(910) 483-6611

OBJECTIVE　To benefit an organization that can use an experienced commercial construction superintendent who offers a proven ability to manage all categories of trades professionals while also supervising on-time and within-budget project completion.

EDUCATION　Courses in blueprint reading, concrete technologies, and construction management at various technical colleges.
Extensive management and technical training, U.S. Air Force.

EXPERIENCE　**CONSTRUCTION SUPERINTENDENT.** K.L.Smith Construction Company, Inc., GA and TN (2002-present). Have performed as Construction Superintendent for this company on two different jobs:
10/02-present: Lillington, GA. Oversee 35 people in all trades while scheduling, coordinating, and supervising the addition to and renovation of Food Lion #495.
- As a highly skilled carpenter, assured expert carpentry during every phase of renovation.
- Took over the management of a job which was behind schedule and over budget, and have kept my company from being replaced by a competing firm.

4/02-10/02: Murfreesboro, TN. Oversaw up to 70 people in all the trades while scheduling, coordinating, and overseeing all phases and aspects of the construction of Kroger #539.
- Took over a job which was six weeks behind schedule and met all schedule dates; opened the store as originally scheduled, and kept my employer from being replaced.

MANUFACTURING TECHNICIAN. Maytag Cleveland, Cleveland, TN (1996-01). For a manufacturing facility which employs 2,250 people, advanced in a track record of promotion to Oven Cell Technician from Automatic Press Operator, Automatic Press Helper, and Conventional Press Helper.
- Skillfully operated an overhead gantry crane, two separate 500-ton presses, an 800-ton press, and a one-of-a-kind cavity-automated weld line; learned to troubleshoot and repair weld line and parts stackers, including fiber optics and robotics.
- Operated a 300-ton steel stamping press producing quality parts; played a key role in assisting Die Engineering in changing its work methods to become a "one man automatic press" operation; advised technicians on scrap removal methods.
- Became skilled at tool and die troubleshooting operating a 500-ton steel stamping press.
- Gained extensive experience in inspection and quality control.

FIELD SUPERINTENDENT. X&Y Construction, Nashville, TN (6/95-9/95). Scheduled, coordinated, and oversaw construction of a new Bob Evans Farms Restaurant.

JOURNEYMAN CARPENTER. Manning Construction Company, Cleveland, TN (2/95-6/95). Worked as a Journeyman Carpenter on an historic renovation project in Chattanooga; recreated and remodeled a 138-year-old structure according to historic guidelines.

ASSISTANT SUPERINTENDENT. Smith Bros. Construction Co., Inc. (8/93-1/95). At an Athens, GA site, supervised the construction of a perimeter square shopping center while performing as Assistant Superintendent and Job Superintendent.

JOURNEYMAN CARPENTER. Nelson Co., Cleveland, TN (7/92-7/93). Performed journeyman carpentry duties.

PERSONAL　My strengths are my scheduling ability and my quality control skills.

CONSTRUCTION SUPERVISOR

Dear Sir:

With the enclosed resume, I would like to make you aware of my versatile background and of the experience and knowledge I can offer to an organization in need of a technically proficient and creative professional.

As you will see, I served with pride in the U.S. Army where I earned advancement to supervisory and leadership roles and excelled as an instructor, counselor, and mentor for my subordinates and peers. In every job I have held, I have quickly become recognized as a person who could take on any assignment or task and a find way to improve productivity, quality, and bottom-line profitability. Adjusting to rapidly changing priorities, schedules, and environments has also been a major factor in my success in implementing changes which bring about results.

One of the strong points I would like to emphasize is that I am an innovator who can work from blueprints, technical guidelines, or instructions but who also has a talent for improvising and finding solutions to any problems which occur or situations which require a fast and creative solution. As a professional soldier trained in the areas of airborne operations, jungle warfare, Ranger School, and as a sniper, I was a leader and pace setter in pressure-filled situations. Known for my personal integrity and honesty, I was entrusted with a Top Secret security clearance.

If you can use an experienced and mature professional with a high level of energy and enthusiasm, I hope you will contact me to suggest a time when we might meet to discuss your needs. I can assure you in advance that I could rapidly become an asset to your organization.

Sincerely,

Brian Donaldson

BRIAN DONALDSON

1110½ Hay Street, Fayetteville, NC 28305   •   preppub@aol.com   •   (910) 483-6611

OBJECTIVE

To offer technical skills and creativity along with the ability to follow blueprints or to improvise solutions which result in quality products while responding quickly.

EDUCATION

Completed over 100 credit hours of general studies, Liberty University, Lynchburg, VA, and Lincoln State University, UT.

Attended courses in residential/commercial wiring and air conditioning/refrigeration, Texas Central College; while serving in the U.S. Army, was selected to attend specialized schooling leading to certification in parachute freefall and jumpmaster techniques, Ranger school, jungle warfare, sniper school (honor graduate), and advanced leadership.

EXPERIENCE

LEAD INSTALLER. Holmes Heating and Air, Lincoln, UT (2002-present). Oversee a crew and personally install residential and commercial HVAC systems; conduct site surveys.

PARACHUTE RIGGER. Irvin Aerospace, Mills, UT (2001-02). Provided technical expertise for a project which was recently cancelled: followed blueprints while building and then installing satellite recovery systems which consisted of nine 156-ft. diameter parachutes.

SHOP FOREMAN. Lincoln Communications, Lincoln, UT (2000-2001). Oversaw all operational aspects of the wood shop for this busy local advertising and sign company; built a variety of wood specialty items, from redwood signs to furniture for the office.
- Demonstrated ability to construct wood furnishings from verbal descriptions alone.
- Supervised two shop workers; built signs from blueprints.

Earned a reputation as a skilled professional who could handle pressure and see to the details of completing any project on time and to high standards, U.S. Army:
CONSTRUCTION SUPERVISOR. Ft. Lewis, WA (1999-00). Recognized as a cost-conscious professional; ordered, tracked, and managed equipment and materials for numerous construction projects at a 400-student military training center for supervisory personnel.
- Researched and determined competitive prices for everything constructed, installed, or renovated at the school to include purchasing items from local civilian sources if their price and quality were better than items available through government channels.
- Utilized computerized systems to track equipment and material costs and man-hours.
- Supervised teams working at different construction sites simultaneously.

OPERATIONS SUPERVISOR and **SENIOR INSTRUCTOR.** Ft. Lewis, WA (1998-99). Handpicked for this leadership role with dual areas of emphasis as an instructor/mentor and coordinator of plans for training, transportation, food and lodging, and airborne operations.
- Played a vital role in the development of new courses in land navigation and field training project planning and management.

SUPERVISOR FOR TRAINING AND OPERATIONS. Korea (1996). Was promoted to provide leadership in a headquarters company and advise on collective training issues for the 260-person organization; maintained training records. Earned this promotion based on my skills as leader of a sniper team (1995-96) which achieved increases in test scores as marksmen and in physical training.

PERSONAL

Certified FAA Senior Rigger/Static Line/Accelerated Freefall Jumpmaster. Class A CDL.

Exact Name of Person
Title or Position
Name of Company
Address (number and street)
Address (city, state, and zip)

CONTROLLER

An impressive background and a track record of exceptional results as shown on her resume ought to fetch numerous interviews.

Dear Exact Name of Person: (or Sir or Madam if answering a blind ad)

With the enclosed resume, I would like to formally make you aware of my interest in exploring employment opportunities within your organization.

As you will see from my resume, I have excelled in a variety of assignments which required outstanding accounting, customer service, and management skills. In my current position as Controller, I prepare monthly financial statements and year-end financials while also supervising ten people in the accounting department including an assistant controller as well as the MIS and accounts payable/receivable personnel. I wrote this 30-year-old company's first policies and procedures manual. While in control of $5 million in inventory, I developed procedures which led the company to process inventory by barcode at its nine locations.

In my prior job, I rose to Chief Financial Officer for a diversified corporation with holdings in the construction industry and restaurant business. For one of the company's divisions, I was personally responsible for leading the limited partnership's reorganization out of Chapter 11 bankruptcy and, after leading the company out of bankruptcy, the company posted a 7% net profit within the first year.

I am knowledgeable of software including Depreciation Solution, Computer Systems Dynamics (CSD) programs, and Microsoft Office 97. I have demonstrated my capabilities in operational areas including contract development and negotiation, debt structure reorganization, and information systems/data processing administration.

If you can use a hardworking professional with knowledge in numerous operational areas, I hope you will contact me to suggest a time when we might meet to discuss your needs and how I might serve them. I can provide outstanding personal and professional references. Thank you in advance for your time, and I would appreciate your holding my interest in your company in the strictest confidence at this point.

Yours sincerely,

Michelle Bazaldua

MICHELLE BAZALDUA

1110½ Hay Street, Fayetteville, NC 28305 • preppub@aol.com • (910) 483-6611

OBJECTIVE   To contribute to an organization that can use a skilled accounting professional with experience related to financial analysis and financial statement preparation, auditing, cash management, AR/AP, general ledger, payroll, collections, and automated systems.

EXPERIENCE   **CONTROLLER.** Quality Building Supply, Springfield, VA (2000-present). Prepare monthly financial statements and year-end financials while supervising ten people in the accounting department including an assistant controller, AP and AR personnel, and the MIS Director.
- For this 30-year-old company, wrote its first policies and procedures manual.
- Implemented new computer systems for automated payroll with swipe cards.
- Am in control of over $5 million in inventory; developed procedures in processing inventory by barcode for the company's nine locations.
- Implemented new software called CSD, a program for the building supply industry.

For The Jason G. Roth Company, was promoted from Controller to Chief Financial Officer, and worked in two main divisions of the company (1985-99):

1991-99: CHIEF FINANCIAL OFFICER & GENERAL MANAGER. Stone Mountain, GA.
- For a chain of three premier restaurants, was personally responsible for leading the limited partnership's reorganization out of Chapter 11 bankruptcy; personally renegotiated the company debt structure and reduced food, labor, and liquor costs by as much as 12% within six months.
- After leading the company out of bankruptcy, achieved a 7% net profit within the first year.
- Supervised all business operations at three establishments which employed more than 150 employees while producing annual sales of $4.6 million.
- Was the hands-on manager in charge of daily operations, marketing and promotions, purchasing, inventory control, and alcohol management.
- Was in charge of transition planning as the businesses were readied for sale to a new management team; directed the liquidation of assets not included in the sale.

1985-1991: CONTROLLER and PROPERTY & PROJECT MANAGER. Lester Springs, GA. For the Real Estate Development Division, oversaw on-site and off-site construction of new buildings and tenant improvements in addition to performing all financial and property management functions for 32 industrial properties valued at $128 million.
- Collaborated with the owner and architects during the preliminary planning stages of each project; took bids, awarded contracts, and provided oversight of the construction phase through completion.
- Marketed properties, negotiated leases, and handled all property management duties.
- Was in charge of all accounting for this entire real estate portfolio; in addition to managing investment instruments, negotiated secured/unsecured loans up to $41 million.
- Oversaw cash management, mortgage management, and auditing.
- Served as liaison to company attorneys and accountants.
- Supervised projects valued at $61 million, saving $1.2 million as general contractor.
- Generated more than $7 million in net profits through the careful management of company-owned stocks, bonds, and mutual funds.

ACCOUNT CLERK II. County of Siddell, In-Home Supportive Services, Siddell, GA (1982-85). Prepared regular financial reports for the State of Georgia while also reviewing, auditing, and approving grants valued at $10.8 million on a bimonthly basis.
- Initiated and implemented the county's first computerized Medicare issuance system.

EDUCATION   **Associate of Arts Degree in Accounting,** Hazelton Junior College, GA.

PERSONAL   Knowledgeable of software including Depreciation Solution, CSD, and Microsoft Office.

Date

Exact Name
Title or Position
Name of Company
Address (number and street)
Address (city, state, and zip)

Dear Exact Name of Person: (or Dear Sir or Madam if answering a blind ad)

If you want to job hunt in industries other than the one you're in, keep the Objective on your resume all purpose and versatile. Notice the Personal Section. Sometimes you can show off an accomplishment in the Personal Section which doesn't seem to fit in anywhere else on the resume. It may still be an accomplishment which could make the prospective employer react to you in a positive fashion.

With the enclosed resume, I would like to indicate my interest in your organization and my desire to explore employment opportunities.

As you will see from my enclosed resume, as Credit Manager of a large building supply company, I have played a key role in the growth of the company from two stores with sales of less than $15 million to five stores with more than $40 million in sales. I have been in charge of approving all new accounts for all stores, and I have implemented internal controls which have reduced the number of days of sales outstanding by more than 20 days. Although I am held in high regard by my current employer, the business is in the process of merging with a larger regional company, so I am taking this opportunity to explore opportunities with other area firms.

I hope you will welcome my call soon to arrange a brief meeting at your convenience to discuss your current and future needs and how I might serve them. Thank you in advance for your time.

Sincerely yours,

Phillip Harris

Alternate last paragraph:
I hope you will call or write me soon to suggest a time convenient for us to meet and discuss your current and future needs and how I might serve them. Thank you in advance for your time.

PHILLIP HARRIS

1110½ Hay Street, Fayetteville, NC 28305 • preppub@aol.com • (910) 483-6611

OBJECTIVE	To add value to an organization that can use a well-organized manager who is skilled in developing new systems and procedures for profitability enhancement, establishing new accounts and managing existing ones, and administering finances at all levels.
EDUCATION	**Bachelor of Science in Business Administration (B.S.B.A.) degree**, concentration in Finance, Western Tennessee University, 1991. • Member, Beta Kappa Alpha Banking and Finance Fraternity. • Was active in intramural softball, basketball, and arm wrestling. • Worked throughout college in order to finance my college education. Completed **A.I.B. in Consumer Lending,** Pitt Community College, 1996.
EXPERIENCE	**CREDIT MANAGER.** All Purpose Building Supply, Raleigh, NC (2000-present). Was specially recruited by the company to assume this position which involved establishing a credit department with three employees. • Played a key role in the growth of the company from two stores with sales of less than $15 million, to five stores with sales of more than $40 million. • Reduced the number of days of sales outstanding by 20+ days. • Was in charge of approving all new accounts for five stores. • Developed and maintained an excellent working relationship with all customers. • Formulated and implemented key areas of company policy by authoring credit policies; directed activities including account adjustments, skip tracing, liening, and billing. • Coordinated with the corporate attorney; prepared cash flow projections and provided the controller with financial information for profit-and-loss statements and balance sheets for the company owners. • Implemented procedures that lowered chargeoffs and increased collection activity while accounts receivables grew from $2 million to $7.5 million.

CONSUMER LOAN OFFICER. East Coast Federal Savings & Loan, Raleigh, NC (1996-00). Was promoted to responsibilities for handling activities in these areas:

commercial lending	consumer lending
collections	credit card approval
credit investigations	marketing of consumer loans

LOAN OFFICER & COLLECTION REPRESENTATIVE. NCNB National Bank of North Carolina, Raleigh, NC (1991-95). After excelling as a Collection Representative, was promoted to Loan Officer, in charge of lending money for consumer purchases and performing credit investigations.
- As a Collection Representative, collected past due accounts, cross-referenced bank records versus automobile dealerships' records, and investigated consumer account payment records while also handling foreclosures, repossessions, insurance claims, and skip tracing of delinquent accounts.
- Performed liaison with banking auditors and legal personnel.
- Gained expertise in all aspects of banking and lending.

SALESMAN/ACCOUNT REPRESENTATIVE. Premier Building Supply, Oakland, TN (1988-91). Worked at this construction industry supply company in the summers and breaks during the years when I was earning my college degree.
- Learned to deal with people while selling building materials, light fixtures, garden supplies, and hardware; graduated into responsibilities for handling major accounts.

PERSONAL   In high school was a member of the National Math Honor Society and the Science Club and set my school's record in the shot put while also excelling in football and wrestling.

Exact Name of Person
Title or Position
Name of Company
Address (no., street)
Address (city, state, zip)

ELECTRICIAN Dear Exact Name of Person (or Dear Sir or Madam if answering a blind ad):

I would appreciate an opportunity to talk with you soon about how I could contribute to your organization through my expertise related to installing, troubleshooting, and repairing electrical and electronic equipment and controls. I offer an outstanding reputation as a skilled troubleshooter and problem solver, and I can provide very strong personal and professional references.

As you will see from my enclosed resume, I currently work as a Maintenance Electrician. I am proficient in using programmable logic controller status indicators and a Unix computer system for monitoring and troubleshooting, and I have played a key role in minimizing costs through my expert ability to troubleshoot and repair plant equipment and systems including process controls, production machinery, and motor controls.

In a prior job as a Maintenance Electrician, I learned ladder relay logic and digital gate logic while also becoming proficient with programmable logic controllers. I am skilled in performing set-ups, adjustments, and repairs to mechanical, electrical, pneumatic, and hydraulic systems. In previous experience I excelled as an Electronics Technician with the U.S. Navy and was promoted ahead of my peers to management positions.

You would find me in person to be a congenial individual who works well independently and as part of a productive, motivated team.

I hope you will call or write me soon to suggest a time convenient for us to meet and discuss your current and future needs and how I might serve them. Thank you in advance for your time.

Sincerely yours,

Simon L. Sez

Alternate last paragraph:
I hope you will welcome my call soon to arrange a brief meeting at your convenience to discuss your current and future needs and how I might serve them.

SIMON L. SEZ

1110½ Hay Street, Fayetteville, NC 28305   •   preppub@aol.com   •   (910) 483-6611

OBJECTIVE   In the process of relocating to Delaware to join my wife, I am seeking employment with an organization that can use an Industrial Plant Mechanic or Electrician (Commercial or Residential) who can provide outstanding personal and professional references.

CERTIFICATIONS   Industrial Mechanic
Electrical Installer and Electrical Systems Maintenance

SKILLS   Experienced industrial plant maintenance mechanic with the ability to work within general instructions or guidelines while installing, maintaining, and repairing a variety of electrical machinery, systems, circuits, equipment and controls including:

lighting systems gauges & valves	actuators and motor controls
switches and breakers	paging systems
gear boxes & motor control centers	pumps, generators, & boilers
uninterrupted power supply	central air conditioning systems

- Interpret and use blueprints, wiring diagrams, engineering drawings, and building plans.
- Excellent working knowledge of the NEC.
- Am a licensed **Trencher Operator** (Ditch Witch) and **Forklift Operator**.
- Proficient in **welding:** Oxyacetylene, arc, heliarc, stainless/carbon steel, aluminum

EXPERIENCE   **ELECTRICIAN.** VA Medical Center, Laredo, TX (2000-present). Maintain and repair all electrical systems, office equipment, and small appliances throughout the Center including building service systems, i.e., 250 KW and 600 KW generators, lighting, ventilating and environmental systems, engineering services equipment, kitchen, canteen and laundry equipment.

- Maintain medical equipment including electric motors, lighting, infrared systems, hydraulic systems, air and fluid pumps, medical air and vacuum systems.
- Install and alter telephone and computer cable systems.

ELECTRICIAN. Colony Feed Products, Laredo, TX (1999). Was responsible for maintenance, repair, installation, troubleshooting, and alteration on electrical systems, machinery, motors, and circuits throughout compound of Colony Feed Products Company.

- Followed blueprints and wiring diagrams of starter controls and light circuits; replaced or repaired damaged electrical systems.
- Installed light sockets and power supply systems, switches, outlet boxes in/outdoor.
- Measured, cut, threaded, bent, and assembled/installed rigid conduit and armored cable nonmetallic cable which connected to various out motors/panel boxes.
- Inspected electrical systems to prevent deterioration and downtime of machinery.

INDUSTRIAL MECHANIC/ELECTRICIAN (SUPERVISOR). Barker Poultry, Laxton, NM (1996-98). Supervised eight maintenance personnel on the second and third shifts while serving as the only electrician on both shifts; maintained all electrical systems throughout the plant and was responsible for the entire production line.

- Inspected, maintained, and repaired electric motors and motor control centers on trolley lines, electric forklift trucks, and tow motors, including the drive gear boxes.
- Fabricated and welded machinery and parts.
- Installed conduit and wiring throughout the plant.

EDUCATION   *Midtown Technical Community College,* Laxton, NM.
Electrical Installation and Maintenance (76 hours); Industrial Mechanics (70 hours)

- Excelled academically and was named to President's List, 1995-96.

Exact Name of Person
Exact Title
Exact Name of Company
Address
City, State, Zip

ELECTRICIAN

Dear Exact Name of Person (or Dear Sir or Madam if answering a blind ad):

With the enclosed resume, I would like to make you aware of my interest in exploring employment opportunities with your organization as an electrician.

Experience as an electrician

I have worked on a variety of projects as an electrician. For several years, I have worked in full-time and part-time capacities for Pearson Construction on commercial, industrial, and residential properties. On a full-time assignment during 2001 and 2002, I worked as Top Electrician's Helper at the Baltimore Airport. I also worked on a project at the Port Authority in Baltimore and on projects at power plants, coal-fired plants, and steam plants.

Experience in HVAC

You will see from my resume that I offer six years of experience in heating, ventilating, and air conditioning (HVAC) work. From 1992-2000 I worked in the HVAC field, and I was promoted to Crew Leader in charge of three people. In that capacity I dealt with local inspectors and supervised projects from start to finish, from the initial cutting of holes, through installing trunk lines and pouring concrete, to complete wiring of units and related fixtures.

Excellent safety record and ability to pass background investigation

On two separate occasions, I have passed rigorous background investigations. I passed a rigorous 10-year background investigation in order to work as Top Electrician's Helper at the Baltimore International Airport. I also passed a rigorous background investigation prior to my employment as an Electronics Technician in the Radio Shop of the New Jersey Highway Patrol. I am a nonsmoker and nondrinker and have established an outstanding safety record in the HVAC field and in the electrical field.

If my background and skills interest you, I hope you will contact me to suggest a time when we could meet in person to discuss your needs. I can provide outstanding references at the appropriate time. Thank you.

Yours sincerely,

Nicholas Cage

NICHOLAS CAGE

1110½ Hay Street, Fayetteville, NC 28305 • preppub@aol.com • (910) 483-6611

OBJECTIVE
I want to contribute to an organization that can use a skilled electrician who offers an outstanding safety record along with experience in industrial, commercial, and residential properties.

LICENSES & CERTIFICATIONS
Universal Freon License.
New Jersey State Board of Refrigeration Examiners
Technician Certification: Type 1. Certification #NJ–444-5555
Air Conditioning Contractors of America
Technician Certification: Type II & Type III. Certification #4-44-4444
Fork Life Operator Authorization.

TECHNICAL SKILLS
Bucket trucks: Skilled in the operation of two types of bucket trucks: Bronco and Hi-Ranger.
Trenchers: Skilled in the operation of two types of trenchers: Vermeer and Ditch Witch.
Wiring: Knowledgeable of residential, industrial, and commercial electrical wiring practices.
- Proficient in installation and bending of all conduit types.
- Skilled in blueprint reading and scale applications. Experienced in installation and troubleshooting of lighting fixtures, receptacles, as well as fire and alarm system components.

Electronics knowledge: Experienced in installing, troubleshooting, and repairing devices such as:

Two-way radios	Automotive strobe lights	Hazard and safety lights
Radar units	Vascar computers	Scanners

HVAC (Heating, Ventilating, and Air Conditioning): Experienced in installing commercial and residential units, from start to finish, including package and split units.
- Offer six years of experience in HVAC; highly experienced in servicing and troubleshooting of nearly all types of units including controls such as thermostats and zone system dampers.

EDUCATION
Completed 1 ½ years of college, Medford Community College, Medford, NJ.
Graduated from Medford Senior High, Medford, NJ, 1992.

EXPERIENCE
ELECTRICIAN. Pearson Construction, Medford, NJ (2000-present). Work on a variety of commercial, industrial, and residential projects.
- Passed a rigorous 10-year background investigation in order to work on a project at the Port Authority in Baltimore, MD and at Baltimore International Airport.
- Was Top Electrician's Helper at the Baltimore International Airport, where we renovated a concourse and on projects at power plants, coal-fired plants, and steam plants.

ELECTRONICS TECHNICIAN. New Jersey Highway Patrol-Radio Shop, Medford, NJ (Sept 2000-May 2001). Passed a rigorous background investigation before employment.
- Repaired equipment and couplers, radars, scanners, and Vascar computers that measure the speed at which automobiles travel. Troubleshot stubborn electronics problems.

INSTALLATION TECHNICIAN & SHEETMETAL MECHANIC & CREW LEADER. Crawford Heating and Air, Medford, NJ (1992-2000). Was promoted to **Crew Leader** , and supervised three people while assigning and supervising work. Dealt with local inspectors.
- Supervised projects from start to finish, from initial cutting of holes, through installing trunk lines and pouring concrete, to complete wiring of units and related fixtures.

PERSONAL
Perfect safety record. Nonsmoker and nondrinker. Stable married individual. Excellent references.

Date

Exact Name of Person
Title or Position
Name of Company
Address (no., street)
Address (city, state, zip)

ELECTRICIAN Dear Exact Name of Person (or Dear Sir or Madam if answering a blind ad):

I would appreciate an opportunity to talk with you soon about how I could benefit your organization through my ability to plan and organize work, supervise employees, and see that work is completed in a timely and efficient manner.

As you will see from my resume, I offer experience in the areas of electrical wiring and installation and also in food service management. I have succeeded in both fields while earning a reputation as a hard worker who can be counted on.

I have achieved excellent results in supervising as many as 24 employees in fast-paced hospitality environments including military dining facilities, major hotel restaurants, and a residential center for the blind and senior citizens. I have managed ordering, food preparation, planned and prepared meals, and worked as a cook.

Through training and experience as an electrician, I am skilled in using electronic test equipment and repairing small appliances as well as in installing residential and commercial wiring.

I hope you will welcome my call soon to arrange a brief meeting at your convenience to discuss your current and future needs and how I might serve them. Thank you in advance for your time.

Sincerely yours,

Orville P. Handson

Alternate last paragraph:
I hope you will call or write soon to suggest a time convenient for us to meet and discuss your current and future needs and how I might serve them. Thank you in advance for your time.

ORVILLE P. HANDSON

1110½ Hay Street, Fayetteville, NC 28305   •   preppub@aol.com   •   (910) 483-6611

OBJECTIVE

To contribute through my ability to plan and organize work and supervise employees for maximum effectiveness and through my specialized experience in residential/commercial wiring installation and food service management.

EXPERIENCE

Gained experience as an Electrician with several companies, Yancy, NY:
Mycon, Inc. (1999-present). Handle a variety of work including installing panel boxes and transformers, hanging lights, and running wire.

Shoe Hill Construction (1998). Became familiar with business operations and worked on numerous projects by installing panel boxes, lights, and transformers, and laid wire.
* Made suggestions which resulted in reducing labor costs 18%.

Smith's Electric (1997). Gained knowledge of emergency generators, including how they operate and how to make repairs on them.
* Participated in installing pipe and wiring on various commercial projects and wiring for a new computer system.

DINING FACILITY MANAGER. Dragon Services, Fayetteville, NC (1993-97). Had the final say in all operational areas while supervising 24 employees in a facility which prepared three full meals a day for personnel at Ft. Bragg, the nation's largest military base.
* Managed facility; ordered supplies, maintained records, and sanitized all equipment.

OPERATIONS MANAGER. Hilton Hotel, James, NY (1987-92). Ensured food service facilities operated smoothly and efficiently.
* Became skilled in supervising and dealing with people from a variety of socioeconomic levels, walks of life, ages, and nationalities.

FOOD PREPARATION SUPERVISOR. Elmhurst Rest Stop, Elmhurst, NY (1985-87). Oversaw a staff of 16 preparing meals for approximately 120 residents and staff in a shelter for the blind and at a camp sponsored by the shelter.
* Earned a reputation as a hard worker willing to contribute a great deal of effort.

GENERAL MANAGER. ABC Electronics, Far Rockaway, NY (1980-85). Successfully owned and operated my own business repairing stereo equipment and TVs as well as installing antennas.

Other Experience: Served in the U.S. Army in various areas including radio/telephone operation; installation and minor repair; dining facility management; and vehicle driver and dispatcher.

EDUCATION & TRAINING

Completed one year of Mechanical Engineering, Delaware State College, Dover, NJ.
Excelled in approximately 800 hours of course work in Electrical Wiring and Installation, Frederick Technical Community College, NY.
Received a diploma in Hotel and Food Service Management after completing a nine-month course sponsored by the State of New York.
Additional training in electronics, sanitation for food service, and general contracting for the federal government..

PERSONAL

Recipient of several community service awards; held leadership positions with the Boy Scouts.

CAREER CHANGE

Date

Exact Name of Person
Exact Title
Exact Name of Company
Address
City, State, Zip

ENGINEER Dear Exact Name of Person (or Dear Sir or Madam if answering a blind ad):

With the enclosed resume, I would like to express my interest in exploring employment opportunities with your organization.

Management and problem-solving skills refined in military service

As you will see from my resume, I offer strong management skills which I have recently refined in the U.S. Army's Special Operations community. As an Engineer Advisor, I traveled worldwide to provide leadership during a variety of projects, and I have communicated in both Portuguese and Spanish while training individuals from Central and South America.

Management skills refined in civilian employment

Prior to entering the U.S. Army, I worked in the hospitality industry, and I was promoted to Assistant Beverage Manager of the Marriott Corporation. For three years I worked in beverage ordering and inventory control for high-volume ballroom operations, and I dealt with dozens of liquor and beverage vendors and distributors as I ordered inventory. I gained strong bottom-line management skills in that job as I reconciled inventory usage and shrinkage and continuously developed more cost effective ways to provide quality customer service.

If you can use a highly motivated manager who thrives on solving problems through people, I hope you will contact me soon to suggest a time we might meet to discuss how I could contribute to your organization. I can provide excellent professional and personal references at the appropriate time. Thank you for your time and consideration.

Sincerely,

David Irving

DAVID L. IRVING

1110½ Hay Street, Fayetteville, NC 28305 • preppub@aol.com • (910) 483-6611

OBJECTIVE I want to contribute to an organization that can use a Special Forces-trained professional with exceptionally strong management, organizational, and problem-solving skills which have been refined through unique worldwide assignments which required a top-notch leader and communicator.

EDUCATION **College: B.S. in Business Management,** Colorado State University, Denver, CO, 1991.
Military training: Completed challenging military training programs including these:
Special Forces Qualifications Course (1 ½ years)
Individual Terrorism Awareness Course (INTAC)
Primary Leadership Development Course (top 10%)   Basic NCO Leadership Course
Airborne School   Spanish School (Honor Grad)

LANGUAGES Proficient in Spanish

HONORS Received numerous medals, letters of commendation, and other honors recognizing exemplary performance, including an Army Commendation Medal honoring the leadership I provided to a 12-member Brazilian contingency force that visited the U.S. for two weeks.

EXPERIENCE **ENGINEER ADVISOR.** U.S. Army Special Forces, Ft. Campbell, KY (1996-present). As the Engineer Sergeant in the Special Operations community, advised a Company Commander on engineering-related issues. Have traveled extensively to coordinate numerous projects in Central and South America.
- **Highlights of special projects:** Planned and supervised projects related to combat engineering, light construction, and specialized combat operations. Constructed and used improvised munitions. Coordinated administrative and logistical activities for 78 projects in Colombia. Supervised 1,800 Colombian soldiers in airfield defense and force protection. Provided leadership during the construction of a two-story building containing classrooms for 1,500 Bolivian students. Played a key role in planning and implementing humanitarian assistance projects in Bolivia.
- **Written communication:** Prepared the engineer portions of area studies and operations plans.
- **Employee training and personnel administration:** Spoke in Spanish as I organized and trained foreign soldiers to prepare them to participate in internal defense projects in South America and Central America. Trained Bolivian special anti-narcotic police agents in booby traps and demolitions.
- **Maintenance management:** Maintained $2.5 million in logistical supplies and equipment for 3,500 Colombian soldiers during a special project.

BALLROOM ASSISTANT BEVERAGE MANAGER. Marriott Corporation, Denver, CO (1991-95). Began as a Bellman working in Guest Services; excelled in greeting guests and providing for their transportation and storage needs.
- **Management:** Was promoted to Assistant to the Beverage Manager for Ballroom Operations; for three years worked in beverage ordering and inventory control for high-volume ballroom operations.
- **Vendor relations and purchasing:** Dealt with dozens of liquor and beverage vendors and distributors; ordered inventory, and reconciled inventory usage and shrinkage.

PERSONAL Held **Secret security clearance.** Unlimited personal initiative. Excellent references.

CAREER CHANGE

Date

Mrs. Veronica Lane
Owner
Braselton Gallery
185 Hazelwood Drive
Hilton Head, SC 99877

ENVIRONMENTAL COMPLIANCE INSPECTOR

This professional has decided that the city where she is relocating does not have the high-powered environmental work in which she has been involved. So she is choosing her upcoming relocation as the ideal time to switch careers to the art gallery field. She has long had an interest in art gallery work, public relations, and public affairs and feels that her skills and personality would be well expressed in this new environment.

In terms of career change, this is true: You don't know if it's possible until you try!

Dear Mrs. Lane:

With the enclosed resume, I would like to make you aware of my interest in exploring employment opportunities with your organization. I have recently relocated to South Carolina with my husband because of his new position, and I have much to offer an organization that can use a versatile hard worker with strong communication, management, computer operations, and budget skills. I am interested in the management position we recently discussed on the telephone.

In my most recent work experience, I have worked in the environmental compliance field and recently functioned as the only Environmental Compliance Inspector for my employer in Dallas, TX. In that role I acted as spokesperson for environmental issues and was involved in training employees at all levels. Continuously involved in quality assurance activities, I conducted announced and unannounced inspections to determine compliance with regulations.

Although I have excelled in my recent job, I have decided to explore opportunities outside the environmental field at this next phase in my career. You will notice from my resume that I offer strong computer knowledge. I am skilled in database management using Microsoft Access, and I am proficient with all Microsoft programs. I have worked effectively in situations where I was a bookkeeper, budget assistant, computer program analyst, and administrative assistant.

I believe one of my main strengths is my ability to adapt easily to new environments as I have a natural problem-solving orientation. Known for my attention to detail in all matters, I excel in situations in which excellent analytical and problem-solving skills are required. I also offer the ability to act as a spokesperson for an organization utilizing the public speaking and problem-solving skills which have been refined through experience.

If you can use a versatile and adaptable professional with knowledge in numerous areas to become a part of your team, I hope you will contact me to suggest a time when we might meet in person to discuss your needs. I can provide outstanding references at the appropriate time.

Sincerely,

Amy Vanderbilt

AMY VANDERBILT

1110 1/2 Hay Street, Fayetteville, NC 28305 • preppub@aol.com • (910) 483-6611

OBJECTIVE

To benefit an organization that can use an articulate, experienced professional with exceptional planning and organizational skills who offers a versatile background related to customer service, public relations, bookkeeping, and project management.

**EDUCATION &
CERTIFICATION**

Completed two years towards a B.S. in Business Management, University of Virginia. Attended numerous courses related to Environmental Laws and Regulations, Hazardous Material Waste Handling, and CPR/First Aid.

COMPUTERS

Completed formal coursework for Microsoft applications and the Windows operating system. Knowledgeable of Windows and Microsoft Access, Excel, Word, and Works.
- Skilled in database management using Microsoft Access.
- Have created presentations with PowerPoint.

EXPERIENCE

1994-2000: ENVIRONMENTAL COMPLIANCE INSPECTOR. Advanced from Environmental Assistant (1994-98) to Environmental Compliance Inspector with Bristol Corporation (1998-2000), Dallas, TX. Recently resigned this position in order to relocate with my husband.
- As the only inspector in Dallas for this major corporation, conducted announced and unannounced inspections of facilities to determine compliance with environmental regulations; provided guidance and made recommendations for corrective action, then prepared formal reports of the inspection.
- On my own initiative, updated the environmental compliance checklist/inspection form which was four years out of date.
- Was extensively involved in training personnel at all levels, from executives to entry-level personnel; conducted classes and briefed executives and personnel.
- Acquired expertise in quality assurance and environmental compliance inspection.
- Have acquired vast expertise related to environmental issues while serving in a highly visible capacity as the spokesperson for environmental compliance.
- Received the highest possible evaluations on all performance appraisals; was praised for "consistently exercising sound judgment," for my "hard work in improving compliance."

COMPUTER ANALYST. Department of Defense, Ft. Hood, TX (1993). Handled data entry and computer systems support for a project that computerized inventory data for eight schools.

ADMINISTRATIVE ASSISTANT. Department of Defense, Ft. Dix, NJ (1992-93). Maintained a student database using Lotus 1-2-3 while also handling purchase requisitions and assisting in contract modifications; worked closely with the Public Affairs office, and was Acting Public Affairs Officer in the absence of the Director.

BUDGET ASSISTANT. Womack Army Community Hospital, Ft. Bragg, NC (1991). Managed expenditures of the Supplemental Care Program utilizing automated accounting system, and performed audits of medical facility treatment activities and pharmacy inventory.

BUDGET ASSISTANT. U.S. Army, Belgium (1988-90). Maintained ledgers of fund distribution for major units while gathering data for budget analysts, confirming accuracy of reports, as well as reconciling and balancing ledgers.

PERSONAL

Have earned three Sustained Superior Performance Awards. Known as a service-oriented professional with strong analytical and problem solving skills. Excellent references available.

**EQUIPMENT
OPERATOR**

Dear Sir or Madam:

With the enclosed resume, I would like to express my interest in exploring employment opportunities with your organization and make you aware of my versatile skills and talents. I am in the process of permanently relocating to Idaho for family reasons, and I would appreciate the opportunity to discuss job openings which might utilize my versatile skills.

As you will see from my enclosed resume, I have excelled in several functional areas. While serving my country in the U.S. Army, I was promoted ahead of my peers to mid-management. I served with distinction as a Computer Operator, and I became known for my exceptionally strong mathematical and computational skills. I became accustomed to operating in an environment in which there was "no room for error" as I was involved in performing precise mathematical calculations used to calculate targets in live firing projects.

While serving my country, I was also cross-trained as a Vehicle Operator and Communications Operator. I became skilled in operating a 12-ton tracked vehicle and safely transporting people and equipment in all types of terrain and weather. I also worked as a Communications Operator and became skilled in using field telephones, digital message systems, and radio transmitters/receivers.

After military service, I went to work as a Maintenance Worker I and I have been promoted to Maintenance Worker II. Although I am excelling in this job which involves carpentry, plumbing, masonry, and maintenance knowledge, I am seeking to transfer into a job which could make more extensive use of my communication, sales, and customer service skills.

I can provide excellent references at the appropriate time, and I hope you will contact me to suggest a time when we might meet in person to discuss your needs.

Yours sincerely,

Belton Jones

BELTON JONES

1110½ Hay Street, Fayetteville, NC 28305 • preppub@aol.com • (910) 483-6611

OBJECTIVE

I want to contribute to an organization that can use a versatile employee who offers skills related to training and supervising employees, maintaining and operating vehicles, handling sales and customer service, as well as operating computers.

EDUCATION

Completed numerous training programs sponsored by the U.S. Army including programs pertaining to computer operations, radio and telecommunications, management and supervision, and vehicle maintenance.
- Received a Certificate, Primary Leadership Course, 1995. Also received a Certificate from the Computer Operator Course, 1992.

Completed training sponsored by Vernon County, Georgia, pertaining to the management of maintenance operations, 1998-present.

Graduated from Plummer County High School, Butler, ID, 1990.

LICENSE

Hold a current Pesticide License issued by the County of Vernon in GA.

EXPERIENCE

EQUIPMENT OPERATOR & MAINTENANCE WORKER II. Vernon County, GA (1998-present). For the county, perform general carpentry and renovation work related to the construction, repair, or alteration of floors, roofs, stairways, partitions, doors, windows, and screens; build, erect, and repair a wide range of items such as partitions, cabinets, and bookcases; play a key role in the demolition of structures.
- Maintain plumbing systems and change faucet washers, stems, and seals; repair toilets by changing tank bulbs, overflow tubes, and guide wires.
- Perform preventive maintenance and minor repairs on tractors, mowers, string trimmers, power and hand tools, compactors, and other items.
- Perform liaison with the public and communicate the policies of the county; exercise tact and courtesy with the general public.
- Have refined my knowledge of the procedures, materials, and equipment related to the plumbing, carpentry, and grounds maintenance trades.
- Have become skilled in the use and care of a variety of hand and power tools necessary to perform plumbing, masonry, carpentry, and maintenance tasks.
- Read and interpret blueprints and specifications.
- Have received the highest possible evaluation of my performance in the following areas:

Quality of Work	Quantity of Work
Dependability	Attendance and Punctuality
Initiative and Enthusiasm	Judgment
Cooperation	Relationships with Others
Coordination/Scheduling	Safety and Quality Assurance

- Began as a Maintenance Worker I and was promoted to Maintenance Worker II.

COMPUTER OPERATOR. U.S. Army, Ft. Benning, GA (1994-97). Became known for my exceptionally strong mathematical and computational skills while performing precise calculations in a state-of-the-art computerized center which provided precise data used to determine targets for live-fire training projects.
- Advanced to the rank of E-4 (middle management) ahead of my peers; was responsible for training/supervising four people operating a sophisticated computer system.
- Operated a computer while also using graphs, tables, charts, and maps for manual computation.

PERSONAL

Possess an outgoing personality which is well suited to customer service and sales.

Date

Attn: Box 2688
c/o Fayetteville Publishing Company
P.O. Box 849
Fayetteville, NC 28302-0849

FLOORING
INSTALLER

Dear Sir or Madam:

I would appreciate an opportunity to talk with you soon about how I could contribute to your organization through my skills as a hardwood flooring specialist known for my dedication to quality workmanship.

I am very proud of my reputation as a professional who has never had an unsatisfied customer. I have never had to return to a job and fix or repair anything I have done due to poor quality. I will not sacrifice quality or my reputation for excellence.

As you will see from my enclosed resume I also own all the standard tools except for the 12" and 8" drum sanders. My experience includes the installation of all types of pre- and unfinished flooring as well as sanding, finishing, refinishing, layout, trouble-shooting, edging, stairways, and replacement/repair/add-ons.

I hope you will call or write me soon to suggest a time convenient for us to meet and discuss your current and future needs and how I might serve them. Thank you in advance for your time.

Sincerely,

Max G. Nestor, Jr.

MAX G. NESTOR, JR.

1110½ Hay Street, Fayetteville, NC 28305   •   preppub@aol.com   •   (910) 483-6611

OBJECTIVE   To offer experience and well-refined skills to an organization that needs a quality-conscious professional familiar with the equipment and sanding and finishing hardwood flooring.

SPECIAL SKILLS   Through experience and training from some of the finest craftsmen in the area, have become familiar with almost every piece of equipment used in this field including:
- *drum sanders:* Clarke-American 12" and 8"
- *combo belt and drum sanders:* Hummel
- *edgers:* Clarke-American B2 and Super 7
- *buffers:* Clarke 16"
- *other:* hand sanders and vibrators
- *power and hand tools:* power nailers, air nailers, and compressors
- Own all my own tools except for 12" and 8" drum sanders

EXPERIENCE   **JOB PLANNER, INSTALLER,** and **SANDER.** Nestor Wood Flooring and Interiors, Gardner, TN (2000-02). Broadened my knowledge of prefinished wood installation methods working for two companies simultaneously while planning and completing wood flooring installations.
- Removed existing floor coverings such as vinyl or carpet.
- Prepared subflooring for the new installation using manufacturers specifications.
- Completed trim-out work such as baseboards and shoe molds as well as cutting door jambs before the flooring was completed in order to meet flooring specifications.
- Controlled supply inventories and ordered materials as needed.
- Became very aware of the fact that a complete, accurate estimate cannot be completed without actually visiting the site and checking the job carefully so no details are left out.

INSTALLER, SANDER, and **FINISHER.** A.B. Smith Flooring, Gardner, TN (1995-00). Benefited from a combined 35 years of experience while absorbing the professional secrets of crafting hardwood floors and trim work including revitalizing complete staircases.
- Became skilled in all phases of the craft including sanding, filling, staining, matching existing colors, and finishing floors.
- Gained experience in completing work on stairs and risers, side boards, and handrails.
- Saved flooring which had been severely damaged by flooding or fire while learning the special characteristics of woods ranging from oak and maple to heart and white pine.

BUILDING MAINTENANCE SPECIALIST. Handy Group, Inc., Nashville, TN (1994-95). Completed a wide range of repairs on 22 multiunit buildings in an apartment complex including conducting walk-throughs with tenants.
- Worked with plumbing, drywall, carpets, and cabinetry as well as carpentry work.

CARPENTER. Betts Homes, Inc., Charleston, SC (1992-94). Finished framing and trim work as a Carpenter/Punch Man involved in completing repair work for new home warranties.

Highlights of earlier experience: Gained a strong base of experience in the construction business as a Carpenter/Framer with a New York home improvements company and knowledge of inventory control in a plumbing and heating company.

TRAINING   One of the top five students during a U.S. Army Electrical Engineering training program

PERSONAL   Am an adaptable quick learner with a reputation for quality and craftsmanship first.

Exact Name of Person
Title or Position
Name of Company
Address (no., street)
Address (city, state, zip)

**FOREMAN &
SUPERINTENDENT**

Dear Exact Name of Person (or Dear Sir or Madam if answering a blind ad):

I would appreciate an opportunity to talk with you soon about how I could contribute to your organization through my experience in managing people and projects.

As you will see from my resume, I offer considerable construction industry experience. As a teenager in New Jersey, I began working for builders and then became a self-employed contractor of roofing, framing, and siding jobs. After that I served my country with distinction and excelled in numerous challenging assignments. In one job at West Point, I coached the U.S. Military Academy Parachute Team to its first national championship competition in 34 straight years and then to its first national title. That was a thrill for me because, although my predecessor had three national titles and many world competitions to his credit, I led the West Point team to its first national title through strengthening its training program, reorganizing physical facilities for better utilization, and by applying my strong leadership style.

Since leaving the military I have excelled as a foreman and superintendent on residential and commercial jobs, and I offer skills in all aspects of residential and commercial building. I can provide outstanding personal and professional references. I will cheerfully relocate according to your needs.

I hope you will write or call me soon to suggest a time when we might meet to discuss your current and future needs and how I might serve them. Thank you in advance for your time.

Sincerely yours,

Clem K. Hammer

Alternate last paragraph:
I hope you will welcome my call soon to arrange a brief meeting at your convenience to discuss your current and future needs and how I might serve them. Thank you in advance for your time.

CLEM K. HAMMER

1110½ Hay Street, Fayetteville, NC 28305   •   preppub@aol.com   •   (910) 483-6611

OBJECTIVE

To benefit an organization that can use a skilled organizer, resourceful problem solver, and versatile manager with strong communication, negotiating, and motivational abilities.

EXPERIENCE

FOREMAN/ACTING SUPERINTENDENT. Briar Builders, Lincoln, NE (2000-present). Because of my excellent reputation for both personal character and construction expertise, was recruited by this construction industry firm to oversee its residential development activities; handled all duties of a superintendent.

- Purchased lots and coordinated clearing and footings; built multiple single-family homes in the $85,000-$140,000 price range in new residential developments.
- Was actively involved in selling many of the homes we built; coordinated with real estate brokers for the sale of some of the properties.
- Prepared all written materials related to construction including description of materials needed, documents for appraisals and building permits, and other paperwork.
- Hired and supervised workers from every construction trade.

SUPERINTENDENT. PNC Builders, Lincoln, NE (1998-00). Played a key role in this company's enjoying the most profitable period in its history; acted as a superintendent for residential developments and for commercial projects.

- Supervised construction of five commercial office buildings in MT, NE, and WY; my attention to detail and expert management brought these projects in at a cost of 30% less than had been bid by the next highest bidder.
- Negotiated the purchasing of residential lots; prepared documentation for appraisal with VA and mortgage companies, filed building permits, selected and negotiated terms with subcontractors, and supervised all work from land clearing through finished project stage while handling all job costing, accounting, disbursements, and finances.

SELF-EMPLOYED REMODELER. Lincoln, NE (1997-98). After my honorable discharge from military service, performed renovations and remodeling of residential properties; built/remodeled kitchens and bathrooms and designed/built home additions.

Highlights of military experience: U.S. Army, locations worldwide. During the following highlights of my military experience, was promoted ahead of my peers and was selected for difficult assignments which required excellent organizational and management skills.

- **Operations Sergeant.** Was selected for a job at West Point supervising riggers in the repair of parachute equipment; supervised airdrops of people/assets.
- Was handpicked for a position as an **Executive Aide** to a Commanding General.

Other construction industry experience: Began working for builders in New Jersey and then became a self-employed contractor of roofing, framing, and siding jobs; became a skilled carpenter and learned to operate heavy construction equipment while prospecting for customers, negotiating contracts, ordering materials, and preparing payroll.

EDUCATION

Excelled in more than three years of U.S. Army training related to management, industrial safety, and other areas.
Completed the General Contractor's Course, Fayetteville Technical Community College.

PERSONAL

Am known for common sense and honesty. Can provide strong references. Offer exceptionally strong crisis management skills. Held Top Secret security clearance.

Centex Bateson/Simpson
P.O. Box 71459
Ft. Bragg, NC 28307

**GENERAL
FOREMAN**

Dear Sir:

I would appreciate an opportunity to talk with you about joining your organization as a construction superintendent.

As you will see from the enclosed resume, I have been a highly valued part of the construction management team of Zenith Construction Company headquartered in Vermont. Projects for which I have had a supervisory role include dam renovations, the construction of multimillion-dollar office buildings, additions to prisons and hospitals and retail facilities, conversion of a warehouse into high-tech laboratories, and construction of sewer treatment plants.

With a reputation as a take-charge individual who gets along well with others, I am known as a highly safety-conscious professional, and I am proud of my unblemished safety record as a foreman. Knowledgeable of OSHA and all other safety codes and practices, I believe a key factor in being a successful superintendent is continuously keeping an eye on safety as well as on the bottom line. I am skilled at supervising construction activities in order to remain within budgets and on schedule.

I hope you will call or write me soon to suggest a time convenient for us to meet and discuss your current and future needs and how I might serve them. Thank you in advance for your time.

Sincerely yours,

Avery S. Lamb

AVERY S. LAMB

1110½ Hay Street, Fayetteville, NC 28305   •   preppub@aol.com   •   (910) 483-6611

OBJECTIVE

To contribute to an organization that can use a skilled construction superintendent with extensive experience in supervising a wide range of commercial and industrial projects.

EXPERIENCE

Have been a construction foreman on a variety of projects for Zenith Construction Company, VT:

GENERAL FOREMAN. Zenith Construction Company, Ft. Bragg, NC (2000-present). Am handling all the responsibilities of a superintendent while supervising workers, scheduling work, ordering materials, controlling costs, and preparing daily reports related to the construction of three 25,000-sq. ft. military billeting buildings valued at $20 million.
- Despite unexpected problems, met all schedules and remained within budget.
- Supervise the layout crew, excavation, form work, concrete placement and other related activities; perform troubleshooting on rebar and masonry work; involved in all scheduling of subcontractors.

GENERAL FOREMAN. Foundations, Davis, W. VA (1999-00). Handled the duties of a superintendent working within a management structure comprised of multiple superintendents under a general superintendent; supervised the construction of seven buildings in a new 27-building **prison complex**, including a central power plant, food service and laundry.

ACTING SUPERINTENDENT. Central Medical Center, Bedford, MD (1998-99). Was the only Zenith employee on this job supervising **demolition, removal, and replacement of brick veneer** by subcontractors as well as supervising the setting of a 155-ft. steel smoke stack and related mechanical work in an occupied hospital.
- Scheduled major mechanical system shutdown in an operating hospital.

GENERAL FOREMAN. XWYZ, Manford, NH (1998). Set up this project "from scratch" in an upgrade and expansion job; supervised blasting/excavating in an area surrounded by large concrete structures in use as the city sewer plant without causing damage to plant.

GENERAL FOREMAN. Delta Lab, Bladen, ME (1997-98). Supervised tradesmen in the gutting and renovation of a 130,000-sq. ft. warehouse into **high-tech labs**; supervised the massive structural steel reinforcement of the facility and created "airtight" areas which could be used for the production of bacteria; used multiple subcontractors.

GENERAL FOREMAN. S. Maryland Medical Center, Cory, ME (1995-97). Supervised a $12 million **hospital addition** which included complete renovation of the emergency room

LABOR FOREMAN. Whitney's Retail Store, Freeport, ME (1994-95). Became experienced with wood construction on a project that **doubled the size of a retail store** operating 365 days a year, 24 hours a day; scheduled and supervised subcontractors.

FOREMAN. Lange Hydro Project, Rockwood, MD (1993-94). On the **intake structure and powerhouse of an existing dam,** was labor foreman overseeing pile driving, excavations, and concrete work; gained experience working over, beside, and in water.

Other projects for Zenith Construction Co. (1987-93). Worked on commercial projects in the $10 million range which included the Portland Museum of Art, Fourth St. Parking Garage, a warehouse, the Coopers Family Lodge and Waterford Condominiums.

Date

Static Control Components, Inc.
Attn: Supervisor
P.O. Box 152
3115 Hal Siler Drive
Sanford, NC 27331

GENERAL CONSTRUCTION MANAGER

Dear Sir or Madam:

I am sending you a resume describing my background in the communications services industry because I feel there might be a "fit" between your needs and my extensive management skills and telecommunications knowledge.

As you will see, I recently opted for an early retirement from Sprint Virginia Telephone after serving the company with distinction and being offered a further promotion which I declined. In my most recent position as General Manager of Engineering and Construction, I was handling responsibilities similar to those of a CEO at a small or medium-sized company. In the process of managing 300 managers, engineers, supervisors, craft, and clerical employees while also supervising more than 200 contractors performing large-scale fiber optic/copper installations and maintenance, I was in charge of a $32 million budget. When the company merged with Centel in 1993, I took over the physical and human resources of Centel and was given the additional responsibility of reforming Centel's organization into the Sprint Virginia Telephone structure.

Although I have managed major disaster relief efforts and supervised the installation of fiber optic/copper systems all over the Southern region, I take greatest pride in my accomplishments as a manager of human resources. Since my job involved managing unionized and non-unionized employees, I had to demonstrate highly refined interpersonal, problem-solving, and negotiating skills at all times. Although I have never enjoyed the business of terminating or transferring employees, through the years I have handled that responsibility with tact and sensitivity and have been commended for my "style." I also am proud of the fact that I have selected, trained, developed, and promoted employees who have become some of the company's most valuable employees.

If you can use an astute and energetic manager who could contribute to your organization as I have done to Sprint Virginia Telephone, please give me a call and I will make myself available at your convenience. You would find me in person to be a youthful and vigorous manager who could have a great deal to offer your organization. I would consider any part-time, full-time, or consulting assignments as your needs and goals dictate.

Sincerely yours,

Chris F. Builder, Jr.

CHRIS F. BUILDER, JR.

1110½ Hay Street, Fayetteville, NC 28305   •   preppub@aol.com   •   (910) 483-6611

OBJECTIVE

To make contributions to an organization that can use a respected professional with highly refined strategic planning and problem-solving skills who has expertly managed multimillion-dollar budgets, capital expansion projects, and large-scale responses to natural disasters while supervising both unionized and non-unionized personnel.

EXPERIENCE

Recently declined a promotion and took an early retirement after a distinguished career and track record of promotion with Sprint Carolina Telephone:
GENERAL MANAGER, ENGINEERING AND CONSTRUCTION. Fairfax, VA (2000-present). After the company merged with Centel, was promoted to oversee all engineering and construction activities in the South Region, and assumed responsibility for the physical and human resources formerly under Centel management.

Management of Human Resources:
- Managed 300 engineers and professionals including district managers and also provided oversight management of 200 contractors who provided engineering/construction services; negotiated and supervised the proper administration of contracts/agreements.
- Became skilled at union negotiations, handling grievance procedures, and resolving disputes in a timely and fair manner; was entrusted with the independent authority to add or reduce contract work forces and to shift personnel from one district to another.
- After the merger with Centel, had to plan and implement a reduction in force.

Financial Management:
- Planned and administered a $32 million budget within a corporate system which had a "no excuses" philosophy about cost overruns.
- Was the approving authority for procurement of capital equipment, and supervised teams responsible for the installation of fiber optic systems.

Management of Disaster Response Efforts as well as Major Capital Expansions:
- Directed prudent responses to emergency outages and responded to natural disasters such as hurricanes that impacted on outside distribution network and physical plant; Chairperson of the Emergency Restoration Plan and supervised emergency response crews.
- Implemented project management practices such as scheduling tools and Total Quality Management Techniques; supervised the installation of fiber optic systems from Fairfax to Richmond and to Charlotte.

Customer Service and Community/Government Liaison:
- Was keenly responsive to customer service demands with critical deadlines.
- Negotiated with federal, state, local government, and private persons and agencies for right-of-way access and other issues.
- Improved the corporate image through my extensive civic involvement; received the prestigious "Old Faithful Award" for community service given by The President's Club.

Highlights of previous Sprint Virginia Telephone experience: **Division Distribution Manager,** Fairfax, VA (1990-99); **Division Engineer,** Richmond, VA (1987-90); **Division Commercial Supervisor** (1986-87); **District Engineer,** Fairfax, VA. (1980-86).

EDUCATION

Bachelor of Science in Business Administration, Atlantic Christian College, 1980.
Previously studied **Mechanical Engineering** at N.C. State University.

PERSONAL

Possess exceptionally strong interpersonal skills with a highly advanced understanding of the technology behind fiber optics, remote line units, and subscriber carrier concentrators.

Date

Exact Name
Exact Title
Address
Address
City, state zip

GENERAL CONTRACTOR
Dear Sir or Madam:

With the enclosed resume, I would like to introduce you to my more than 20 years of experience in all aspects of the building trades and in small business management. I am skilled at estimating jobs, planning job layout, ordering supplies and materials, scheduling personnel and equipment, hiring and training personnel, and safeguarding tools and equipment. My expertise also includes the ability to run a field level to lay out a house as well as use equipment including air saws, forklifts, and all types of power tools

As an experienced General Contractor in Scottsdale, AZ, I built from the ground up and operated a successful small business which carried out all types of construction

I have recently relocated to your area because I want to live near my aging parents, and I am exploring employment opportunities with large construction firms that can benefit from my technical knowledge and management skills. If you can use my considerable expertise, I hope you will contact me.

Yours sincerely,

Anthony Phillips

ANTHONY PHILLIPS

1110½ Hay Street, Fayetteville, NC 28305   •   preppub@aol.com   •   (910) 483-6611

OBJECTIVE

To contribute to the Cambridge County school system through my strong desire to teach in a program which provides instruction in carpentry and the building trades by applying my extensive experience as well as my management and public relations skills.

EDUCATION & TRAINING

Completed programs of instruction at Scottsdale Technical Community College which included the following:
- Carpentry I and II – all phases of building Blueprint Reading
- Welding
- Small Engine Repair
- Real Estate – buying and selling residential and commercial property

LICENSES & CERTIFICATIONS

Am licensed by the State of Indiana as a General Contractor.
Have been certified as a welder and as a Briggs & Stratton small engine mechanic.

SPECIALIZED EXPERTISE

Offer more than 20 years of experience in all aspects of the building trades and in small business management:

Estimating jobs	Planning job layout
Ordering supplies and materials	Scheduling personnel and equipment
Hiring and training personnel	Safeguarding tools and equipment
Running a field level to lay out a house	
Using equipment including air saws, forklifts, and all types of power tools	

EXPERIENCE

LICENSED GENERAL CONTRACTOR and **GENERAL MANAGER.** Doone Construction Company, Scottsdale, IN (2000-present). Built from the ground up and operate a successful small business which carries out all types of construction jobs to include building new homes and completing residential remodeling projects.
- Have earned a reputation as an honest, reliable, and dependable self-starter.
- Apply my knowledge while building well-made homes to my own high-quality standards.
- Oversee the administrative duties of operating a small business from hiring and training employees, to scheduling in order to ensure jobs are completed on time, to making sure equipment and tools are on site when needed and properly taken care of.
- Manage financial support such as payroll and tax processing and insurance.
- Do job estimates and negotiate contracts.
- Personally developed and polished the skills needed to build a home from the ground up and am effective in passing my knowledge on to others.

Highlights of earlier experience: Displayed inventory control skills as well as the ability to manage human and material resources for maximum productivity, including:
- As a Store Manager for Bailey Shoes: finished a 12-month training program in six months; set a new company record for store grand opening sales levels; was selected as one of five trainers to evaluate the potential of candidates for management jobs within the 163-store chain.
- Supervised two people as a Lead Carpenter for Andrews Construction Company in Shelton, IN: built concrete forms, poured concrete, hung steel, and ran interior trim.
- Served with honor in the U.S. Air Force: had Top Secret security clearance and advanced quickly in rank while providing security for multimillion-dollar equipment.

PERSONAL

Am an active community volunteer who enjoys working with young people as a girls' softball coach and boys' basketball and baseball coach. Meet challenges head on.

Exact Name of Person
Title or Position
Name of Company
Address (no., street)
Address (city, state, zip)

**HEAVY EQUIPMENT
OPERATOR**

Dear Exact Name of Person (or Dear Sir or Madam if answering a blind ad):

I would appreciate an opportunity to talk with you soon about how I could contribute to your organization through my experience in heavy equipment operation and my "accident-free" driving record.

While serving my country in the U.S. Air Force, I became known as a skillful and safe driver and equipment operator. I earned an achievement medal for my contributions as a member of a civil engineering company in Germany. During the war in the Middle East I provided important support while removing 45 inches of snow from runways. Then I kept the runways free of snow and ice accumulation which allowed allied planes to complete their assigned missions.

In the aftermath of the war, I was honored with another achievement medal in recognition of my contributions during efforts to ensure the safe passage of Kurdish refugees along the Iraqi/Turkish border. I took heavy equipment out along remote trails in a heavy downpour of rain and was described as "displaying exceptional courage which reflects favorably on himself and the image of the U.S. Air Force."

I hope you will welcome my call soon to arrange a brief meeting at your convenience to discuss your current and future needs and how I might serve them. Thank you in advance for your time.

Sincerely yours,

Evan A. Scrooge

Alternate last paragraph:
I hope you will call or write me soon to suggest a time convenient for us to meet and discuss your current and future needs and how I might serve them. Thank you in advance for your time.

EVAN A. SCROOGE

1110½ Hay Street, Fayetteville, NC 28305 • preppub@aol.com • (910) 483-6611

OBJECTIVE   To contribute my excellent skills in operating heavy equipment and my safe driving record to an organization that can use a hard-working young professional.

SPECIAL SKILLS   Through training and experience, am qualified to operate and drive vehicles and heavy equipment including, but not limited to, the following:

John Deere 410 backhoe	Case 580-B backhoe
Dump trucks up to 20 tons (automatic)	Caterpillar 130-G motorized grader
8- to 12-ton vibratory roller	Rough terrain forklift
John Deere 4-1/2 cubic yard loader	John Deere 690-C pneumatic excavator

EXPERIENCE   *Developed a reputation as a highly skilled and competent* **Heavy Equipment Operator** *while serving in the U.S. Air Force:*

Sheppard AFB, TX (2001-present). Further developed my operating skills and reputation for dependability while involved in using equipment to solve and repair serious road and airstrip problems.

- Helped construction crews and engineering company personnel with projects including preparations for laying concrete foundations.
- Was singled out for the honor of "best equipment operator in the R.E.O.T. School."

Sembach AB, Germany (1998-00). Earned two Air Force Achievement Medals for my contributions which were officially described as "distinctive" and "invaluable" to a civil engineering company.

- Excavated and removed 100 cubic meters of contaminated soil after an oil/water separator developed a leak: was commended for completing the project ahead of schedule.
- Played an important role in removing 45 inches of snow from runways so that flight lines were able to remain operational and in use in support of the war in the Middle East.
- Was named the community's "Technician of the Month, November 1999."
- Was credited with solving numerous major road and ground problems through my skills, knowledge, and important contributions.
- Helped construct a concrete foundation for a skateboard ramp for the community.

Iraq and Turkey (1998-99). Performed with distinction in the harsh environment and dangerous conditions during the war in the Middle East.

- Was singled out for praise for "exceptional courage" displayed while transporting a front end loader through narrow remote trails in a downpour of rain in order to provide safe transport for Kurdish refugees on the only accessible trail.

TELEPHONE CABLE INSTALLER. Army National Guard, Grove Hill, AL (1996-97). Learned the technical details of installing cable and COMSEC (communication secure) telephones to allow constant contact between various departments and companies.

HEAVY EQUIPMENT OPERATOR. Evans Bridge, Inc., Opelika, AL (1994-95). Operated a variety of equipment including backhoes, loaders, and small terrain forklifts.

- Conducted training for new employees in equipment operation and safety procedures.

TRAINING   Completed military training programs in heavy equipment operation.

PERSONAL   Secret clearance. Offer an "accident-free" driving history despite weather conditions.

SOMC CONUS OFFICE
c/o ABC Consultants, Inc.
Dept. FO-0820
5301 Wisconsin Ave., Suite 210
Washington, DC 20015

HEAVY EQUIPMENT OPERATOR

Dear Sir or Madam:

In response to your recent advertisement for maintenance personnel for overseas opportunities in Saudi Arabia, please accept the following resume as formal indication of my interest in the Engineer Equipment Inspector positions or any other position for which you feel I may qualify.

As you will see from my resume, I offer extensive knowledge of heavy equipment operations as well as a strong supervisory and employee training background.

As you have requested, I am submitting also a copy of my DD214 along with my training certificates.

Thank you in advance for your time and consideration. I look forward to hearing from you soon to arrange a brief meeting at your convenience to discuss your current and future needs and how I might serve them.

Sincerely,

Reed S. Oboe

REED S. OBOE

1110½ Hay Street, Fayetteville, NC 28305　　•　　preppub@aol.com　　•　　(910) 483-6611

OBJECTIVE　　To apply my extensive knowledge of heavy equipment operations for the benefit of an organization that can use my versatile hands-on equipment skills and overseas experience.

TRAINING　　Completed the U.S. Army Corps of Engineers Heavy Construction Equipment Course. Graduated from a four-week leadership course in which 25 to 30 people received concentrated team-building skills for personnel in the engineering field.

EQUIPMENT KNOWLEDGE　　Skilled in operation of a variety of crawler and wheeled tractors with dozer attachments scoop loaders, motorized graders, and towed or self-propelled scrapers, including:

621 Caterpillar scraper	track loaders	D-5 dozers	7-1/2 ton wheeled crane
130-G graders	613 scrapers	YUK-D-4 dozers	950-B bucket loaders
Up to 245 Caterpillar excavators		Rex and fill compactors	
D-7 E & F Caterpillar dozers		Various military vehicles	
Caterpillar mechanical graders		K-3000 compactors/rollers	
JCB dump trucks		Bobcat 753 and 853 scoop loaders	

Offer basic knowledge of munitions such TNT sticks, C-4 plastique, and ammonium nitrate.

EXPERIENCE　　**HEAVY EQUIPMENT OPERATOR.** Forrest County Solid Waste Management, Dallas, TX (2000-present). Use my versatile equipment skills to operate various heavy equipment while loading and unloading trucks using loaders with fork attachments and handling other activities related to compacting and covering trash with dirt.
* Hauled dirt used for covering, leveling, filling, and cutting dirt while maintaining roads and drainage ditches.
* Used excavators to load trucks.
* Ensured traffic in and around the work area was operating according to safety guidelines.
* Known for my ability to work efficiently either independently or as part of a team.

HEAVY CONSTRUCTION EQUIPMENT OPERATOR. U.S. Army, Ft. Bragg, NC (1994-00). Advanced into supervisory roles while gaining experience in equipment operations for different organizations based at Ft. Bragg, the largest U.S. Army base in the world.
* Maintained responsibility for a $3.2 million inventory of heavy construction equipment.
* Earned the Meritorious Service Medal for my performance during the war in the Middle East: established and maintained burrow pits for road construction projects throughout the region.
* Was specially selected to assist the 82nd Airborne Division during the war as the main engineer digging the sites for armament (including missile batteries and guns) and vehicles to be safely located as well as earth berms for the safeguarding of personnel.
* As a member of an airfield assessment team among the first people to jump into Panama, assisted in checking for booby traps and hot-wired vehicles.
* Supervised runway repair teams to build airfields for C-130 and smaller aircraft.
* Refined my supervisory skills to ensure equipment repairs were complete.
* Hauled heavy equipment to construction sites throughout Saudi Arabia.

Highlights of other experience: As a member of the U.S. Army Reserves, gained my initial experience in operating heavy construction equipment, Boulder, CO (1992-94).

PERSONAL　　Member of the 82nd Airborne Association, Disabled Veterans of America and the American Legion. Am single and willing to relocate for year-long overseas assignments.

Date

Exact Name of Person
Exact Title
Exact Name of Company
Address
City, State, Zip

Dear Exact Name of Person (or Dear Sir or Madam if answering a blind ad):

With the enclosed resume, I would like to make you aware of my background in the operation and maintenance of heavy construction equipment as well as of my effectiveness as a supervisor in this field.

As you will see from my resume, while serving in the U.S. Army I earned four Achievement Medals in recognition of my accomplishments. I was also honored with numerous Certificates of Achievement in recognition of my technical competence, leadership abilities, and professionalism. While assigned to maintain and supervise the use of primary earth-moving equipment and support vehicles, I became known as a hard worker who motivated others to pay attention to detail and make certain that every project was completed on time and to high quality and safety standards.

I completed training which included courses in heavy equipment operations, hazardous material handling and transportation, and the operation and maintenance of medium tactical vehicles. I am licensed by the U.S. Army to operate its full inventory of heavy construction equipment.

Earlier experience included joining a National Guard unit while still in high school and gaining versatile skills in carpentry, masonry, vehicle operations, inventory control, and leadership duties. Other jobs emphasized customer service, team work, and vehicle operating skills.

If you can use an experienced heavy equipment operator and supervisor who is known for his high levels of drive, initiative, and energy, I hope you will welcome my call soon when I try to arrange a brief meeting to discuss your goals and how my background might serve your needs. I can provide outstanding references at the appropriate time.

Sincerely,

Paul Scott Simpson

Alternate Last Paragraph:
I hope you will write or call me soon to suggest a time when we might meet to discuss your goals and how my background might serve your needs. I can provide outstanding references at the appropriate time.

PAUL SCOTT SIMPSON

1110½ Hay Street, Fayetteville, NC 28305 • preppub@aol.com • (910) 483-6611

OBJECTIVE

To offer a solid background in the operation and maintenance of heavy construction equipment to an organization that can benefit from my supervisory abilities and reputation.

TRAINING

Completed U.S. Army training which included a seven-week heavy equipment operator's course as well as the Operation and Operator Maintenance of the Family of Medium Tactical Vehicles Course, and hazardous material transportation and handling programs.

SPECIAL SKILLS

Have qualified as an operator for heavy equipment which includes the following:

M998 utility truck	M1088 truck tractor	M1089 tractor trailer
M931A2 5-ton tractor trailer	35 KW generator	950B scoop loader
613 BNS scraper	613BWDS water distributor	130GNS road grader
M818 5-ton tractor trailer	M1078 cargo truck	M1094 dump truck
M101A1 ¾-ton cargo trailer	M105A2 1-1/2-ton cargo trailer	M796 trailer bolster
HP15T tilt trailer	Hercules 11-wheel roller	CFM compressor
SP848 sheepsfoot roller	M172A2 25-ton 250 cargo trailer	

EXPERIENCE

SUPERVISORY HEAVY EQUIPMENT OPERATOR. U.S. Army, Ft. Benning, GA (2000-present).

- Was awarded several medals and honors for my accomplishments while maintaining and operating primary earth-moving equipment and the vehicles needed to haul them.
- Supervised as many as nine subordinates in the operation and maintenance of combat engineering equipment and vehicles worth millions of dollars.
- Earned respect from my superiors for my skill at helping others see the whole process so they could work together as a team to get the job done on schedule.
- Was frequently singled out for my attention to detail and dedication to finding more efficient ways to get the work done.
- Earned four Army Achievement Medals for "meritorious achievements" which included the following actions:

    "Dedication to duty, technical competence, and leadership" during a roadway project in a project during which two roads and six culverts were completed,
    "Professionalism, hard work and dedication" as a team leader,
    "Taking quick actions" which saved a civilian's life,
    "Effectiveness" in instructing 200 ROTC cadets at a summer camp

- Was awarded a Certificate of Commendation for participating in "Operation Uphold Democracy" in Haiti.

Highlights of other experience:

CARPENTER and **MASON.** U.S. Army National Guard, Horseheads, NY (1996-2000). Gained respect for my adaptability and skills in areas which included team leadership, training, driving a supervisor's vehicle, and maintaining inventories of tools, weapons, and vehicles in addition to my primary duties as a carpenter and mason.

SENIOR DELIVERY DRIVER and **COOK.** Picnic Pizza, Horseheads, NY (1991-96). Learned to work with the public while taking orders for, making, and delivering pizzas; became skilled in handling money while accepting payments and running a cash register.

PERSONAL

Will travel or relocate. Offer the ability to handle multiple simultaneous duties on time and to high standards. Can work with and relate to people from other cultures.

Date

TO: Alyeska Pipeline
BY E-MAIL
RE: Quality Assurance Lead

Dear Sir or Madam:

With the enclosed resume, I would like to make you aware of my interest in the position of Quality Assurance Lead which you recently posted on your website. I am submitting my resume for your consideration, and you will see that I offer strong skills and extensive experience related to your needs. I would like to be considered for Quality Assurance Lead or for any other positions within your organization where my skills would be beneficial to you. I am in the process of leaving the U.S. Army after a distinguished track record of accomplishment, and I am eager to return to Alaska, which is my home state.

As you will see from my resume, I have recently excelled as a Supervisor and Heavy Equipment Operator with the U.S. Army. I received several medals and awards in recognition of my management abilities and technical knowledge while supervising eight people involved in the construction and repair of horizontal construction projects including roads, drainage, and airfields. I am skilled at operating nearly any type of heavy equipment, and I can repair and maintain all vehicles.

In previous experience with the U.S. Army, I worked as an Aircraft Structural Repair Mechanic and Quality Assurance Inspector. As a Safety Manager and Quality Assurance Inspector for 12 years, I established and maintained a record of zero safety incidents because of my dedication to quality results and ability to train employees in safe practices. I have always been able to achieve availability rates well above the standards required because of my skill in troubleshooting complex problems and my ability to train associates in safety, quality assurance, and attention to detail in all matters.

I can provide excellent references at the appropriate time, and I can assure you in advance that I offer a reputation for integrity and reliability. If you can use my considerable skills and talents to further your goals, please contact me to suggest a time when we might meet to discuss your needs. I look forward to returning home to Alaska, and I hope I have the opportunity to discuss employment opportunities with you.

Sincerely,

Clint Brissom

CLINT BRISSOM

1110½ Hay Street, Fayetteville, NC 28305 • preppub@aol.com • (910) 483-6611

OBJECTIVE   To contribute to an organization that can use a versatile professional with proven management and supervisory skills along with extensive technical knowledge related to construction.

EDUCATION   **Technical:** Completed U.S. Army Heavy Equipment Operator Course, the U.S. Army Advanced Aviation Systems Course, and the 40-hour HAZMAT Course.
Received **ASE Certification,** Automotive Maintenance Technician Course, College of the Desert.
Received Certification, Air Conditioning Repair Course, SnapOn Technical Community College, CA.
Trained as **Vehicle Emissions Inspector and Repairman**, Alaska and California.
Management: Completed U.S. Army Primary Leadership Development Course; refined my skills in time management, logistics, scheduling, management, and other areas.
College: Excelled academically (3.5 GPA) in completing more than three years of college courses towards B.S. in Psychology, University of Anchorage and Anchorage State University.

EXPERIENCE   **SUPERVISOR & HEAVY EQUIPMENT OPERATOR.** U.S. Army, Ft. Campbell, KY (2001-present). In a job equivalent to Foreman, was awarded several medals and honors for my accomplishments while involved in the construction and repair of horizontal construction projects including roads, drainage, and airfields; supervised maintenance and operation of primary earth-moving equipment and the vehicles needed to haul them.
- Supervised eight subordinates in the operation and maintenance of engineering equipment and vehicles worth millions of dollars.
- Earned respect from my superiors for my skill at helping others work together as a team
- Was frequently commended for my attention to detail and my efficiency.

AIRCRAFT STRUCTURAL REPAIR MECHANIC & QUALITY ASSURANCE INSPECTOR. U.S. Army, Ft. Richardson, AK (1990-01). Was promoted ahead of my peers into supervisory positions; was selected for positions as a Quality Assurance Inspector, Safety Manager, and Training Chief.
- Managed maintenance scheduling and administration related to the structural repair and maintenance of 22 advanced rotary-wing aircraft.
- During one major project for 1½ months, supervised 22 individuals.
- Received respected medals for my management achievements and technical accomplishments in both peacetime and in combat situations.
- Became skilled at operating, maintaining, and repairing ground support equipment.
- As a Safety Manager and Supervisor for 12 years, accumulated a record of zero safety incidents because of my dedication to quality results and ability to train employees.
- Maintained operational readiness rates at 90% (20% above the required standard).

SPECIAL SKILLS   Qualified as an operator for ground support equipment and heavy equipment, to include:

M998 utility truck	M1088 truck tractor	M1089 tractor trailer
M931A2 5-ton tractor trailer	20 KW generator	950B scoop loader
613 BNS scraper	613BWDS water distributor	130GNS road grader
10+ ton crane	M1078 cargo truck	M1094 dump truck
M101A1 ¾-ton cargo trailer	M105A2 1-1/2-ton cargo trailer	M796 trailer bolster
HP15T tilt trailer	Hercules 11-wheel roller	CFM compressor
SP848 sheepsfoot roller	M172A2 25-ton 250 cargo trailer	

PERSONAL   Work well in environments which require making prudent decisions in unusual circumstances.

Date

Exact Name of Person
Title or Position
Name of Company
Address (number and street)
Address (city, state, and ZIP)

**INDEPENDENT
CONTRACTOR**

Dear Exact Name of Person (or Dear Sir or Madam if answering a blind ad):

I would appreciate an opportunity to talk with you soon about how I could contribute to your organization through my reputation as a talented manager with strong abilities in motivating employees and guiding them to meet high performance standards by setting an example of true professionalism and dedication to excellence.

While serving my country in the U.S. Air Force, I consistently earned the respect and praise of my superiors for my ability to take on challenges and excel in the tough jobs. I thrive on solving problems and on using my ability to maximize the potential of each employee, thereby achieving higher levels of productivity while eliminating methods which waste valuable time, money, and human resources.

Presently I operate two independent businesses. I am a licensed real estate agent while also involved in running a paint contracting company with four employees. Throughout my military career I displayed my adaptability and versatility in two main fields of concentration: the development and management of training programs and the supervision of supply operations.

I would like to emphasize that my strongest abilities are in building teams, providing quality training, and motivating others to excel and maximize their own individual talents. I possess sound judgment and decision-making skills along with the ability to react quickly and handle the pressure of deadlines and stressful situations.

I hope you will welcome my call soon to arrange a brief meeting at your convenience to discuss your current and future needs and how I might serve them. Thank you in advance for your time.

Sincerely yours,

Rhoda C. Walnut

Alternate last paragraph:
I hope you will call or write me soon to suggest a time convenient for us to meet and discuss your current and future needs and how I might serve them. Thank you in advance for your time.

RHODA C. WALNUT

1110½ Hay Street, Fayetteville, NC 28305   •   preppub@aol.com   •   (910) 483-6611

OBJECTIVE

To offer superior managerial and motivational abilities to an organization in need of a creative problem solver who excels in increasing productivity and morale while guiding employees to outstanding results through a keen talent for bringing out the best in others.

EXPERIENCE

INDEPENDENT CONTRACTOR. Lexington, KY (2000-present). Am simultaneously involved in two independent business activities: market and sell residential real estate and operate a paint contracting company where my contributions include making estimates and scheduling four workers in cooperation with other contractors.

With a reputation as a talented manager of human, material, and fiscal resources, advanced in supply/logistics as well as training program development/supervision, U.S. Air Force:
MANAGER OF SUPPORT SERVICES. Clark AFB, TN (1997-2000). Described as a solid leader who could be counted on to solve difficult problems, supervised 38 flight services/supply specialists supporting 80 permanent as well as 15 other types of transient aircraft.
- Located sources for parts for a 15,067-line-item inventory valued in excess of $98 million.
- Took on a problem area, and in five months had succeeded in increasing parts availability from 36 to 65%; reduced unavailable parts rates 14%.
- Implemented strong measures for following up on difficult-to-locate parts and maintained 80% availability in one area where the Air Force's standard was 75%.
- Revitalized the awaiting-parts program and freed $400,000 in daily operating expenses.
- Established a training and job rotation system which produced thoroughly cross trained personnel and eliminated production losses due to absences for training.
- Reduced critical spares unavailability 20% by locating and correcting data base errors.

TRAINING AND MOBILITY PROGRAM MANAGER. Clark AFB, TN (1995-96). Transformed a substandard operation into one recognized for outstanding achievements while building a new atmosphere of cooperation and team work; managed a special equipment inventory in a program which prepared for rapid response to worldwide emergencies.
- Implemented a data base capable of monitoring assets valued in excess of $25 million.
- Was credited with making a broad range of improvements, including a comprehensive training plan, which greatly increased capabilities.
- Handpicked for a quality assessment team, developed a unit self-assessment plan.

INSTRUCTOR. Pope AFB, NC (1992-94). Consistently produced first-rate results as the senior instructor and role model for 400 basic trainees annually.

MANAGER, SUPPLY RECEIVING DEPARTMENT. Germany (1990-1991). Known for my initiative, technical supply knowledge, and expertise as a motivator, supervised ten people.
- Prepared discrepancy reports; worked with stock control personnel to solve problems.
- Eliminated sea and land shipment detention charges which had been $30,000 in 1990.
- Guided my section to recognition with a monthly incentive award six times in one year.

EDUCATION & TRAINING

Studied Business Management, Central Texas College.
Completed extensive training in logistics and personnel management; am currently studying for a real estate broker's license at the Fayetteville (NC) Real Estate Academy.

PERSONAL

Anticipate the potential for problems and have a keen ability to develop remedies.

Date

Exact Name of Person
Title or Position
Name of Company
Address (number and street)
Address (city, state, and ZIP)

**INDEPENDENT
REAL ESTATE BROKER**

Dear Exact Name of Person (or Sir or Madam if answering a blind ad):

Can you use an enthusiastic, results-oriented sales professional who offers outstanding communication skills, a talent for reading people, and a reputation for determination and persistence in reaching goals?

With a proven background of success in sales, I have displayed my versatility while selling and marketing a wide variety of products and services including residential real estate and land, new and used automobiles, and financial products/investment services. In one job I trained and supervised a successful team of mutual fund and insurance sales agents. Most recently as an Independent Real Estate Broker with a Pond Realty office in Langley, VA, I achieved the $3 million mark in sales for 2002 While excelling in all aspects of the business, I have used my experience and knowledge to create marketing strategies and tools which reached large audiences and generated much business.

Earlier experience gave me an opportunity to refine my sales and communication abilities as well as gain familiarity with business management including finance and collections, inventory control, personnel administration, and customer service. Prior to owning and managing a business which bought, reconditioned, and marketed automobiles, I was one of Edwards Buick's most successful sales professionals, earning the distinction of being "Salesman of the Month" for 13 consecutive months and "Salesman of the Year."

If you can use a seasoned professional with the ability to solve tough business problems, maximize profitability, and increase market share under highly competitive conditions, I would enjoy an opportunity to meet with you to discuss your needs and how I might serve them. Known for my resourcefulness, I can provide outstanding personal and professional references.

I hope you will welcome my call soon to arrange a brief meeting at your convenience. Thank you in advance for your time.

Sincerely,

Dirk N. Aetna

DIRK N. AETNA

1110½ Hay Street, Fayetteville, NC 28305 • preppub@aol.com • (910) 483-6611

OBJECTIVE

To offer a track record of success in sales and managerial roles where outstanding communication skills and the ability to close the sale were key factors in building a reputation as a highly motivated professional oriented toward achieving maximum bottom-line results.

EXPERIENCE

INDEPENDENT REAL ESTATE BROKER. Pond Realty, Langley, VA (2000-present). Reached the $3 million personal sales level for 2002 while providing a range of experience which has played a key role in boosting overall sales and profitability of a thriving agency in this highly competitive market.

- Have become known for my strong interpersonal and communication skills while coordinating with potential buyers, lending institutions, construction professionals, sellers, and others.
- Negotiate all aspects of financial transactions; deal with mortgage company representatives to arrange financing and with attorneys to handle real estate closings.
- Utilize my expert marketing abilities; create sales strategies and preparing direct mail materials to capture the interest of prospective clients and generate new business.
- Have become skilled in all aspects of property evaluation and am skilled in comparing newly available homes with those having comparable features.
- Handle the details of researching information and completing paperwork for sales of new and existing homes as well as land.

SALES AND MARKETING REPRESENTATIVE. Self-employed, Langley, VA (1992-99). Trained and then supervised the efforts of as many as 12 agents while also personally marketing and selling mutual funds and insurance.

- Refined my abilities in a competitive field and excelled in developing sales and marketing techniques which resulted in increased sales.

Highlights of earlier experience: Gained versatile experience in sales, inventory control, and customer service in jobs including the following:

FINANCE AND OPERATIONS MANAGER: Became highly effective in handling finances, marketing, and sales as the owner of a business with six sales professionals, a title clerk, a bookkeeper, and 12 employees in the body shop (Genie Auto Shop, Richmond, VA).

- Created marketing and advertising plans and products which were highly effective.

SALES REPRESENTATIVE: For a major automobile dealer, consistently placed in the top three of 22 sales professionals (Edwards Buick, Richmond, VA).

- "Salesman of the Month" for 13 consecutive months and once as "Salesman of the Year."

FIELD SALES MANAGER: Became the youngest person in the company's history to hold this position after only a year (Fuller Brush Company, Plattsburgh, NY, and Phoenix, AZ).

- Became skilled in earning the confidence of potential customers and achieved a highly successful rate of positive responses from four out of each five people I approached.

TRAINING

Completed corporate training programs in areas such as real estate law, brokerage, finance, and securities as well as life, accident, and health insurance.
Am licensed as a real estate salesman, broker, and life/accident/health insurance agent.

PERSONAL

Am known for my ability to see "the big picture" while managing the details. Offer a proven ability to develop strategic plans that maximize profitability and market share in competitive environments. Am a results-oriented, persistent individual.

Exact Name of Person
Title or Position
Name of Company
Address (no., street)
Address (city, state, zip)

INTERIOR DESIGNER   Dear Exact Name of Person (or Dear Sir or Madam if answering a blind ad):

I would appreciate an opportunity to talk with you soon about how I could contribute to your organization through my sales and communication skills, interior design expertise, as well as my initiative and ability to work independently.

As you will see from my resume, I have been working since I was 16 years old, and I financed 80% of my college education through summer and part-time jobs. A highly motivated self-starter, I was nominated for numerous honors at Maryville University because of the leadership I provided on campus, to my sorority, and in the community. I am especially proud of the fact that, as my sorority's elected president, I transformed a poorly performing organization with serious financial problems into a respected entity which won the "most improved chapter" award.

I have found that my leadership is a valuable asset in business, too. I have a knack for motivating people, and I am respected for my ability to troubleshoot difficult problems and satisfy even the fussiest customers. You would certainly find me to be a hard worker who would enjoy contributing to your goals, and I would be delighted to provide outstanding personal and professional references at the appropriate time.

I hope you will welcome my call soon to arrange a brief meeting at your convenience to discuss your current and future needs and how I might serve them. Thank you in advance for your time.

Sincerely yours,

Joy Ann Honour

Alternate last paragraph:
I hope you will call or write me soon to suggest a time convenient for us to meet and discuss your current and future needs and how I might serve them. Thank you in advance for your time.

JOY ANN HONOUR

1110½ Hay Street, Fayetteville, NC 28305   •   preppub@aol.com   •   (910) 483-6611

OBJECTIVE   To contribute to an organization that can use a creative and dynamic young professional with expertise related to interior, commercial, and residential design who offers very strong leadership, motivational, communication, and sales skills.

EDUCATION   **Bachelor of Science (B.S.)** degree in Human Environmental Sciences, Maryville University, Maryville, SC, 1995.
- As elected president of my sorority, Delta Zeta, transformed a disorganized operation into the "most improved chapter in NC and SC"; was personally named "Outstanding President for NC and SC" and inducted into the Greek Hall of Fame.
- Was elected Student Legislator, Student Government Association; was elected Secretary of the legislature's Rules and Judiciary Committee.
- Was nominated for several prestigious awards for campus, community, and sorority leadership; received the respected Artemis Award.
- Personally financed 80% of my college education through part-time and summer jobs.

MEMBERSHIP   Member, American Society of Interior Designers since 1989; presently an Allied Practitioner.

EXPERIENCE   **INTERIOR DESIGNER.** The Decorator Store, Charleston, SC (1998-present). Have worked with this family-owned business since I was 16 years old, and have become an expert in all aspects of residential interior design in a shop that is well known for its creation of quality window treatments.
- Hired and supervised other employees.
- Am known for my skill in working with "fussy" clients in this very custom business.
- Applied my leadership skills by helping this store to expand from its solid niche in window treatments into interior design consultation services.
- Have become skilled in figuring the actual fabrication of window treatments.
- Used my sales and organizational skills to improve customer relations/service.
- Because of my strong communication and motivational skills, am the interior designer who troubleshoots stubborn problems when they arise.

INTERIOR DESIGN INTERN. U.S. Government, Directorate of Engineering and Housing — Design Branch, Ft. Bragg, NC (May 1997-August 1997). Received a letter of praise and appreciation and was complimented for my initiative and independence while excelling in an internship which required me to design an entire building; specified carpets, tile, and paints; performed some architectural sketching; redesigned a map.
- Worked on interior design recommendations for the new medical center at Ft. Bragg.
- Studied the design of local churches.
- Received an "A" for my internship; invited to participate in meetings on the new hospital.

COMPUTER OPERATOR. Maryville Technical Community College, Maryville, SC (June 1996-August 1996). Processed information for a tire recycling project using the Apple computer; data processed the results of others research, and inputted mailing lists.

TYPIST. World Travel, Maryville, SC (June 1996). Typed letters, delivered tickets, and set up displays of travel brochures; took pride in doing very small jobs to the best of my ability.

PERSONAL   Believe my leadership qualities are very valuable as they help me sell and motivate people. Am interested in gaining expertise in every aspect of interior design.

Date

Exact Name of Person
Title or Position
Name of Company
Address (number and street)
Address (city, state, and zip)

INTERIOR DESIGNER   Dear Exact Name of Person (or Sir or Madam if answering a blind ad):

I would appreciate an opportunity to talk with you soon about how I could contribute to your organization through my education and experience in interior design.

As you will see from my resume, I am presently the Acting Interior Designer for the UNC Hospital in Chapel Hill where I oversee repair, renovation, and construction projects throughout the hospital system. Originally accepted for a 200-hour internship, I found myself in a position where my supervisor was absent half of the time and I was training myself. I took over when she left and am currently holding this job on an interim basis.

This opportunity has given me the chance to prove myself at a level not usually enjoyed by a young person at this stage of her career. I have taken on a wide range of projects throughout the facilities while becoming skilled at budget analysis, preparing specifications, ordering products to be used in various projects, and overseeing the actual renovations and repairs.

While in college I was an instrumental player in efforts to gain FIDER (Foundation for Interior Design Education Research) accreditation for my school and was a member of the first class to graduate with this accreditation in place.

I am a customer service-oriented good listener known for my ability to handle pressure and deadlines. Through my creativity and knowledge, I have a great deal to offer to an organization that can use a detail-oriented and mature young professional.

I hope you will welcome my call soon to arrange a brief meeting to discuss your current and future needs and how I might serve them. Thank you in advance for your time.

Sincerely,

Bettina K. Charles

Alternate last paragraph:
I hope you will call or write me soon to suggest a time convenient for us to meet and discuss your current and future needs and how I might serve them. Thank you in advance for your time.

BETTINA KAROL CHARLES

1110½ Hay Street, Fayetteville, NC 28305   •   preppub@aol.com   •   (910) 483-6611

OBJECTIVE

To offer creativity and knowledge of residential and industrial interior design to an organization that can use a detail-oriented communicator who thrives on challenges.

EXPERIENCE

INTERIOR DESIGNER. UNC Hospitals, Chapel Hill, NC (1999-present). Oversee the details of coordinating repair and construction projects as well as facility enhancements.

- Hired for a 200-hour internship, stepped into the designer's job when it was unexpectedly left vacant and worked with the department supervisor to restructure the position.
- Assisted in restructuring the facility enhancement portion of the budget ($450,000) including combining corrected figures into a concise report for hospital administrators.
- Handled operational areas ranging from ordering products to overseeing installation and repair.
- Consulted with physicians, nurses, and other involved staff members to get their input into design projects for areas which directly affected them.
- Participated in meetings in preparation for design competition at IIDA, the International Institution of Designers of America.
- Oversaw a wide variety of projects throughout the hospital, including:
  burn center: wall coverings, lockers, and seating for the staff locker rooms
  food and nutrition lounge: seating specs and color scheme determination
  pulmonary unit: artwork specs and installation, budget analysis for seating in treatment areas, and finish selections for seating
  patient education offices: site analysis, space planning, and budget analysis
  pediatric waiting room: specs and budget analysis for seating renovations, provided assistance with artwork donation collection and installation
  imaging department: specs, budget, and procurement of flooring

INTERIOR DESIGN ASSISTANT and **SALES ASSOCIATE.** Occasional Designs, Greenville, NC (1996-98). Became familiar with all aspects of the business while assisting clients and guests, creating displays as well as keeping them updated and fresh-looking, assisting with office operations, and learning about the various suppliers.

- "Sold" myself and my potential to management through the creative idea of working free for two weeks and proving myself so that I was soon offered a permanent position.
- Learned about color, arrangement, and space planning while assisting designers in selecting fabric, wallpaper, window treatments, carpet, and all other aspects of design.
- Refined my communication skills and became adept at understanding what a client wanted so that those needs could be communicated in turn to a decorator.
- Utilized my creativity while designing ads and helping with advertising sales projects.

WAITRESS/HOSTESS. Applebee's in Raleigh and Durham, NC (1990-95). Learned to be patient and cheerful while dealing with customers; worked closely with cooks, other wait staff, and bartenders.

EDUCATION

Earned a **B.A. degree in Interior Design**, East Carolina University, Greenville, 1996.

- Was instrumental as a member of the class which completed all the preliminary work resulting in gaining the program FIDER (Foundation for Interior Design Education Research) accreditation; this degree program is the model for the university's future.

AFFILIATIONS

Member, ASID, American Society of Interior Design; selected for membership in NKBA (the National Kitchen and Bath Association) after judging a competition.

Date

Exact Name
Exact Title
Address
Address
City, state zip

Dear Sir or Madam:

    With the enclosed resume, I would like to introduce you to my more than 20 years of experience in as a Journeyman Roofer.

    In my most recent position, I was credited with increasing production levels an impressive 25% while installing shingles on both flat and touchdown-style roofs; I achieved perfect accountability for an average of $2,000 in materials and flashing while also maintaining and controlling $2,000 worth of tools used on each job. I certainly understand the importance of minimizing waste and providing customers with quality installation which will be guaranteed for up to ten years.

    I have recently relocated to your area because I want to live near my aging parents, and I am exploring employment opportunities with large construction firms that can benefit from my technical skills. If you can use my considerable expertise, I hope you will contact me.

Yours sincerely,

Lenny Watts

LENNY WATTS

1110½ Hay Street, Fayetteville, NC 28305   •   preppub@aol.com   •   (910) 483-6611

OBJECTIVE

To offer an organization my strong management skills, my experience in the construction industry, as well as my ability to handle multiple projects and priorities.

EDUCATION & TRAINING

Have completed approximately two years of college course work with a concentration in Business Administration.

Completed the **Wisconsin Construction Contractors Education Series** course which emphasized Wisconsin laws, business employment and Equal Opportunity law, foreclosures, and basic contract law, Human Resource Development Center, Gladstone, WI, 2000.

Received U.S. Army courses related to loading aircraft, hazardous cargo handling, safety, quality assurance, leadership development, and training/counseling techniques.

COMPUTERS

Offer computer skills with Windows; Microsoft Word, Excel, and Quicken

EXPERIENCE

Am advancing my knowledge level and skills in the construction industry:
JOURNEYMAN ROOFER. Smithson Roofing, Canby, WI (2001-present). Am credited with increasing production levels an impressive 25% while installing shingles on both flat and touchdown-style roofs; learned to operate forklifts.
- Achieve perfect accountability for an average of $2,000 in materials and flashing while also maintaining and controlling $2,000 worth of tools used on each job.
- Understand the importance of minimizing waste and providing customers with quality installation which will be guaranteed for up to ten years.

FOREMAN and **JOURNEYMAN ROOFER.** North Molalla Roofing, Molalla, WI (2000-01). Increased production 40% while meeting schedules for installing shingles and materials, including detail flashing, with a minimum of waste.

APPRENTICE/JOURNEYMAN ROOFER. Clark's Roofing, Clackamas, WI (1998-00). Learned OSHA regulations relative to the industry, operation of roofing equipment, procedures for accounting for materials, and tool and vehicle maintenance procedures.
- Was hired for this job after a ten-month apprenticeship with Parkinson Construction.

Advanced in supervisory roles with the U.S. Army:
SUPERVISOR & TEAM LEADER. Ft. Campbell, KY (1994-98). Earned two Army Commendation Medals for my contributions and leadership during training, daily operations, and under combat conditions during the war in the Middle East.
- Held multiple responsibilities for ensuring personnel were trained to high standards and that weapons and vehicles were properly maintained and operationally ready.
- Supervised physical security support activities for housing, office, and support facilities.
- Completed **Ranger School**, the military "stress test" which only 50% of students complete.

VEHICLE MECHANIC and **DRIVER.** Ft. Campbell, KY (1991-94). Became recognized as a skilled mechanic while controlling tools and parts, carrying out and supervising maintenance, and road testing motorcycles.
- Selected to attend the Army-sponsored **Motorcycle Safety Course**.
- Handpicked to attend a U.S. Air Force **Air Load Planning Course**.

PERSONAL

Was frequently cited by my superiors as possessing "sound judgment, strong initiative, a high degree of knowledge, and exceptional abilities." Meet challenges with enthusiasm.

Date

Exact Name of Person
Exact Title
Exact Name of Company
Address
City, State, Zip

**LANDFILL
MANAGER**

Dear Exact Name of Person (or Dear Sir or Madam if answering a blind ad):

With the enclosed resume, I would like to make you aware of my interest in exploring employment opportunities with your organization.

With a reputation as a respected executive with vast experience in the waste disposal and construction industries, I have worked for only two companies in the past 20 years. Early in my career, I worked for Waste Materails, Inc., and I excelled in jobs which included Landfill General Manager, District Landfill Manager, and Regional Landfill Manager.

Since 1987, I have excelled in a track record of promotion with Brighton Industries, and I most recently served as General Manager of a 3,200-ton-per-day MSW landfill, where I provided oversight for 15 employees and 20 contract workers. The company was recently sold, and I have decided not to continue with the new owners.

In previous positions with Brighton Industries, I served as District Manager in Alabama, Maryland, Michigan, and Ohio. In Ohio, I formed a new company for landfills and managed daily operations while also working with the local community to expand the landfill. On one occasion, I formed a new company and hired supervisory personnel for a district with four transfer stations, 11 residential routes, and recycling for two Ford assembly plants. In Maryland, I took over a year-old landfill losing $7 million yearly and took initiatives which restored profitability of a five-year, $67 million contract. I have managed dozens of construction projects.

If you can use a seasoned problem solver and decision maker with vast knowledge of construction and waste disposal, I hope you will contact me to suggest a time when we might talk in detail about your needs. I offer an outstanding industry reputation and can provide excellent references.

Yours sincerely,

Roger Prilliams

ROGER PRILLIAMS

1110½ Hay Street, Fayetteville, NC 28305 • preppub@aol.com • (910) 483-6611

OBJECTIVE

I want to contribute to a company that can use the vast knowledge and skills I have gained while working at the executive level in the construction and waste disposal industries.

CERTIFICATIONS SWANA Landfill Certified; State of Alabama Landfill Certified

EXPERIENCE

Excelled in the following advancement based on achievements, Brighton Industries.
2002-present: GENERAL MANAGER. Roseboro, AL. Took over management of a 3,200-ton-per-day MSW landfill; managed 15 employees and 20 contract workers.
- This company was recently sold and I decided not to continue with the new owners.

1998-02: DISTRICT VICE PRESIDENT OF ALABAMA LANDFILLS. Bartow, AL. Took over the management of five landfills after the company purchased them; re-permitted all five landfills, restructured operations, and boosted profitability. Managed a $14 million budget and 40 people.

1994-98: DISTRICT MANAGER. Richmond, VA. Took over a year-old landfill losing $7 million yearly; took initiatives which restored profitability of a five-year, $67 million contract.
- Built and operated a 225-acre site; construction included a multi-layer liner system with leachate and methane gas collection systems, and lined leachate ponds; extensive erosion/sediment control.
- Handled contracts with the county, including bidding/awarding of work to subcontractors.
- Provided oversight for 33 employees and 100 subcontractor employees at a landfill.

1993-94: DISTRICT MANAGER. Detroit, MI. Formed a new company which included a leasing property for maintenance, an office, and a container rebuild shop; hired supervisory personnel for a district with four transfer stations, 11 residential routes, and recycling for two Ford assembly plants.
- Employees included personnel separating cardboard, pallets, and metal from the waste stream.

1992-93: DISTRICT MANAGER. Cleveland, OH. Formed a new company for landfills and managed daily operation of Glenwillow Landfill; worked with the local community in expanding the landfill. Purchased property and built office, scalehouse, and maintenance buildings as well as a new entrance, interior roads, and drainage while overseeing generate site aesthetics.
- For the Warner Hill Landfill, handled the complete closure plan including final grades, gas and leachate collection systems, as well as final cover and monitoring plan.

1991-92: REGIONAL LANDFILL OPERATIONS MANAGER. Linthicum, MD. Managed operations of 9 operating landfills in MI, OH, MD, VA, WV, and PA as well as Ontario and Quebec. Monitored 11 closed sites in the region with remedial work including leachate collection systems and disposal, methane gas systems, final cover, closure plans; handled permitting, design, negotiations.

1987-90: GENERAL MANAGER. Pompano Beach, FL. At the Central Disposal Landfill, managed permitting, design, construction, methane gas and recovery, both collection and treatment plants. Also oversaw building maintenance and beautification projects.

EDUCATION

Two years of college course work in civil engineering at various institutions.

Exact Name of Person
Title or Position
Name of Company
Address (number and street)
Address (city, state, and zip)

**LEASING
CONSULTANT**

Dear Exact Name of Person (or Sir or Madam if answering a blind ad):

I would appreciate an opportunity to talk with you soon about how I could contribute to your organization through my experience in apartment lease/rental operations as well as through my reputation as a people-oriented, enthusiastic, and energetic young professional.

Known as quick learner, I can be depended on for personal integrity, resourcefulness, and dedication to excellence in everything I attempt. As you will see from my enclosed resume my most recent jobs have been as a Leasing Consultant in Colorado Springs, CO. For ABC Investments, Inc., I was entrusted with managing a large 280-unit property and a smaller 78-unit property. Earlier with Alpha Financial Services, Inc., I earned advancement after only a month with the company and have gained a strong interest in continuing to grow and provide excellent services in this field.

I hope you will welcome my call soon to arrange a brief meeting to discuss your current and future needs and how I might serve them. Thank you in advance for your time.

Sincerely,

Pearl N. Golden

Alternate last paragraph:
I hope you will call or write me soon to suggest a time convenient for us to meet and discuss your current and future needs and how I might serve them. Thank you in advance for your time.

PEARL N. GOLDEN

1110½ Hay Street, Fayetteville, NC 28305   •   preppub@aol.com   •   (910) 483-6611

OBJECTIVE   To offer my knowledge and experience in the area of property management and apartment rental and leasing operations to an organization that can use an enthusiastic young professional known for well-developed customer service and human relations skills.

EXPERIENCE   **LEASING CONSULTANT.** ABC Investments, Inc., Colorado Springs, CO (1998-present). Was credited with increasing the occupancy rate for the company's rental units while managing a 280-unit property and a smaller 78-unit property.

- Organized the operations of the property management office and provided excellent customer service through my professionalism in providing the highest quality services.
- Maintained records on leased apartments and prepared weekly and monthly reports.
- Balanced records of rent received as well as other cash income.
- Displayed a mature and professional manner while managing the office to include answering phones, walking prospective renters through unoccupied units, and completing lease arrangements.
- Was entrusted with full charge of the office when the Property Manager was away and counted on for sound judgment and decision-making skills.
- Made up flyers promoting the complex and took them to various local companies for display; resulting in increasing awareness of the complex, thereby producing more leased units.
- Earned units toward my CAM — Certified Apartment Manager — designation.

LEASING CONSULTANT. Alpha Financial Services, Inc., Colorado Springs, CO (1996-98). Demonstrated interest, enthusiasm, and strong communication and "people" skills which led to my advancement to this position after only a month with the company.

- Learned the proper and ethical ways to succeed in this business and was given increasingly more responsibility in showing, leasing, and managing rental/leased properties.

TEACHER and **EARLY CHILDHOOD EDUCATION SPECIALIST.** Manana/La Casa Unified School District, Manana, CA (1995). Planned and oversaw age-appropriate classroom activities; supervised three aides while ensuring each child was learning in a safe and interesting environment.

- Refined my planning and time management skills while earning 24 units in Early Childhood Education.

SITE DIRECTOR. Poco Hills Family YMCA, Manana, CA (1991-94). Originally hired as a Counselor, took on full responsibility for an after-school program for 35 school-age children at its start up.

- Was selected from a group of four counselors to provide leadership and supervision for all phases of the new program.
- Planned activities and ensured that social, emotional, and physical developmental needs of the children were being met and that they were in a safe and healthy environment.

EDUCATION   Completed 1-1/2 years of college course work with concentrations in Child Development and Nursing, Mt. San Antonio College, Walnut, CA.

TRAINING   Attended a training program sponsored by the Apartment Association of Colorado Springs, CO, with an emphasis on legal and motivational training as well as resident relations.

PERSONAL   Am a quick learner and work well with people as a member of a team or independently.

MAINTENANCE MECHANIC

Dear Sir or Madam:

With the enclosed resume, I would like to make you aware of my interest in applying for the position as Forklift Mechanic on the 1B shift.

As you will see from my resume, I am qualified by Wal-Mart to operate the RC, Slip, and Clamp forklifts, and I previously repaired, tested, and maintained 4K, 6K, and 20,000-lb. forklifts while serving my country as an Aviation Support Equipment Mechanic and Inspector in the U.S. Navy. As an Equipment Repair Specialist, Mechanic, and Inspector, I won numerous awards in recognition of my accomplishments in decreasing downtime, boosting organizational efficiency, and developing new systems that streamlined efficiency. I trained and developed personnel who became knowledgeable of operational inspection techniques, and I was singled out by the Navy for jobs as Work Center Safety Officer and Inspector because of my excellent technical knowledge and unquestioned reliability.

A skilled maintenance professional, I am proficient at maintaining hydraulic systems, reading schematics, and troubleshooting electrical systems. While in the Navy, I excelled in numerous schools and courses which refined my technical knowledge and troubleshooting abilities, and I became skilled in repairing, maintaining, and testing not only forklifts but also all types of ground support equipment.

After leaving the Navy and prior to joining Wal-Mart, I worked as a Maintenance Mechanic for a private company where I was involved in building, installing, and repairing industrial equipment used in institutions such as jails and hospitals.

I am a responsible and hard-working individual who prides myself on my ability to make any activity function more efficient and I would enjoy the opportunity to apply my strong technical knowledge for the benefit of Wal-Mart as a Forklift Mechanic.

Sincerely,

Jackson Mitchell

JACKSON MITCHELL

1110½ Hay Street, Fayetteville, NC 28305　•　preppub@aol.com　•　(910) 483-6611

OBJECTIVE

I want to further contribute to the Wal-Mart organization as a 1B Shift Forklift Mechanic through my extensive preventive maintenance, safety, and quality assurance background.

LICENSES

Qualified and licensed by Wal-Mart to operate the RC, Slip, and Clamp forklifts

SKILLS

Skilled maintenance professional; maintain hydraulic systems; skilled in reading schematics; troubleshoot electrical systems

EDUCATION

Through training/experience while serving in the U.S. Navy, became skilled in repairing, maintaining, and testing **forklifts (4K, 6K, & 20,000-lbs.)** and aircraft ground support equipment including:

tow tractors	liquid oxygen carts	hydraulic units
gas turbine compressors	fire fighting unit	mobile electric power plants

Completed ASE Class "A1" School; ASE GTC-85 Turbine Engine Course; ASE GTCP-100 Gas Turbine Engine Course.

Completed a six-week arc and gas welding course at a community college.

EXPERIENCE

UNLOADER. Wal-Mart, Hope Harbour, FL (2000-present). Began as a Staple Stock Unloader on 2A shift in June 2002 and then moved to DA Unloader on 1B.

- Safely and skillfully operate all three forklifts used by Wal-Mart.

MAINTENANCE MECHANIC. X & Z Equipment, Tallahassee, Goldsboro, and Mt. Olive, FL (1999-02). For a private company, serviced and maintained coin-operated laundry equipment; built laundromats and installed large, commercial laundry equipment in institutions.

- Functioned as the company's mechanic, and troubleshot maintenance problems in multiple cities where the company installed and serviced equipment.
- Also maintained the owner's 49-unit trailer home park's plumbing system and well.
- Made regular visits to laundromats owned by the company to collect receipts, make bank deposits, complete maintenance and repair, and handle any customer service or operational problems; often supervised other employees.

Served my country in the U.S. Navy and was promoted ahead of my peers because of my exceptional skills related to preventive maintenance, quality assurance, and safety:

AVIATION SUPPORT EQUIPMENT MECHANIC & INSPECTOR. NAS Whidbey Island, WA (1998). Won several medals in recognition of my achievements in reducing downtime and boosting organizational efficiency, and cited as a major contributor to the air station's selection for the 1998 Installation of Excellence Award.

- Was selected to oversee a support activity in which 2,300 items of equipment for 22 customer units were properly issued, received, and accounted for.
- Trained personnel to be thoroughly knowledgeable of operational inspection techniques.
- Implemented a system which made scanning repair/maintenance boards easier to read at a glance and streamlined maintenance tracking activities.
- Was singled out for the critical position of Work Center Safety Officer.

EQUIPMENT REPAIR SPECIALIST. NAS China Lake, CA (1997). Repaired and did preventive maintenance on gas turbine compressors and ground support equipment.

PERSONAL

Responsible and hard-working individual who excels in technical problem solving.

CAREER CHANGE

Date

MARKETING CONSULTANT

Dear Sir or Madam:

With the enclosed resume, I would like to make you aware of my interest in exploring employment opportunities with your organization.

In my current position as a Marketing Consultant, I have been working outside the construction field, but I am attempting to return to a suitable opportunity in the construction industry.

In my previous job as Department Chairman, Carpentry and Cabinetmaking, at Davidson Technical Community College, Davidson, VA, I taught a one-year general construction and business course combining classroom and practical field experience; involved students in projects which included forming and pouring concrete as well as carpentry/cabinetmaking. I built a dynamic program which, soon after I took over as chairman, was attracting twice as many students as previously; developed programs which have become recognized as "the best" offered by the state's 52 community colleges.

I have also acted as General Contractor on construction projects with control over architectural details as well as framing, foundation, and trim work.

If you can use a versatile construction industry professional with strong supervisory and communication skills, I hope you will contact me to suggest a time when we might meet to discuss your needs. Thank you in advance for your time.

Sincerely,

Marcus Knolsen

MARCUS KNOLSEN

1110½ Hay Street, Fayetteville, NC 28305 • preppub@aol.com • (910) 483-6611

OBJECTIVE

To benefit an organization that can use a powerful motivator with proven skills in managing and streamlining business operations for maximum profitability along with a track record of success as an entrepreneur, college instructor and administrator, and general contractor.

EDUCATION

B.S. degree in Physical Education, Davidson State University, VA.

EXPERIENCE

MARKETING CONSULTANT. Success Unlimited, West Palm Beach, FL (1999-present). Travel throughout the U.S. and occasionally to Europe as a Sales and Marketing Consultant for a network marketing organization which sells and distributes top-quality nutritional products.

- Have combined my enthusiastic support of the company's products with my highly effective motivational style in building a nationwide organization of thousands of distributors whom I have recruited, trained, and motivated.
- Have utilized to great advantage my ability to deal effectively with people at all socio-economic levels, from doctors to painters; take pride in the fact that I have helped many individuals build a profitable full-time business while helping others to develop a business providing extra income.
- Utilize my considerable business management experience to train distributors in all aspects of business management, from inventory control to customer relations.
- Began part-time in 1992, and within six months built my business up to the point that it became a full-time job.
- Am one of only nine distributors in the U.S. on the company's National Advisory Board.

DEPARTMENT CHAIRMAN, CARPENTRY, AND CABINETMAKING. Davidson Technical Community College, Davidson, VA (1992-99). Taught a one-year general construction and business course combining classroom and practical field experience; involved students in projects which included forming and pouring concrete as well as carpentry/cabinetmaking.

- Built a dynamic program which, soon after I took over as chairman, was attracting twice as many students as previously; developed programs which have become recognized as "the best" offered by the state's 52 community colleges.
- Acted as General Contractor on construction projects with control over architectural details as well as framing, foundation, and trim work.
- Led students in completing projects up to 5,000 square feet and worth $250,000.
- Increased the program's scope to cover business and computers.

GENERAL CONTRACTOR. Thomas Smith Construction Company, Raeford, VA (1990-92). Developed a successful company which specializes in custom-built single-family and multi-family homes priced up to $200,000; also handle multimillion-dollar commercial building projects.

- Handled bidding of projects, negotiation, contracts, and subcontractor coordination.

SPECIAL SKILLS

Familiar with construction including sheet rock, plumbing, roofing, painting, electrical work, masonry, painting, concrete, cabinetmaking, reading blueprints, carpentry, and supervision.

PERSONAL

Outstanding personal and professional references upon request. Strong work ethic.

CAREER CHANGE

Date

Dear Sir or Madam:

With the enclosed resume, I would like to inquire about employment opportunities in your organization and make you aware of my extensive background related to sales and marketing, customer service, and management.

Sales, Customer Service, and marketing background

As you will see from my resume, I have most recently excelled in handling sales and customer service responsibilities in both the financial services and automobile sales field. In my earliest positions as an Auto Sales Representative, I refined my communication and negotiating skills and then advanced in a track record of accomplishment as a Sales Manager and then General Sales Manager. In my current job in the financial services field, I am excelling as a Mortgage Consultant in a highly competitive marketplace, and I am known for my excellent communication and negotiating skills.

Experience in contracting and purchasing

In a previous job, I refined my decision-making and problem-solving skills as an Assistant Contract Officer. I was authorized to approve contracts under $500,000 for the procurement of goods and services, and I was commended for my ability to maintain excellent working relationships while overseeing strict quality assurance related to the expenditure of public money.

Military and security background

As a young airman in the Air Force, I proudly served my country and was entrusted with one of the nation's highest security clearances: Top Secret. After military service, I worked in the law enforcement and corrections field and continued to serve my country in the National Guard in administrative capacities.

I can provide outstanding references at the appropriate time, and I would enjoy an opportunity to talk with you in person about your needs. If you can use a versatile young professional who is accustomed to excelling in multifaceted complex assignments, I hope you will contact me. Thank you in advance for your time.

Yours sincerely,

Mark R. Graham

MARK R. GRAHAM

1110½ Hay Street, Fayetteville, NC 28305   •   preppub@aol.com   •   (910) 483-6611

OBJECTIVE

I want to contribute to an organization that can use an accomplished sales professional who offers a proven ability to establish strong working relationships, generate profitable bottom-line results, and provide outstanding customer service.

EDUCATION

College: Completed three years of college at these institutions: studied **General Studies** and **Sociology**, Boston College, MA; studied **Business Administration**, Northeastern University, MA; and studied **Business Administration**, Boston Business College, MA.
Military Training: Completed technical training and professional development courses sponsored by the U.S. Air Force; areas studied included administration and operations management.
Sales: Completed numerous courses related to sales and customer service sponsored by my employers.

EXPERIENCE

Sales and Financial Field:
MORTGAGE CONSULTANT. New England Mortgage, Brookline, MA (1997-present). As a mortgage consultant for a regional mortgage brokerage company, provide services related to debt consolidation while refinancing VA, FHA, conforming, and nonconforming loans.

GENERAL SALES MANAGER. Peter David Used Cars, Lexington, MA (1995-97). Was recruited by the founder of the company to serve as his General Sales Manager; supervised up to 10 sales professionals including assistant sales managers.
* Trained sales professionals in winning techniques related to sales and customer service.
* Helped my sales staff become skilled at "closing the sale" and negotiating final details.

SALES MANAGER. Revere Chrysler-Suzuki, Lexington, MA (1994-95). Was credited with being a major force in helping the company achieve gross sales of $32 million a year along with an extremely healthy after-tax income.
* Resigned from this job when I was recruited by my former employer, Peter David, to become his General Sales Manager.

Corrections and Law Enforcement Field:
CORRECTIONAL OFFICER. (1990-94). Worked in a 1,000-man corrections facility in Maryland State Penitentiary, Potomac, MD and in the Bethesda City Jail, Bethesda, MD.

Contracting and Finance Field:
ASSISTANT CONTRACT OFFICER. Defense Control Administrative Services, Bethesda, MD (1985-90). Was authorized to approve contracts under $500,000 for the procurement of goods and services for the U.S. government; refined my communication and negotiating skills while fine-tuning the details of complex contracts.

Military Service:
ADMINISTRATIVE SPECIALIST. Strategic Air Command, Andrews AFB, MD (1980-84). Held a Top Secret security clearance and was entrusted with receiving Top Secret documents and other classified documents. Was promoted rapidly from Airman to Sergeant.

PERSONAL

Enjoy helping others and being in business situations in which my product knowledge can help consumers make a wise decision about products and services. Have proven my ability to provide the finest customer service in a highly competitive marketplace.

CAREER CHANGE

Date

BY FAX TO: Mrs. Maryanne Snider
District Manager
Pfizer

Dear Mrs. Snider:

**MORTGAGE LOAN
SPECIALIST**

This sales professional is
actually seeking to transfer
her skills into a new
industry. She is hoping to
convince employers in the
pharmaceutical industry
that she could excel in
pharmaceutical sales
through applying the same
highly motivated nature
which has helped her
achieve outstanding results
recently in banking and
earlier in the human
services field.

    With the enclosed resume, I would like to make you aware of my interest in employment as a **Pharmaceutical Healthcare Representative** with Pfizer. I believe you are aware that Don Smith, one of your Healthcare Representatives, has recommended that I talk with you because he feels that I could excel in the position as Pharmaceutical Healthcare Representative.

    As you will see from my enclosed resume, I offer proven marketing and sales skills along with a reputation as a highly motivated individual with exceptional problem-solving skills. Shortly after joining my current firm as a Mortgage Loan Specialist, I was named Outstanding Loan Officer of the month through my achievement in generating more than $20,000 in fees.

    I believe much of my professional success so far has been due to my highly motivated nature and creative approach to my job. For example, when I began working for my current employer, I developed and implemented the concept of a postcard which communicated a message which the consumer found intriguing. The concept has been so successful that it has been one of the main sources of advertisements in our office and the concept has been imitated by other offices in the company.

    In addition to my track record of excelling in the highly competitive financial services field, I have also applied my strong leadership and sales ability in the human services field, when I worked in adult probation services. I am very proud of the fact that many troubled individuals with whom I worked told me that my ability to inspire and motivate them was the key to their becoming productive citizens.

    If you can use a creative and motivated self starter who could enhance your goals for market share and profitability, I hope you will contact me to suggest a time when we could meet in person to discuss your needs and goals and how I could meet them. I can provide strong personal and professional references at the appropriate time.

Yours sincerely,

Irene S. Lane

IRENE S. LANE

1110½ Hay Street, Fayetteville, NC 28305   •   preppub@aol.com   •   (910) 483-6611

OBJECTIVE	To offer my experience in sales, marketing, and customer service to an organization that would benefit from my aggressive style of developing customer relationships and my desire to work for an organization that seeks to maximize market share and profitability.
EDUCATION	**B.S. in Business Administration,** University of San Diego, CA 1998. • Completed this degree in my spare time while excelling in my full-time job.
EXPERIENCE	**SENIOR MORTGAGE LOAN SPECIALIST.** First Mortgage Services, San Diego, CA (1997-present). Have continuously excelled in this position which requires excellent sales, customer service, decision making, and problem solving skills. • In Jan. 2000 was named Outstanding Loan Officer for generating $20,000 in fees. • Process VA, FHA, conforming, and nonconforming first and second mortgages while handling debt consolidations, refinancing, and other financial arrangements. • Consult with attorneys, VA and FHA officials, appraisers, and other construction and lending officials in matters related to loan conveyances and loan closings. • Research property to assess value, ensure liens, and assess credit worthiness of clients. • Am known for my gracious style of communicating with the public and for my ability to explain technical concepts in language that is understandable to lay people. • Have gained valuable experience in marketing services which are not well understood by the average consumer. **MORTGAGE LOAN SPECIALIST.** Ramsey Mortgage, San Diego, CA (1995-97). Gained expertise in all aspects of mortgage loan processing while becoming an expert in handling slow payments and credit repairs. **ADULT PROBATION SERVICES OFFICER.** California Department of Corrections, San Diego, CA (1990-95). Because of my exceptional work performance, excellent attitude, and superior work performance, was promoted in the following track record: **1994-95: Adult Intensive Probation Parole Officer.** Was promoted to a supervisory position which involved providing guidance and supervising a case load of 50 clients per week. • Earned widespread respect for my ability to establish rapport and cordial relationships with a wide variety of individuals from troubled backgrounds and with turbulent case histories. **1990-94: Adult Probation/Parole Officer.** Took pride in the fact that an extremely high percentage of my clients completed their probation and went on to become well adjusted and productive citizens; was frequently told that it was my leadership and motivation skills which made the difference in their lives. • Provided supervision and guidance for up to 150 clients per month who were on court-ordered probation; completed paperwork and reports in a timely fashion. **DEPUTY CLERK.** County Clerk of Superior Court, San Diego, CA (1988-90). Processed affidavits for court traffic tickets, misdemeanors, and felonies in the Criminal Division; was known for my professional style of interacting with others. **Other sales experience**: Gained sales experience as an Account Representative for a company which sold sleep systems; also worked as a Sales Representative for a company marketing the Canon Facsimile line.
PERSONAL	Enjoy tackling, achieving, and exceeding ambitious goals through my ability to work effectively with others. Excel in prospecting for new business. Resourceful and high energy.

Date

Exact Name of Person
Title or Position
Name of Company
Address (number and street)
Address (city, state, and zip)

OFFICE MANAGER, REAL ESTATE COMPANY

Dear Sir or Madam:

This junior professional was the victim of "downsizing" when the real estate and construction industries fell on hard times. That's why her first job shows an ending date expressed as a year. Notice that nearly all these resumes show just the "year dates" of employment; it is usually not necessary to show the dates of employment with month-by-month details. Sometimes this allows you to "edit" your career and leave a job off your resume which you held for only a few months.

With the enclosed resume, I would like to make you aware of the considerable business, management, and customer service skills I could put to work for you.

As you will see from my resume, I am skilled in all aspects of office management and am proficient with software including accounting programs such as Quicken Pro as well as WordPerfect and the Windows programs including Word, Excel, and Access. In one of my first professional positions, I was promoted rapidly by a children's entertainment company to responsibilities which involved traveling to conventions to book shows and negotiate contracts. The youngest person ever promoted to vice president, I am still a member of the Board of Directors of that company and am respected for my business insights and marketing instincts.

I offer exceptionally strong management skills and have contributed significantly to the bottom line in every job I have ever held. In my most recent position with a real estate company, I handled office responsibilities which had previously been the responsibility of two people, and I made valuable contributions to profitability by reorganizing numerous office systems for greater efficiency. I can provide outstanding personal and professional references from all employers for whom I have worked.

In every job I have held, I have played a key role in the development and implementation of sound business plans while also creating and coordinating innovative marketing and advertising programs. I have also been involved in financial analysis, projections, and business plan modeling as well as the preparation and analysis of reports used for strategic and operational business purposes.

You will see from my resume that I have completed three years of college with a cumulative GPA of 3.87. I am pursuing completion of that degree in my spare time. I am a highly motivated individual with a reputation as am ambitious self-starter, and much of my college work was completed while I excelled in sales and other jobs.

If you can use a versatile young professional known for outstanding management, marketing, customer service, organizational, communication, and public relations skills, I hope you will contact me to suggest a time when we might meet.

Sincerely,

Claudine Walbert

CLAUDINE WALBERT

1110½ Hay Street, Fayetteville, NC 28305 • preppub@aol.com • (910) 483-6611

OBJECTIVE

To benefit an organization that can use a hard worker and fast learner with extensive computer operations experience, a background in business management and business development, along with skills in marketing and advertising.

EDUCATION

With a 3.87 GPA, have completed three years of college studies in Economics, Indiana University, Bloomington, IN; am pursuing completion of the degree in my spare time.

SPECIAL SKILLS

Skilled in utilizing a variety of software for maximizing business performance:
WordPerfect   Quicken Pro   One Write Plus
Windows, including Word, Excel, and Access   Quick Books
- Experienced in accounts receivable and payable as well as inventory control
- Operate multi-line telephone systems
- Excel in newsletter development and graphic layout

EXPERIENCE

OFFICE MANAGER. Craven and Associates, Tampa, FL (2000-present). For a real estate company, functioned as the "right arm" to the owner as he concentrated his energies in sales while I managed all business and office functions; completed Real Estate School.
- Performed strategic business planning and development while also coordinating all marketing and advertising activities; designed effective advertising.
- Handled all areas of accounting including payables and receivables.
- Processed all the company's real estate contracts and performed liaison with customers.
- Scheduled appointments for clients with the builder, interior decorator, insurance company, and closing attorney.
- As Office Manager, performed work previously done by two people; saved the company money by reorganizing office procedures and the filing system for greater efficiency.

MANAGER. Fred Astaire Dance Studio, Tampa, FL (1996-00). Made significant contributions to the bottom line of this company which specialized in teaching the art of Ballroom dancing; handled all accounting matters, including the preparation of weekly and monthly reports, while also planning and implementing innovative campaigns to boost the numbers of students.
- Developed and implemented business plans that increased the customer base.
- Coordinated marketing and advertising activities.
- Prepared/analyzed reports pertaining to business development and strategic planning.
- Hired, trained, and supervised new employees including dance instructors.
- Played a key role in diversifying the types of dance instruction offered to include Country Western and Latin as well as Ballroom.
- Planned dance competitions and special events including parties; became known for my meticulous attention to detail in all matters.

MANAGER. Common Sense Business Systems, Tampa, FL (1995-96). For a small wholesale distribution company, excelled in handling numerous roles simultaneously; in this one-person office, handled sales, customer service, accounting, inventory control, and liaison with the parent company.

PERSONAL

Have a cheerful, outgoing personality that is well suited to customer service.

CAREER CHANGE

Date

Exact Name of Person
Title or Position
Name of Company
Address (no., street)
Address (city, state, zip)

PAINTER   Dear Exact Name of Person (or Dear Sir or Madam if answering a blind ad):

Can you use a dynamic and highly motivated young professional who offers a track record of outstanding sales and managerial results based on hard work, enthusiasm, and persistence?

As you will see from the resume I am enclosing, I worked full-time while earning my B.S. degree at East Carolina University. In every job I have held — ranging from warehouse co-manager, to shift supervisor, to painter — I have prided myself on doing every task to the best of my ability.

I feel my highly motivated nature and enthusiastic personality are especially suited to sales situations, and you will also see from my resume that I have excelled in selling both life and health insurance products as well as pest control services. In one job as an Insurance Salesman for U.S. Life & Casualty, I was in charge of a territory including Greenville, NC, and surrounding counties and I rapidly became skilled at prospecting for customers, telemarketing, overcoming objections, and closing the sale. I excelled in that and other jobs while attending college full time.

I offer a mature understanding of what it takes to succeed in sales, and I am aware that discipline, patience, and persistence are critical. I believe I demonstrated those qualities at a young age when I achieved the Eagle rank in Boy Scouts, an accomplishment which few attain.

I hope you will welcome my call soon to determine if there is a time when we could meet in person so that I could show you that I am a highly motivated, ambitious person who could become a valuable part of your team. Thank you in advance for your time.

Sincerely yours,

Larry E. Remington

LARRY E. REMINGTON

1110½ Hay Street, Fayetteville, NC 28305　　•　　preppub@aol.com　　•　　(910) 483-6611

OBJECTIVE

I want to contribute to an organization that can use a dynamic and results-oriented young professional who offers proven sales, marketing, and communication skills along with an enthusiastic and highly motivated nature.

HONORS

Achieved Eagle Scout rank in 1988; this is the highest award in Boy Scouts and is attained by only 2% of those who join Scouts.
- Elected President, Vocational Industrial Clubs of America (DECA), in high school.
- Elected Vice President, Pi Kappa Phi Fraternity, in college.
- Elected Philanthropy Chairman for Pi Kappa Phi Fraternity.

EDUCATION

B.S. degree, Community Services, East Carolina University, Greenville, NC, 2002.
- Worked full-time in the jobs described below in order to finance my college education.

LICENSES

Licensed in NC to sell Life and Health Insurance.
Licensed pest controller in NC.

EXPERIENCE

PAINTER. CANDO Custom Paint, Greenville, NC (2000-02). Worked full time in this job while putting myself through college; was known for my professional attitude and expert workmanship on both industrial and residential sites.

SHIFT SUPERVISOR. A.B.C.Z., Inc., Greenville, NC (1998-99). While financing my college education, worked up to 15 hours a day at a local pool hall/bar near my college campus; handled management responsibilities including supervising waitresses on the shift, overseeing the serving of alcohol, and accounting for all money made on my shift.

SALES REPRESENTATIVE. Brown's Pest Control, Greenville, NC (1997). After obtaining my pest control license, excelled in selling pest control services based on the professional inspections I conducted.
- Gained experience in selling a service and in communicating the technical details of pesticides and chemicals in language which the general public could understand.
- Rapidly became one of the company's most productive sales representatives.
- Was able to step into an unfamiliar industry and become a valuable employee.

INSURANCE SALESMAN. U.S. Life & Casualty Company, Charlotte, NC (1995-99). Obtained my Life and Health Insurance License; became one of the company's top salesmen.
- Was in charge of a territory including Greenville, NC, and surrounding counties.
- Learned valuable techniques in selling financial services and in explaining abstract concepts to people.
- Refined my skills in prospecting for customers, telemarketing, overcoming objections and closing the sale as well as in servicing customers.
- Rapidly acquired expert product knowledge related to financial instruments.

CO-MANAGER, WAREHOUSE. Quality Carpets, Fayetteville, NC (1993-95). Managed forklift operators and other personnel in this busy warehouse.
- Cut carpet material, loaded and unloaded trucks, and drove a forklift.
- Learned to work under tight deadlines where priorities were constantly changing.

PERSONAL

Excel at dealing with people and am skilled at building rapport with people of all ages and backgrounds. Believe that my enthusiastic nature is a valuable asset in sales situations.

Date

**PLANT RECLAMATION
MANAGER**

Dear Sir or Madam:

I would appreciate an opportunity to talk with you soon about how I could contribute to your organization through my experience in project management and safety program development and execution as well as my specialized skills related to scheduling complex operations.

Throughout my years as a U.S. Air Force officer, I was consistently described as a true professional who sets the standard. My training included more than a year of competitive technical courses as well as advanced management programs. My technical orientation includes a great deal of exposure to computers and other types of electronics equipment.

My present position involves overseeing all phases of operations in a well-established company in the demolition industry. I am achieving excellent results in this job while handling a wide variety of activities including health and safety program development and compliance and job estimating. With oversight for 40 employees using millions of dollars worth of heavy machinery and equipment, I ensure success through my ability to communicate with people at all levels as well as through the application of my problem-solving and troubleshooting skills.

Known as a mature and dependable leader and manager, I also offer a reputation as an enthusiastic and highly energetic individual with a creative mind and the ability to think on my feet. I am highly skilled at motivating and encouraging others to perform up to my high standards and enjoy being a contributor to well-functioning teams.

I hope you will welcome my call soon to arrange a brief meeting at your convenience to discuss your current and future needs and how I might serve them.

Sincerely yours,

Gerry H. Pace

GERRY H. PACE

1110½ Hay Street, Fayetteville, NC 28305　　•　　preppub@aol.com　　•　　(910) 483-6611

OBJECTIVE

To offer my reputation as an enthusiastic manager with a strong technical background and a talent for building teams and completing multiple projects simultaneously.

EXPERIENCE

OPERATIONS MANAGER. Plant Reclamation, Richmond, CA (2000-present). Provide total oversight for all phases of projects completed by 40 employees using millions of dollars worth of heavy machinery and equipment; juggled the demands of "wearing three hats" by also acting as the Director of Health and Safety and as a Job Estimator.

- Personally guided the company in maintaining the lowest injury/accident rate of any organization in the demolition/reclamation industry nationwide.
- Revised the company's health and safety-related standard operating procedures.
- Became very knowledgeable of OSHA (Occupational Health and Safety Administration) guidelines and with procedures which ensured compliance.
- Gained a broad base of experience related to heavy equipment operations and maintenance as well as construction and demolition operations.

Earned a reputation as a talented and technically oriented manager with a knack for producing results as a U.S. Air Force officer:

TECHNICAL AND SAFETY OPERATIONS MANAGER. Seymour Johnson AFB, NC (1997-99). Advised a chief executive on both ground and flight safety issues while also working closely with maintenance and other support personnel.

- Developed a specialized program which greatly eliminated the dangers of birds impacting on aircraft and which was rated as "the best ever seen" by Air Force inspectors.
- Applied my expertise while investigating incidents and used the information gained to prepare reports which laid out changes to procedures, regulations, and policies.

COMBAT NAVIGATOR. Saudi Arabia (1995-96). Won numerous awards for my direct contributions to the success of allied efforts during the war in the Middle East.

- Saved countless lives by personally locating and destroying seven SCUD missile sites, over 30 Iraqi tanks, and flew more than 65 sorties over Iraq and Kuwait.

SCHEDULING MANAGER. Seymour Johnson AFB (1993-94). Became highly proficient in handling the details of complex scheduling operations in an organization where each day's scheduling changes impacted on future operations; scheduled 240 sorties weekly.

TECHNICAL OPERATIONS MANAGER/NAVIGATOR. Moody AFB, CA (1992). Was officially evaluated as "unflappable" and capable of "thinking on his feet," also became known as a skilled and confident speaker in a job which involved making frequent briefings to executives in an organization with an obligation to respond immediately worldwide.

EDUCATION & TECHNICAL TRAINING

B.A., Geography, University of California, Berkeley.

Excelled in 66 weeks of intensive programs, including the accident investigation/safety course sponsored by the University of Southern California.

Completed a 40-hour hazardous waste operations course.

Have completed 1,500 hours of flight time as a navigator.

Proficient with PCs and computer networks, Windows, and dBase.

PERSONAL

Have a Top Secret security clearance; am very well-organized and detail oriented. Have a talent for being able to communicate with people at all levels.

Date

Box 1741
Fayetteville Publishing Company
PO Box 849
Fayetteville, NC 28302

PLUMBER   Dear Sir or Madam:

With the enclosed resume, I am responding to your ad for A Plumbing Specialist.

As you will see from my resume, I offer the strong mechanical aptitude you are seeking and, in fact, have earned a reputation for being "able to fix anything." I credit my mechanical know-how to starting work at a young age. From the time I was 16 years old, I worked in a plumbing business as a plumber's helper and, even though I worked part-time every day after school, I managed my time well enough to graduate from Donavan Senior High School as an Honor Graduate and as president of the Vocational Industrial Clubs of America (VICA) for two years.

After high school, I continued to work as a plumber and in 2000 I was promoted to manage the plumbing supply business where I began working as a youth. When I took over as manager, the business had profitability problems. I have transformed it into a very profitable operation while instituting inventory controls, reorganizing accounts payable/receivable, and altering purchasing policies and procedures. I am currently designing and implementing a safety program to assure absolute compliance with OSHA standards. Through my management experience, I have acquired excellent customer service skills.

Although I am highly regarded by my current employer, I have the goal of becoming a maintenance foreman in a large construction firm one day, and I am positive I have the mechanical knowledge, natural intellect, and management ability to advance into such a position.

If you can use a talented and versatile young professional such as myself, please call me at home and I would be delighted to make myself available to you for a personal interview. I can provide exceptionally strong personal and professional references. Thank you in advance for your time in considering my resume for employment with your company.

Sincerely yours,

Andre D. Kitchen

ANDRE D. KITCHEN

1110½ Hay Street, Fayetteville, NC 28305 • preppub@aol.com • (910) 483-6611

OBJECTIVE

I want to offer The Kelly-Springfield Tire Company my extensive experience in all aspects of plumbing installation, repair, and operations management along with my skill in reading and fabricating from sketches and prints.

LICENSES & CERTIFICATIONS

Completed the Plumbing Code Level #3 course, and am preparing to sit for the state exam in order to become a licensed plumber.

Certified in backflow prevention testing and repair, certification #020-G; certified by Public Works Commission in 1995 and recertified in 1997 and 1999.

EDUCATION

- Made a perfect score on both the math and reading assessment portions of the General Manufacturing Certification Program, Fountain Technical Community College.
- An **Honor Graduate** from Donavan Senior High School, Fountain, IA; achieved a 3.8 GPA on a 4.0 scale.
- Was able to excel academically and socially as a leader even though I held a part-time job as a plumber's helper from the time I was sixteen and throughout high school.
- Was elected president of Vocational Industrial Clubs of America (VICA) for two years.
- Named **Student of the Year** in Industrial Cooperative Training I and II, 1995 and 1996.

SPECIAL SKILLS

- Skilled in all types of plumbing repairs and new installation.
- Proficient in cutting and threading steel pipes and fitting the same.
- Experienced in managing accounts receivable/payable, purchasing, and sales.
- Skilled in operation of equipment including generators, electric drain cleaning machines, electric pipe threaders and cuttings, tamping machines, and flaring tools.

EXPERIENCE

PLUMBER. Chatham County Schools, Fountan, IA (2000-present). Perform plumbing repairs for schools and administrative buildings throughout the school system.
- Install boilers and install/repair heat and return lines for boilers and heating systems.
- Install commercial dishwashers and kitchen equipment in cafeterias.
- Employed part-time on the building security force at the Chatham County Civic Center.

MANAGER. ABC Plumbing Supply Company, Inc., Fountain, IA (1994-00). Began working after school as a plumber's helper at 16 years of age. Was promoted to manage the company after excelling as a plumber's helper and then plumber in this plumbing supply business; transformed it from an unprofitable operation into one that made substantial profit.
- After analyzing procedures and practices, instituted new inventory controls that eliminated waste and loss, and also dramatically altered purchasing policies/procedures.
- Reorganized the accounts payable and receivable departments.
- Was always willing to tackle weekend or night plumbing repair jobs to meet customer needs in addition to my regular management responsibilities.
- Designed and implemented a safety program to assure absolute compliance with all OSHA standards and other regulations regarding the plumbing trade.
- Performed commercial and residential rough-in, top-out, and setting out of plumbing fixtures in new homes and buildings.
- Repaired plumbing in offices, schools, restaurants, apartments, and homes.

PERSONAL

Known for my knack for being able to fix anything! Am single; would relocate. Offer strong customer service skills that have been refined through management experience.

Exact Name of Person
Title or Position
Name of Company
Address (no., street)
Address (city, state, zip)

PROJECT MANAGER   Dear Exact Name of Person (or Dear Sir or Madam if answering a blind ad):

Can you use an experienced project manager who offers a background in both manufactured housing as well as "spec" and custom residential construction?

As you will see from my resume, I worked full-time while earning my B.S. degree in Civil Engineering, Construction Option, at North Carolina State University.

In my current position, I am supervising the major remodeling of residential housing while also managing projects related to site-built and manufactured housing. In my previous position, I developed a profitable construction business which became known for on-time delivery and integrity. I began in the construction industry as a Carpenter's Helper, and then I accepted a position as a Rental Unit Maintenance Manager.

Although I am held in high regard in my current position, my wife and I are relocating to your area, and I am seeking an employer that can use my construction knowledge and project management experience.

I hope you will welcome my call soon to determine if there is a time when we could meet in person so that I could show you that I am a highly motivated, ambitious person who could become a valuable part of your team. Thank you in advance for your time.

Sincerely yours,

Larry E. Remington

GIL BARRY WESTERN

1110½ Hay Street, Fayetteville, NC 28305   •   preppub@aol.com   •   (910) 483-6611

OBJECTIVE   To benefit an organization that can use a smart, cost-conscious businessman who has demonstrated the ability to grow and manage a profitable construction company through my project management skills and knowledge of both commercial and residential construction.

EDUCATION   **Bachelor of Science in Civil Engineering, Construction Option**, North Carolina State University, Raleigh, NC, 1990; worked full-time while earning my degree.

EXPERIENCE   **PROJECT MANAGER**. Brahms Construction Company , Inc., Charlotte, NC (2000-present). For both site-built and manufactured housing at three family residential subdivisions, am responsible for all budgeting, quantity surveys, material purchasing, subcontractor scheduling, permit procurement, inspection scheduling, construction supervision, as well as coordination among interior decorators, realtors, and home buyers.
- Scheduled, supervised, and assured completion of all warranty work.
- Supervised major remodeling of residential rental units.

PRESIDENT/MANAGER. Second Avenue Renovation, Charlotte, NC (1989-present). Developed a profitable construction business and established a base of very satisfied customers while managing projects of varying sizes and complexity and completing jobs on time and within budget.
* Succeeded in this business by developing a personal reputation for quality, honesty, and reliability; now generate a significant portion of new business through word-of-mouth referrals and repeat customers.
* Became skilled in all aspects of project supervision, including management of subcontractors, liaison with suppliers, coordination with inspectors, supervision of employees, and communication with customers.
* Developed expertise related to all phases of site development as well as all aspects of planning and laying out new homes and additions.

RENTAL UNIT MAINTENANCE SUPERVISOR. Worsted Properties, Raleigh, NC (1985-89). Became knowledgeable about most areas related to the installation and upkeep of electrical and plumbing systems/fixtures while supervising construction, repairs, and maintenance performed on a diversified inventory of rental apartments and houses.
- Boosted profits and cut costs by reducing the time vacant units were "down" for repairs.
- Gained experience in property maintenance, public relations, and coordination.
- In a simultaneous job as **Night Manager** for Sophie's Subs in Raleigh, increased kitchen productivity by 25%, thereby reducing the need for additional workers.

CARPENTER'S HELPER. Allen Framing Contractors, Raleigh, NC (1984-85). Achieved an exceptionally high volume of production, reducing the need for additional crew.
- Was involved in the production and transportation of wall components for a 200-unit apartment complex.
- Learned to use power and air tools as well as surveying practices and instruments.
- Learned the basic principles of concrete construction and was a highly productive worker while building and setting forms for concrete construction.

PERSONAL   Offer a proven ability to relate effectively to all participants in a construction project. Am known as a talented planner, organizer, and scheduler with excellent skills.

Exact Name of Person
Exact Title
Exact Name of Company
Address
City, State, Zip

PROJECT MANAGER   Dear Exact Name of Person (or Dear Sir or Madam if answering a blind ad):

With the enclosed resume, I would like to make you aware of my interest in exploring employment opportunities with your organization.

While completing my B.S. degree in Urban and Regional Planning from West Virginia University, I was aggressively recruited by the largest industrial materials supplier in the world , Smith Enterprises, Inc., upon college graduation, and I rapidly advanced from inside sales to outside sales. As an inside sales representative, I managed 85 accounts worth $3 million and increased the profit margin by 15%. I restored confidence in some of the company's largest regional accounts, and I established outstanding relationships with all customers. After being promoted to outside sales with the Builder Sales Division, I took over an underperforming territory and, within four months, tripled sales.

I was recruited for my current job as Project Manager with a construction company by a customer whom I served while at Smith. Quality Construction created a new position especially for me, and I have been instrumental in developing sales of a new division to the $1 million per annum level. I excel in working with customers, subcontractors, city and state officials, as well as insurance personnel. I am in charge of 300 independent subcontractors who all work for me on various projects, and I have earned the confidence of veteran construction industry professionals because of my technical construction knowledge.

I gained considerable construction industry experience while in college as I worked up to 30 hours a week as a Carpenter and Residential Framer. I also managed crews for various jobs, and am skilled at utilizing a wide variety of construction industry tools and can safely operate various vehicles and equipment. One of the accomplishments of which I am proud is the fact that I financed all of my college education through loans and part-time jobs in the construction industry.

If you can use an aggressive young professional with a wealth of knowledge related to the construction industry, I hope you will contact me to suggest a time when we might meet to discuss your needs. I can provide outstanding personal and professional references at the appropriate time, but I ask that you please not contact my current employer until after we have a chance to meet and discuss your needs.

Yours sincerely,

Nathan Dawson

NATHAN DAWSON

1110½ Hay Street, Fayetteville, NC 28305 • preppub@aol.com • (910) 483-6611

OBJECTIVE

I want to contribute to an organization that can use an experienced young professional with extensive sales, customer service, and management experience.

EDUCATION

Bachelor of Science (B.S.) degree in Urban and Regional Planning, West Virginia University, Blacksburg, WV, 1998.
- Acquired technical knowledge of the design of cities, neighborhoods, and traffic flow.
- In a summer internship, designed landscaping including sprinkler systems.

COMPUTERS

Experienced with Autocad, ArcInfo, ArcView, 3D Walkthrough, and many other programs.

EXPERIENCE

PROJECT MANAGER. Quality Construction Co., Blacksburg, WV (2002-present). Was recruited by a company which was a customer account of mine when I worked for Smith Enterprises; have excelled in a new position created specially for me and have been instrumental in developing a new division, increasing sales to the level of $1 million per annum in less than a year; the owner recently hired a second Project Manager to help with the work.
- Am in charge of 300 independent subcontractors working for me on various projects; have earned the respect of all subcontractors, most of whom are senior construction industry craftsmen.
- As Project Manager, 85% of my work is concerned with the repair of damaged property; perform liaison with many insurers; also work with customers adding to their homes.
- Extensively research covenants and other matters.
- Excel in working with customers, insurance personnel, government officials, and others.

INSIDE AND OUTSIDE SALES PROFESSIONAL. Smith Enterprises, Inc., Blacksburg, WV (1998-02). As a graduating college senior, was recruited by the largest industrial materials supplier in the world which is owned by a British firm and headquartered in Newport News, VA.
- Of the 30 people Smith interviewed at West Virginia, I was the only one invited to the second interview and was hired after an extensive battery of tests.
- Although the company has a standard policy of starting new sales employees in the warehouse and then promoting them to inside sales in one year, I was promoted to inside sales after only two months.

Inside sales achievements: managed 85 accounts worth $3 million and increased profit margin by 15%.
- As **Inside Sales Representative,** took over a corporate account worth $1.7 annually to Smith and restored confidence which had been lost through my predecessor's lack of follow through; established outstanding relationships.
- Inherited the $200,000 Smithfield Packing account which was "on the ropes" and quickly restored the customer's confidence in Smith's products and customer service.
- Handled debits/credits; was the primary contact for industrial firms within a 60-mile radius including Monsanto, Smithfield Packing, Lundy's, Carolina Foods, and others.

Outside sales achievements: took over an underperforming territory producing $17,000 and, within four months, increased sales to $53,000.
- As **Outside Sales Representative,** established strong rapport with all customers.
- Managed a two-person installation crew, a one-person showroom staff in Blacksburg, a two-person showroom staff in Pinehurst, and two employees in Sanford.

PERSONAL

Highly motivated hard worker with unlimited personal initiative. Excellent references.

CAREER CHANGE

Date

PROJECT MANAGER

This individual has been working outside his preferred functional area lately, and he is attempting to return to a position as Project Manager.

Dear Sir or Madam:

I am writing to express my interest in exploring employment opportunities with your organization.

As you will see from my resume, I offer extensive experience in the construction industry and in the electrical field. I am a self-motivated individual with an extensive background which includes supervision of workers, knowledge and application of tools and equipment, mechanical and preventive maintenance management, and overall knowledge of all construction-oriented activities and procedures. My experience also includes heavy/highway building categories.

I strive for pride and quality in all I do, and I offer an outstanding safety record as a supervisor and as an operator of all types of construction equipment and vehicles. I am known for my ability to train and motivate workers to strive for the highest standards of efficiency, profitability, and safety. I personally offer a strong bottom-line orientation and am a skilled project manager who is experienced in bringing jobs in on time and within budget.

If you can use a skilled construction industry professional with versatile supervisory, sales, and customer relations skills, I hope you will write or call me to suggest a time when we might meet to discuss your needs and how I might serve them. I can provide excellent personal and professional references at the appropriate time, and I am sure it would be a pleasure to talk with you in person.

Yours sincerely,

Alex English

ALEX ENGLISH

1110½ Hay Street, Fayetteville, NC 28305   •   preppub@aol.com   •   (910) 483-6611

OBJECTIVE   To benefit an organization that can use an experienced construction industry professional who offers an extensive safety and project management as well as supervisory experience.

LICENSE & SKILLS   Have held an Electrical Contractor's license (now expired); am preparing to take the exam. Operate the full range of construction equipment including backhoes, bulldozers, loaders, hydraulic cranes, forklifts, scrapers, and other equipment.

EXPERIENCE   **WAREHOUSE MANAGER.** ABC Electric Company, Inc., Garner, NM (April 2002-present). Responsible for delivery of material and equipment to job sites. Am personally responsible for controlling and accounting for vast quantities of material while also supervising the maintenance and upkeep of all vehicles and equipment.

INDEPENDENT SUBCONTRACTOR. Norris Dump Truck, Garner, NM (2000-02). Founded "from scratch," then owned and operated a business which functioned as a subcontractor to area firms; hauled dirt, rocks, gravel, and other material to construction sites.

PROJECT MANAGER. Silver's Electrical, Midland, MI (1998-99). Worked primarily on a project for UpJohn Pharmaceuticals in Kalamazoo, MI through a major firm which subcontracted my services.
- Managed all electrical work with 26-person crew.
- Bid on jobs; maintained change order records, contract documents, and billings.
- Worked on several large contracts related to instrumentation and controls as well as air emission control projects.
- Contracted waste treatment plant and heat trace project.

PROJECT MANAGER. Commercial Automation Solutions, Inc., Garner, NM (1997-98). Prebid meetings with estimators prior to job bids, and set up contract documents, bonds, insurance, and other documentation defining roles and relationships.
- Established and coordinated a schedule of values, billing jobs, and order material.

PROJECT MANAGER, ELECTRICAL SERVICES. Electric Corporation, Garner, NM (1997). Ordered material for jobs; scheduled jobs with owners and general contractors to meet completion dates.
- Recruited, interviewed, and hired workers to perform electrical work.
- Priced all change orders.

SELF-EMPLOYED ELECTRICAL CONTRACTOR & TELECOMMUNICATIONS TECHNICIAN. CO and NM (1986-96). Performed commercial and industrial installations in New Mexico and Arizona on sites which included office buildings, shopping centers, and duct banks. Installed secondary and primary underground feeders for contract with CP&L. Provided on-call maintenance for AT&T for pay phones and credit card phones.

Military service: U.S. Army 2nd Division, 82nd Airborne. Received two Purple Hearts, one Bronze Star, and one Silver Star.

EDUCATION   Completed extensive training related to building codes, electrical work, mechanical work, and computer operations.

PERSONAL   Excellent personal and professional references are available upon request.

Date

Mr. Gene Latshaw
President
Latshaw Construction
111 Layton Lane
Charleston, SC 99999

PROJECT MANAGER

Dear Mr. Latshaw:

Thank you for your recent expression of interest in my experience. With the enclosed resume, I would like to make you aware of my interest in confidentially exploring management opportunities with your organization.

As you will see from my resume, since 1990 I have worked for the same construction company, where I was crosstrained as a Project Manager, Quality Control Manager, and Foreman. I have managed numerous projects, and I am the Project Manager for all U.S. government and City of Charleston projects. I am experienced in managing projects including airport expansions as well as projects to establish and renovate utilities and roads. I am extremely experienced in managing construction projects on military bases, and I am accustomed to working with quality control technicians form the Corps of Engineers and other regulatory agencies such as OSHA. I am proficient with all aspects of construction administration including negotiating contracts and subcontracts, creating master project schedules, preparing bids for government jobs, and writing purchase orders for materials. Early in my employment, I was crosstrained as an Estimator and Quality Control Foreman.

I have received numerous letters of appreciation and awards for outstanding performance, and I have earned respect for my emphasis on safety, my ability to motivate employees, and my strong bottom-line orientation. I have contributed significantly to my employer's bottom line. For example, I have improved net profit on government jobs from a 15% average to a 35% average. On one $1.6 million job which I managed, the company made a 48% profit.

If you would like to discuss your needs with me, I hope you will contact me to suggest a time when we could meet in person to talk. Thank you.

Yours sincerely,

Michael Taft

MICHAEL TAFT

1110½ Hay Street, Fayetteville, NC 28305   •   preppub@aol.com   •   (910) 483-6611

OBJECTIVE

To benefit an organization that can use a construction industry Project Manager with previous experience in positions including **Quality Control Manager, Foreman, and Estimator.**

TECHNICAL KNOWLEDGE

Knowledgeable of OSHA and EMSHA.
Very knowledgeable of construction activities and procedures at government facilities.

EDUCATION

Bachelor of Science (B.S.) in Business Administration, Charleston State University (a campus of the University of South Carolina), Charleston, SC, 1994
Associate in Applied Science (A.A.S.), Charleston Technical Community College, 1992.

TRAINING

Completed extensive training by military and civilian organizations including the following:
Asphalt Driving Workshop, Department of the Army
Construction Quality Management, U.S. Army Corps of Engineers
Project Productivity Improvements, Carolinas AGC
Hot Mix Asphalt Construction, Department of Transportation
Alcohol and Controlled Substances Training for Supervisors, J.J. Keller & Assoc.
Employment and Labor Law Seminar, Carolinas AGC
Supervisory Training, APAC and Carolinas AGC
One-Minute Manager and *Seven Habits of Highly Effective People* and other seminars

EXPERIENCE

PROJECT MANAGER. Davidson Construction & Engineering, Charleston, SC (1990-present). Began as an **Estimator,** and then was crosstrained in other aspects of the construction business. Worked as a **Laborer** and became familiar with all construction trades. Also worked as a **Quality Control Manager** and **Foreman.**
Highlights of projects: Have managed dozens of projects, and am the Project Manager for all U.S. government and City of Charleston jobs.
- **Renovating and building roads:** For the City of Charleston, managed projects which involved the milling of asphalt on road, the raising the lowering of structures, establishing curbs, gutters, and sidewalks, and resurfacing of existing roads.
- **Airport expansion:** Managed a $1.5 million expansion of the Charleston Regional Airport. Supervised 25 individuals who included foremen, pipe layers, asphalt grade crews, as well as striping and sealcoat crews. Built a general aviation ramp. Finished the project three months ahead of schedule and under budget.
- **Utilities:** Managed a $2 million project at a military base. Developed a site for the U.S. military, and was involved in establishing utilities such as water and sewer. Installed all utilities including water, sewer, storm drains, and erosion control. Supervised paving of surfaces. Managed a project which ran very smoothly while supervising 35 people.
- **Extensive supervisory experience:** On numerous occasions, supervise 75 people including 10 foremen when the company's chief project manager is away.
- **Proficiency with government paperwork:** Have become proficient in writing subcontracts, writing purchase orders for materials, creating master project schedules using CPM, preparing bids for government jobs, and coordinating with quality control technicians from the Corps of Engineers.
- **Bottom-line results:** Have improved net profit on government jobs from a 15% average to a 35% average. The company made a 48% profit on one $1.6 million job.

PERSONAL

Excellent references on request. Have received numerous letters of appreciation and awards.

Date

Exact Name of Person
Title or Position
Name of Company
Address (no., street)
Address (city, state, zip)

PROPERTY MANAGER   Dear Exact Name of Person (or Dear Sir or Madam if answering a blind ad):

I would appreciate an opportunity to talk with you soon about how I could contribute to your organization through my experience and personal qualities.

I am in the process of relocating to Charleston, although I am assisting my current employer in the process of hiring and training my replacement. You will see from my resume that I have most recently excelled in a track record of advancement with Jones Realtors, where I began as a receptionist answering phones for 48 realtors and was immediately groomed for promotion into the sales force. I obtained my N.C. Real Estate License in 1998 and, as a Realtor, I became a million-dollar producer within 12 months. Since 2000 I have worked as a Property Manager for the company and have brought more than 125 new rental properties into management while personally managing an inventory of 200 houses.

You would find me in person to be a vibrant, highly motivated individual who can become a valuable asset to any organization. I can provide outstanding references.

If you can use a top producer with extensive experience in most aspects of the real estate and property management business, I hope you will call or write me to suggest a time when we can meet. I will make myself available for a personal interview at your convenience. Thank you in advance for your time.

Yours sincerely,

Esther N. Adley

Alternate last paragraph:
I hope you will welcome my call soon to arrange a brief meeting at your convenience to discuss your current and future needs and how I might serve them. Thank you in advance for your time.

ESTHER N. ADLEY

1110½ Hay Street, Fayetteville, NC 28305 • preppub@aol.com • (910) 483-6611

OBJECTIVE

I want to contribute to an organization that can use a highly motivated self-starter who offers strong public relations and communication skills along with experience in managing people, property, finances, and daily business operations.

EXPERIENCE

Began with Jones Realtors company in 1997, and have excelled in handling both sales/marketing and property management responsibilities on a large scale:
2000-present: PROPERTY MANAGER. Jones Realtors, Property Management Department, Wichita, KS (2000-present). Have excelled as a property manager for one of the area's most well-known real estate/property management firms; am responsible for an inventory of between 180 to 200 residences.

- *Maintenance Management*: Supervise maintenance activities; coordinate and schedule staff and independent contractors; obtain estimates for work to be performed and monitor major repairs as work proceeds.
- *Public relations*: Screen potential residents and conduct rental showings.
- *Inspections and inventory*: Conduct bi-annual inspections of every property and conduct house inventories; order goods and materials as needed.
- *Administration*: Prepare reports for top management while also preparing lease renewals, inspection reports, and other paperwork.
- *Court liaison*: Handle evictions and represent the company in small claims court.
- *Negotiation*: Mediate between owners and tenants as needed in situations where disputes arise over damages, security deposits, or rent owed.

1997-2000: REALTOR. Jones Realtors, Wichita, KS. Became a $1.2 million-dollar producer within 12 months! Gained valuable skills in sales, marketing, and contract negotiating while acquiring expert knowledge of most aspects of the real estate business.

- Earned a reputation as a skilled and aggressive salesperson who was committed to client satisfaction.
- Began with the company as a Receptionist in 1997 answering the phone for 48 realtors, and started obtaining my real estate license after only three days on the job; and was groomed by management for rapid promotion into the sales force.

OFFICE ADMINISTRATOR. Southwest Real Estate Corp., Killeen, TX (1995-96). Handled a wide range of activities for this real estate company. Processed sales contracts and revisions; verified sales prices, financing, option pricing, and lot premiums with approved documents; deposited and accounted for all earnest money received; prepared sales, closings, and construction reports; maintained land files including settlement statements and title insurance commitments.

PROPERTY MANAGEMENT OFFICER/MEDICAL SUPPLY SPECIALIST. U.S. Army, locations worldwide (1990-94). As Property Management Officer, ordered and received all nonmedical supply items for the Logistics Division; maintained all files of local purchase items ordered and received; maintained quarterly budgets. Also ordered and received medical supplies for nine medical units and three dental clinics.

EDUCATION

Only six credit hours short of a two-year degree, Charles University, KS.
Completed Real Estate Dynamics Course, Psychology of Selling Course, and Time Management Seminar sponsored by real estate organizations.

PERSONAL

Familiar with Excel, Lotus 1-2-3, Word, and the Multiple Listing Service System (MLS).

PROPERTY MANAGER

Dear Sir or Madam:

I am writing to express my strong interest in a position as a Property Manager with your company. With the enclosed resume, I would like to make you aware of my background as an articulate professional with an extensive track record of success in customer service, sales, and management which could be of benefit to your organization.

As you will see from my resume, my involvement in sales and customer service environments extends throughout my career, from my earliest positions as Assistant Manager at Handy City, through jobs in the airline and car rental industries, to my current position as a Property Manager. In addition, my maturity and responsibility have led to consistent advancement into supervisory positions, where I have excelled as a trainer and manager, leading by example while providing the highest possible levels of customer service.

Through the years, I have built a reputation as an energetic, reliable employee. I feel that my dedication to ensuring the continued success of my employers, as well as my outstanding communication and motivational skills, have been the keys to my advancement throughout my career.

If you can use a Property Manager whose sales and customer service skills have been proven in a challenging environments, I hope you will write or call me to suggest a time when we might meet in person to discuss your goals and how my background might serve your needs. I can provide outstanding references at the appropriate time.

Sincerely,

Samuel A. David

SAMUEL AMOS DAVID

1110½ Hay Street, Fayetteville, NC 28305　　•　　preppub@aol.com　　•　　(910) 483-6611

OBJECTIVE　　To benefit an organization that can use an experienced manager with exceptional communication and organizational skills who offers a track record of accomplishment in customer service, training and staff development, and management.

EDUCATION　　Completed three years of college course work towards a Bachelor of Science in Communications; maintained a 3.2 cumulative GPA.

EXPERIENCE　　**PROPERTY MANAGER.** Mountain Rentals, Huntsville, SD (2000-present). Responsible for all aspects of the management for 40 rental properties, including maintenance and upkeep of the physical structure and grounds, inspection and cleaning of individual units, showing of rental properties to potential clients, and collections.
- Conduct exit inspections to determine if tenants have caused damage to the property clean and inspect individual units prior to showing them to prospective tenants.
- Perform minor carpentry, electrical, and plumbing repairs; hang, prepare, patch, and repair sheet rock; prepare and paint interior walls and ceilings.
- Oversee major and minor renovations to the interior and exterior of the buildings, as well as landscape maintenance and lawn care.

ASSISTANT BRANCH MANAGER. Efficiency Car Rental, Huntsville, SD (2000-2001). Supervised and trained two manager trainees; in the absence of the Branch Manager, managed the operation of this local car rental company with a $500,000, 85-car inventory.
- Completed a number of administrative reports, tracking the number of cars rented as well as the per diem cost to the customer and profit to the company on each vehicle.
- Provided exceptional customer service, delivering vehicles to customers and providing detailed information about rental rates, mileage, and insurance
- Ensured that all vehicles were cleaned and prepped prior to delivery to the customer.

ASSISTANT BRANCH MANAGER. Satisfaction Rent-A-Car, Huntsville, SD (1996-2000). While training and directing six manager trainees and a training assistant, assisted in overseeing all aspects of the operation of this busy car rental company with a 200-vehicle inventory worth more than a million dollars.
- Was responsible for scheduling all preventive maintenance, as well as major and minor repairs for all vehicles in the fleet.
- Conducted daily inventory of all vehicles and mechanical inspections at vehicle turn-in.

STATION AGENT. Atlantic SouthEast Airlines, Huntsville, SD (1996-1998). While simultaneously pursuing my college education and working in the above position, took on a second, part-time job assisting Atlantic SouthEast passengers at Huntsville Regional Airport by verifying their flight and/or checking them in on the computer. Loaded/unloaded cargo and filled out baggage claim reports; acted as a signal man during take-off and landings.

Highlights of earlier experience: Began my career in sales and customer service by quickly advancing to **ASSISTANT MANAGER** in my first position with Handy City; managed six employees in the Building Materials department, overseeing inventory control and quality assurance, as well as ensuring that the department met all sales quotas. Coordinated directly with the manager in developing and maintaining compliance with budget forecasts.

PERSONAL　　Am single and can travel or relocate to meet the needs of my employer.

Date

Mr. Vincent Nair
Human Resource Manager
Billows & Klein Recruiters
5881 North Delaware Street.
Miami, Florida 39023

PURCHASING MANAGER

Dear Mr. Nair:

With the enclosed resume, I would like to introduce myself and make you aware of the considerable experience in purchasing, contracting, property management, finance, and operations management which I could put to work for you. I am currently in the process of relocating to the Florida area where my extended family lives, and I would appreciate an opportunity to talk personally with you about how I could contribute to your organization.

With my current employer, I have been promoted to Senior Purchasing Manager. I am responsible for the property management of more than 5,000 houses and apartments, including a fleet of 72 service vans. I also prepare and resourcefully utilize a budget of more than $1.6 million annually for repair parts, outside services, support equipment, and materials. On my own initiative, I have totally streamlined the bidding process. In consultation with the System Manager, I implemented a new computer program to track bids, thereby transforming a previously disorganized manual process into an efficient computerized system. Additionally, I streamlined purchasing procedures while taking over a job which had previously been done by two people. Using available software, I have also established accounting and budgeting programs for a small business.

In all my previous jobs, I have been recognized—sometimes with cash bonuses—for developing new systems which improved efficiency and customer service. For example, while working for the U.S. Embassy in Miami, I created a computerized method of financial reporting which greatly enhanced the budgeting and fiscal accountability functions. In another job as a Purchasing Agent, I exceeded expected standards while handling critical functions including making decisions on the most advantageous sources, assisting in bidding solicitations, and evaluating quotations for price discounts and reference materials.

I have never been in a job where I did not find creative and resourceful ways to cut costs, improve bottom-line results, and strengthen relationships with customers.

I hope you will call or write me soon to suggest a time convenient for us to meet and discuss your needs and how I might serve them. Thank you for your time.

Sincerely,

Robert Rountree

ROBERT ROUNTREE

Until 12/15/02: 1110½ Hay Street, Fayetteville, NC 28305   (910) 483-6611
After 12/16/02: 538 Pittsfield Avenue, Orlando, FL 58401

OBJECTIVE

To contribute to an organization that can use a resourceful purchasing manager who is skilled in contract negotiation, operations management, and personnel administration.

EDUCATION

Completed one year of master's degree work in Urban Management, Texas State University, Mercerville, TX, 1995-96.
Earned B.S. in Health Education, University of Washington, Washington, DC, 1991.
Received A.A. in General Education, Miami Dale Community College, Miami, FL, 1986.
Completed executive development and non-degree-granting training programs in:

Cost Accounting	Managerial Accounting	Procurement
Computer Operations	Inventory Control	Budget Administration

COMPUTERS

Lotus 1-2-3, Excel, WordPerfect, Managing Your Money, Windows, others

EXPERIENCE

SENIOR PURCHASING MANAGER. Briley & Co., Ft. Hood, TX (2000-present). Have acquired a broad understanding of government contracting procedures while achieving an excellent track record of promotion in the finance and purchasing field.

- Was originally employed as a Purchasing Agent to replace two buyers; have been promoted to Senior Purchasing Manager in charge of five associates.
- Am responsible for an annual budget of approximately $2.1 million of which $1.6 million is used by me to purchase repair parts, outside services, support equipment, and materials.
- Responsible for property management: within a $150,000 monthly budget oversee maintenance and repairs performed on 5,000 housing units and a fleet of 72 vans.
- In a formal letter of appreciation, was commended for saving at least $400,000 annually by combining my extensive purchasing knowledge with my creative problem-solving skills.
- On my own initiative, streamlined the bidding process; developed a new system for obtaining price quotes from potential vendors and worked with the System Manager in developing a computer program to track quotes: this transformed the manual quotation to an efficient new process which reduced the time necessary to prepare quotes.
- Established excellent working relationships with vendors all over the country, and am known for my ability to quickly find difficult-to-obtain parts for critical needs.
- Knowledgeable of government contracting and new product testing.

CONSULTANT & VICE PRESIDENT OF FINANCE. Branson Enterprises, Miami, FL (1991-99). Played a key role in helping the owner build a new business; established budgeting and accounting systems. Negotiated the details of the company's largest contract.

PURCHASING MANAGER. Contracting Division of the U.S. Air Force, Washington, DC (1989-91). Handled critical functions including making decisions on the most advantageous sources, assisting in bidding solicitations and acceptance, and evaluating quotations for price discounts as well as delivery/transportation costs. Developed outstanding relationships and received a Laudatory Best Operation performance appraisal with cash bonus.

PROCUREMENT OFFICER. The American Embassy in Miami (1986-89). Began working for the Embassy as a Warehouse Manager and, holding a **Top Secret** security clearance, excelled in managing warehouse operations and in relocating warehouse contents to new facilities.

- Because of problem-solving ability, was promoted to Procurement Officer; took over a disorganized operation and created a computerized method of reporting Local Operational Funds (LOF) which enhanced efficiency of the budgeting and fiscal functions.

PERSONAL

Outstanding personal and professional references. Will cheerfully travel/relocate.

CAREER CHANGE

Date

Exact Name of Person
Title or Position
Name of Company
Address (no., street)
Address (city, state, zip)

REAL ESTATE AGENT

This talented individual has succeeded at real estate sales, but he yearns to make a career transition back into a management position in a large organization. Although he has excelled in sales, he has decided that he prefers management.

Dear Exact Name of Person (or Dear Sir or Madam if answering a blind ad):

I would appreciate an opportunity to talk with you soon about how I could contribute to your organization through my versatile management experience, organizational and program development skills, and reputation for excellence in counseling, motivating, and leading employees to achieve superior results.

As you will see by my resume, I offer a background which includes 20 years of service in the U.S. Army, culminating in executive roles as a Lieutenant Colonel. Throughout my military career, I was involved in planning and carrying out large-scale projects with international implications. In my last military assignment, I managed a $4.5 million annual operating budget at the headquarters of an organization with four separate but interlocking divisions. In one earlier job I developed operating procedures for a unique aviation unit operating teams which rotated from the US and the Persian Gulf. This program involved joint cooperation with the U.S. Navy at high levels and managing more than 200 specialists operating and maintaining aircraft and equipment valued at more than $61 million.

I am a versatile professional able to adapt to rapid change, pressure, and deadlines while maximizing human and material resources to their fullest extent. I am proud of my reputation as an unquestionably honest individual and straightforward speaker. I have been successful in building teams of the highest quality by giving employees my trust and respect for their own abilities and decision-making skills.

My managerial and supervisory experience is enhanced by strong technical skills. I am familiar with data processing practices and several widely used software programs.

Additionally I offer what I feel is a rather unusual educational background. My B.S. degree is in Resource Management and I am a licensed Real Estate Broker. Since retiring from the Army, I have earned an associate degree in General Occupational Technology and in June 1995, will receive a second A.A.S. degree in Banking and Finance.

I hope you will welcome my call soon to arrange a brief meeting at your convenience to discuss your current and future needs and how I might serve them. Thank you in advance for your time.

Sincerely yours,

Perry A. Admiral

PERRY A. ADMIRAL

1110½ Hay Street, Fayetteville, NC 28305　　•　　preppub@aol.com　　•　　(910) 483-6611

OBJECTIVE　　To offer experience in multilevel management to an organization in need of an intelligent, mature executive with a history of attaining exceptional results while directing large-scale operations in a variety of functional areas as a senior military officer.

EDUCATION　　**B.S., Resource Management,** Troy State University, Ft. Rucker, AL, 1978.
A.A.S., Banking and Finance, Tampa Technical Community College (TTCC), Tampa, FL, June 1995.
- Graduated with honors by maintaining a 3.9 GPA.

A.A.S., General Occupational Technology, TTCC, 1994.
- Achieved a perfect 4.0 GPA and was inducted into the National Vocational and Technical Honor Society.

EXECUTIVE & TECHNICAL TRAINING　　Completed the military's graduate-level Command and General Staff College and other graduate-level schools for top executives.
Attended 80 hours of course work in selling, evaluating, and managing real estate, Huff Real Estate School, Tampa, FL, 1993.

EXPERIENCE　　**REAL ESTATE AGENT, PROPERTY MANAGER,** and **STUDENT**. Tampa, FL (2000-present). While earning two associate degrees and an FL Real Estate Broker's License, handled the details of rental property management and real estate sales.

Retired from the U.S. Army with the rank of Colonel after a distinguished career directing daily operations, training, planning, and the execution of programs for organizations with as many as 10,000 employees and up to $61 million worth of equipment in locations throughout the world. Consistently earned respect for my ability to handle a myriad of details and numerous complex projects simultaneously in areas including personnel, security, operations, resource and budget management, public affairs, and aviation.
DEPUTY DIRECTOR. The Pentagon, Washington, DC (1990-99). Directed staff activities and developed and managed the $4.5 million annual operating budget at a corporate headquarters for four 1,000-person divisions, each with separate but coordinating missions, and which provided intelligence support for the military's central command.
- Inspired personnel to achieve exceptional performance ratings and praise for their professionalism and spirit of team work despite the drawback of severe turnover rates.

DIRECTOR OF OPERATIONS AND PLANNING. Persian Gulf (1987-90). Planned, coordinated, and managed a special task force with a sensitive mission in the Persian Gulf: had oversight for approximately 200 people operating in excess of $61 million worth of helicopters which were rotated regularly in teams between the U.S. and the Persian Gulf.

GENERAL MANAGER. Germany (1983-85). Turned an average company into a top performer by providing a leadership style which inspired employees to have a sense of pride; managed a 219-person aviation company with $52 million worth of equipment including 37 vehicles and 45 helicopters.

COMPUTER　　Knowledge of software including Lotus 1-2-3, PageMaker, Microsoft Word, and Windows.

PERSONAL　　Hold FAA Commercial, Single-Engine Helicopter license with 3,500 hours of flight time. Known for honesty and integrity, held a Top Secret security clearance.

Exact Name of Person
Exact Title
Exact Name of Company
Address
City, State, Zip

**REAL ESTATE
APPRAISER**

Dear Exact Name of Person (or Dear Sir or Madam if answering a blind ad):

With the enclosed resume, I would like to make you aware of my interest in exploring opportunities which will take advantage of my knowledge related to mortgage lending as well as my experience related to banking, credit unions, and financial services. As you will see from my resume, I am in the process of relocating to the Atlanta area. Although I am well-respected in my present position, I have made the decision to move closer to the area where many members of my extended family make their homes.

As you will see from my resume, I offer a distinguished track record of accomplishments with credit unions. As a Vice President with a credit union, I enjoyed a history of promotion to increased responsibilities as a credit union executive. I was promoted to Vice President to handle a variety of strategic responsibilities for four branches with total assets of $31 million. Among my accomplishments were significantly outperforming the annual yields for all credit unions, diversifying the total loan portfolio, reducing delinquencies, and increasing capital. While achieving excellent results in all areas of operations, I was instrumental in leading the credit union to a five-star rating from Bauer Financial Reports, Inc., and a superior rating from I.D.C. Financial Publishing, Inc. Earlier as a Loan Manager, I played a key role in the rapid growth of assets of a credit union to $23 million from $10 million.

In 2001 I made a career change into real estate sales and then into the specialized field of real estate appraisal. This experience has allowed me to gain insight into the mortgage lending process from a different angle and has added to my strong background related to lending and financial services.

You would find me to be a congenial professional who is skilled at motivating employees to excel in their jobs and who is experienced in interacting with federal examiners, auditors, risk management professionals, and others with fiduciary responsibilities.

Because I am frequently in the Atlanta area exploring employment and housing options, I would be available for personal interviews at almost any time at your convenience. I hope you will contact me if you can make use of my experience and expertise.

Sincerely,

George Eddy

GEORGE EDDY

1110½ Hay Street, Fayetteville, NC 28305   •   preppub@aol.com   •   (910) 483-6611

OBJECTIVE   To offer a versatile background which has included managing banking and credit union operations as well as real estate sales and appraisal to an organization that can use my ability to create new services, design software programs, and motivate employees to excel.

EDUCATION   **Real Estate Appraisal and GRI Courses,** Finger Lakes Community College, 2002 and 2001.
Credit Union Executive Program, Credit Union National Association, with course work in areas including accounting, marketing, credit/collections, business law, money and banking, and financial counseling. Other college courses in computers and trust services.
Associate's Degree, Business Administration, Kings College, Weymouth, GA.
Certified Financial Counselor, Georgia State University.

EXPERIENCE   **REAL ESTATE APPRAISER.** Crestview and Associates, Weymouth, GA (2001-present). After achieving success in real estate sales, transferred my skills to this specialized area of appraising commercial properties as well as residential property, land, farms, and estates for banks, attorneys, and individuals for mortgage lending purposes.
- Developed expertise in the area of research, and became knowledgeable of USPAP regulations and laws governing the appraisal process.
- Expanded computer knowledge and skills with Windows Marshall and Swift, Appraise It, Deed Plotter, and Sketch-it programs.

VICE PRESIDENT. LaFayette Mutual Federal Credit Union, LaFayette, SC (1988-01). Began as Assistant Vice President and was promoted to handle varied strategic responsibilities while managing 10 employees and indirectly overseeing 29 people in a credit union with four branches and assets of $31 million.
- Developed written policies and procedures for approval by the Board of Directors while managing areas including credit union and office operations, loans and collections, cash flow, business development, insurance and credit card operations, and security.
- Produced an annual yield on loans of 14.95% which significantly outperformed the annual yield of 11.45% for all credit unions.
- Diversified the total loan portfolio: increased secured loans to 45%, decreased unsecured loans to 55%, and increased outstanding loans from $6 to $20 million.
- Became skilled in interacting with a wide range of professionals from federal examiners, to risk management professionals, to others with fiduciary responsibilities.
- Involved in the process of troubleshooting software programs used by the four branches, provided expertise during the conversion to a Data General system.
- Developed an insurance program to provide collateral protection.
- Was instrumental in achieving a five-star rating from Bauer Financial Reports, Inc., and a superior rating from I.D.C. Financial Publishing, Inc.
- Reduced delinquencies to 1.06% and increased capital to 12.3%.

Other experience:
LOAN MANAGER. Marshall Federal Credit Union, Marshall, NJ. Was praised by the board of directors for "never less than excellent" performance; supervised up to 18 people including eight loan officers in a site with an annual loan volume of $14 million.
- Played a key role in the rapid growth of assets from $10 to $23 million.

AFFILIATIONS   Dispute Resolution Center Chairman. Chamber of Commerce board of directors.

Exact Name of Person
Exact Title of Person
Name of Company
Address (number and street)
Address (city, state, and zip)

**REAL ESTATE
APPRAISER**

Dear Exact Name of Person: (or Sir or Madam if answering a blind ad.)

Can you use an enthusiastic, results-oriented sales manager who offers outstanding communication skills, a talent for reading people, and a reputation for determination and persistence in reaching goals?

With a proven background of success in sales, I have displayed my versatility while selling and marketing a wide variety of products and services including residential real estate and land, new and used automobiles, and financial products/ investment services. In one job I trained and supervised a successful team of mutual fund and insurance sales agents. Most recently as a Real Estate Broker and General Manager of a real estate firm, I achieved the $3 million mark in sales for 1998 while training and developing junior associates who have become top producers. While excelling in all aspects of the business, I have used my experience to create marketing strategies which reached large audiences and generated much business.

Earlier experience gave me an opportunity to refine my sales and communication abilities as well as gain familiarity with business management including finance and collections, inventory control, personnel administration, and customer service. Prior to owning and managing a business which bought, reconditioned, and marketed automobiles, I was one of Houston Buick's most successful sales professionals, earning the distinction of "Salesman of the Month" for 13 consecutive months and "Salesman of the Year."

If you can use a seasoned professional with the ability to solve tough business problems, maximize profitability, and increase market share under highly competitive conditions, I would enjoy an opportunity to meet with you to discuss your needs and how I might serve them. I can provide outstanding references.

I hope you will welcome my call soon to arrange a brief meeting at your convenience. Thank you in advance for your time.

Sincerely,

Keith Toomey

KEITH TOOMEY

1110½ Hay Street, Fayetteville, NC 28305 • preppub@aol.com • (910) 483-6611

OBJECTIVE

To offer a track record of success in sales and managerial roles where outstanding communication skills and the ability to close the sale were key factors in building a reputation as a highly motivated professional oriented toward maximum bottom-line results.

EXPERIENCE

REAL ESTATE BROKER & GENERAL MANAGER. Toomey Real Estate, Inc., Myrtle Beach, SC (1994-present). After founding a real estate firm which bears my name, quickly reached the $3 million personal sales level; hired, trained, and now manage three junior real estate brokers who are playing a key role in boosting overall sales and profitability of a thriving agency in this highly competitive market.

- Have become known for my strong interpersonal and communication skills while coordinating with potential buyers, lending institutions, construction professionals, sellers, and others.
- Negotiate all aspects of financial transactions; deal with mortgage company representatives to arrange financing and with attorneys to handle real estate closings.
- Utilize my expert marketing abilities while creating sales strategies and preparing direct mail materials which capture the interest of prospective clients and generate new business.
- Routinely make presentations to other agents and buyers.
- Have become skilled in all aspects of property evaluation and am skilled in comparing newly available homes with those having comparable features.

SALES AND MARKETING REPRESENTATIVE. Self-employed, Myrtle Beach, SC (1988-94). Trained and then supervised the efforts of as many as 12 agents while also personally marketing and selling mutual funds and insurance; refined my abilities in a competitive field and excelled in developing sales and marketing techniques which resulted in increased sales.

Highlights of earlier experience: Gained versatile experience in sales, inventory control, and customer service in jobs including the following:
FINANCE AND OPERATIONS MANAGER: Became highly effective in handling finances, marketing, and sales as the owner of a business with six sales professionals, a title clerk, a bookkeeper, and 12 employees in the body shop (Gene's Auto Shop, Houston, TX).
- Learned small business management while handling sales, finances, and collections.
- Created marketing and advertising plans and products which were highly effective.

SALES REPRESENTATIVE: For a major automobile dealer, consistently placed in the top three of 22 sales professionals (Houston Buick, Houston, TX).
- Was "Salesman of the Month" for 13 consecutive months and "Salesman of the Year."

FIELD SALES MANAGER: Became the youngest person in the company's history to hold this position after only a year with this national company (Fuller Brush Company, Plattsburgh, NY, and Phoenix, AZ).
- Became skilled in earning the confidence of potential customers and achieved a highly successful rate of positive responses from four out of each five people I approached: increased the amount of sales per customer.

STORE MANAGER & SUPPORT SERVICE SPECIALIST: Gained business management experience and learned to handle inventory control and funds (U.S. Navy).

TRAINING

Completed corporate training programs in areas such as real estate law, brokerage, finance, and securities as well as life, accident, and health insurance.
Am licensed as a real estate salesman, broker, and life/accident/health insurance agent.

PERSONAL

Am known for my ability to see "the big picture" while managing the details.

Date

Exact Name of Person
Title or Position
Name of Company
Address (no., street)
Address (city, state, zip)

REAL ESTATE MANAGER

Dear Exact Name of Person (or Dear Sir or Madam if answering a blind ad):

I would appreciate an opportunity to talk with you soon about how I could benefit your organization through my knowledge related to construction and real estate.

In my current position as Real Estate Manager, I was promoted to increasingly responsible roles related to the leasing of rental units, including overseeing maintenance and collecting rent. I was frequently complimented for my poise and "common sense" in handling tenant problems. In the process of excelling in my job, I gained confidence in my ability to sell *anything*!

I am a self-motivated individual with a reputation for always achieving exceptional results. I hope you will welcome my call soon to arrange a brief meeting at your convenience to discuss your current and future needs and how I might serve them. Thank you in advance for your time.

Sincerely yours,

Amanda Kale

AMANDA L. KALE

1110½ Hay Street, Fayetteville, NC 28305　　•　　preppub@aol.com　　•　　(910) 483-6611

OBJECTIVE　　To contribute to an organization that can use a well-organized young professional who is known for my attention to detail, ability to rapidly master new tasks and office procedures, as well as for my excellent clerical and office skills.

EDUCATION　　Studied bookkeeping for small businesses, Wichita Vocational Technical Institute, Wichita, KS, 1989-91.
Graduated from Valley Center High School after completing extensive studies in math, bookkeeping, and typing; Wichita, KS, 1997.

EXPERIENCE　　**REAL ESTATE MANAGER.** Davis Realty, Wichita, KS (2001-03). Was promoted to increasingly responsible roles related to the leasing of rental units, including overseeing maintenance and collecting rent.
- Was complimented for my poise and "common sense" in handling tenant problems.
- Gained confidence in my ability to sell *anything*!

MARKETING EXECUTIVE. Royal Corporation, Wichita, KS (1998-00). Became skilled in speaking to large groups while conducting product demonstrations.
- Recruited new employees for this organization, and trained them in techniques of product demonstration and sales.
- Learned how to "think on my feet" and how to remain enthusiastic, even in the process of presenting the same information over and over again to different groups.

SECRETARY. Specialty Products, Wichita, KS (1997-98). As the only person in this office, refined my ability to juggle numerous tasks that included:

typing	bookkeeping
payroll preparation	computer inputting
greeting customers	preparing invoices
making deposits	preparing the general ledger
setting up for conference meetings	

- Programmed a TRS-80 computer without any prior experience; demonstrated my ability to rapidly master new software and hardware.
- Learned how to maintain calm and collected and keep a smile on my face even when the office got very hectic!

CASHIER. Best Yet Discount Foods, Kellogg & Seneca locations, Wichita, KS (1996-97). Was often commended for my reliability and customer service skills while performing cashiering and bookkeeping functions.

PERSONAL　　Have the ability to learn quickly and efficiently, and have complete confidence that there is nothing I cannot learn and eventually master. Have been told throughout my life that I am a "people person" because I have excellent communication skills and truly enjoy working with employees and customers. Pride myself on my ability to always maintain a professional attitude, no matter what the circumstances.

Date

Exact Name of Person
Title or Position
Name of Company
Address (no., street)
Address (city, state, zip)

REAL ESTATE SALES ASSOCIATE

Dear Exact Name of Person (or Dear Sir or Madam if answering a blind ad):

I would appreciate an opportunity to talk with you soon about how I could benefit your organization through my proven background of managerial experience.

As you will see from my resume, I built a "track record" of consistent advancement ahead of my peers while serving my country in the U.S. Army.

I was involved in managing teams of as many as 44 employees in technical maintenance, inspection, and administrative operations.

During the past three years since leaving military service, I have further applied my creativity and attention to detail while gaining experience in the highly competitive field of real estate sales. Within a year after completing intensive training programs, I reached the prestigious $2 million sales level.

I am a self-motivated individual with a reputation for always achieving exceptional results. Excelling in motivating and developing others, I expect employees to meet my high performance standards.

I hope you will welcome my call soon to arrange a brief meeting at your convenience to discuss your current and future needs and how I might serve them. Thank you in advance for your time.

Sincerely yours,

Monica L. Seller

Alternate last paragraph:
I hope you will call or write soon to suggest a time convenient for us to meet and discuss your current and future needs and how I might serve them. Thank you in advance for your time.

MONICA L. SELLER

1110½ Hay Street, Fayetteville, NC 28305   •   preppub@aol.com   •   (910) 483-6611

OBJECTIVE   To contribute my management expertise to an organization that can use a professional with the proven ability to foresee problems and find solutions.

EXPERIENCE   *Refined my time management skills while further polishing my ability to relate to others as a* **REALTOR/SALES ASSOCIATE,** *Cheyenne, WY:*
T. C. Caldron Realty (2000-present). Am polishing my skills in marketing and selling residential and commercial properties and land.
- Conducted the market analysis of properties to determine their true value while involved in interviewing and counseling prospective buyers and sellers.
- Collected and analyzed financial information in order to qualify prospects.
- Coordinated with other professionals including attorneys, appraisers, lenders, surveyors, and contractors.

Preferred Realty (1995-99). Made important contributions in promoting and marketing while achieving the respected $1 million sales level in less than a year.

Smith & Son Realty (1992-94). Sold commercial and residential properties worth approximately $2 million in two years with the company. Completed training sponsored by the NC Association of Realtors and the University of North Carolina as well as an intensive company-sponsored sales training course.

Earned consistent advancement ahead of my peers while polishing my managerial, supervisory, and leadership abilities, U.S. Army, Ft. Carson, CO:
MAINTENANCE SUPERVISOR. (1990-92). Was the acting department manager for 40 employees maintaining 22 helicopters.
- Was twice selected as an evaluator for a team inspecting California National Guard units.

QUALITY CONTROL SUPERVISOR. (1990). Supervised a team of 14 specialists conducting technical inspections on maintenance, safety, and job proficiency.

SUPERVISORY AIRCRAFT MAINTENANCE SPECIALIST. (1987). Refined my organizational skills overseeing 35 employees maintaining vehicles and ground support equipment.

QUALITY CONTROL SUPERVISOR. (1989). Was selected for advanced schooling and advancement to higher managerial levels on the basis of this job which included supervising 30 administrative employees and 14 aircraft technical inspectors.
- Initiated changes in operating procedures which are now used Army wide.

AIRCRAFT TECHNICAL INSPECTOR. U.S. Army, Germany (1985-88).
Established maintenance and safety policies as the assistant manager of a 45-person organization with 10 vehicles and eight pieces of ground support equipment.
- Displayed knowledge and skills which led to selection for a high-level inspection team.

EDUCATION   Associate's degree in General Studies, Central Texas College, Killeen, TX, 1987.

PERSONAL   Was the "distinguished graduate" of several Army leadership and technical training schools. Always strive for excellence and motivate employees to meet my high standards.

REALTOR   Dear Sir or Madam:

Please excuse the impersonal appearance of this letter, but my husband and I have just relocated permanently to California, are in the final stages of closing on our house, and all the equipment which I would use to personalize this letter to you is in storage until the end of July!

With the enclosed resume, I would like to introduce you to my qualifications and experience and acquaint you with the considerable skills which I have to offer. As you will see from my resume, I most recently worked in Maine as a Realtor, and I handled commercial, residential, and land transactions.

We are permanently settling in California, and I am seeking an organization where I can make a permanent, long-term contribution. My husband has been in the military, but he is on his final tour with only a two-year obligation left to serve. We are eager to "put down roots," and I am confident that I can significantly contribute to your organization.

If you can use a self-starter with unlimited initiative, excellent public relations skills, and a talent for solving stubborn problems, please call or write me at the address or phone number on my resume and I will cheerfully make myself available to you for a personal meeting at your convenience. I can provide outstanding personal and professional references.

I hope to have the pleasure of talking with you in person soon.

Sincerely and best wishes,

Sally Ann Midas

SALLY ANN MIDAS

1110½ Hay Street, Fayetteville, NC 28305   •   preppub@aol.com   •   (910) 483-6611

OBJECTIVE

To contribute through my sales experience to an organization that can use an energetic, hard-working young professional with a strong customer service orientation.

PROFESSIONAL TRAINING

Completed Real Estate School, Bangor Real Estate Academy, 2000, and am a licensed real estate agent/Realtor for the state of Maine.

EXPERIENCE

REALTOR. Hearth and Home Inc., Bangor, ME (2000-02). Handled commercial, residential, and land transactions; worked extensively with VA loans.

SALES REPRESENTATIVE and **OFFICE MANAGER**. Barry's Cleaning, Inc., Fantan, NC (1998-00). Applied my communication skills in maintaining contact with potential and existing customers in order to gain new business while providing quality service to all.
- Earned a reputation as a fast learner and was soon entrusted with preparing bids for jobs with the federal government; typed and prepared support documents.
- Discovered ways to reduce costs while ordering supplies and controlling inventories.
- Gained experience in office operations including answering phones, taking care of accounts payable and receivable, and typing various kinds of paperwork.

HEAVY EQUIPMENT OPERATOR. C.R. Right Construction, Conyers, GA (1997-98). Displayed my adaptability as the "right hand" and assistant to a construction site supervisor: drove heavy equipment to as many as 20 scattered work sites.
- Became known for my dependability in consistently having equipment at the right place at the right time while always "pitching in" and doing whatever needed to be done.

SALES ASSOCIATE. Georgia's Decorating, Inc., East Point, GA (1994-96) Was cited for my ability to "upgrade" sales while providing excellent customer service helping clients choose the right colors, designs, and amounts of paint and wallpaper. Gained customer confidence which resulted in "repeat sales."

RETAIL SALES ASSOCIATE. GenCom, Inc., Atlanta, GA (1992-93). Provided excellent back-up and "service after the sale" in the highly competitive growing field of pager sales: called on prospects to make sales and saw that regular customers were informed of new products as they became available.
* Was honored as the company's "Top Sales Professional" two years consecutively.

Developed and refined leadership and supervisory skills while succeeding in a variety of roles calling for adaptability, U.S. Army National Guard, Atlanta, GA (1985-91):
SUPERVISORY INVENTORY CONTROL SPECIALIST. Supervised 12 employees; prepared paperwork in support of household goods/furniture shipments, took warehouse inventories, and processed documents for personnel being transferred.
SUPPLY TECHNICIAN and **COMPUTER OPERATOR**. Learned to use IBM computers with Lotus software while taking regular inventories and filing/maintaining records.
MEDICAL SPECIALIST. Received specialized training in advanced lifesaving, CPR, and first aid which qualified me to work as a medic. Graduated at the top of my Medical Specialist class and was given the opportunity to work in a major military medical center's labor and delivery department.

PERSONAL

Known as an extremely hard-working quick learner, enjoy the challenge of learning new things. Feel that my greatest strengths lie in sales and in contributing as part of a team.

Exact Name of Person
Title or Position
Name of Company
Address (no., street)
Address (city, state, zip)

**REFRIGERATION &
HEATING
TECHNICIAN**

Dear Exact Name of Person (or Dear Sir or Madam if answering a blind ad):

I would appreciate an opportunity to talk with you soon about how I could contribute to your organization through my expert technical skills in the area of heating, air conditioning, and refrigeration.

As you will see from my resume, I have most recently excelled as a Utilities Equipment Repairer while serving my country in the U.S. Army at the world's largest U.S. military base. Although I now work with a team of people installing, repairing, and servicing a wide range of heating, air conditioning, and refrigeration equipment, I performed this work by myself for a period of 1-1/2 years during a period of severe understaffing. I have become known for my absolute reliability as well as for my unselfish support in training and developing junior technicians.

With a reputation as a highly motivated and intelligent technical professional, I am continuously seeking opportunities to refine my knowledge and skills through formal education and training on my own time. I completed with high honors all the units of study in the Master Course in Air Conditioning, Refrigeration, and Heating Course sponsored by NRI, and I excelled in the Army's Utilities Equipment Repairer Course. I have received several certificates from the EPA and other government agencies certifying my knowledge in specific areas. I have more than 7700 hours in the Apprenticeship Program working toward Journeyman status.

Although I am only 27 years old, I can guarantee that you would find me to be a highly experienced problem solver whom you could count on at all times for excellent customer service skills as well as in-depth technical knowledge. I can provide excellent personal and professional references.

I hope you will call or write me soon to suggest a time convenient for us to meet and discuss your current and future needs and how I might serve them. Thank you in advance for your time.

Sincerely yours,

Hank K. Zucchini

HANK K. ZUCCHINI

1110½ Hay Street, Fayetteville, NC 28305   •   preppub@aol.com   •   (910) 483-6611

OBJECTIVE

I want to contribute to an organization that can use an air conditioning, refrigeration, and heating technician who offers excellent troubleshooting and problem-solving skills.

EDUCATION & CERTIFICATIONS

Completing **Heating and Cooling Course,** Collinswood Technical Community College, 1999.

From the Department of Defense, Environmental Protection Agency Certification Program, received a Certificate for Processing CFC/HCFC Refrigerants, 1997.

Certification from the **Mobile Air Conditioning Society** for completing training in CFC-12 refrigerant recycling and service procedures, 1996.

With High Honors, completed in 1 1/2 years all units of study in the **Master Course in Air Conditioning, Refrigeration and Heating Course** sponsored by NRI, 1994-95.

Received a Diploma as a graduate of the **Utilities Equipment Repairer Cours**e, Ordnance Center and School, Ft. Belvoir, VA, 1993.

Completed courses toward **Associate Degree in Air Conditioning, Refrigeration, and Heating,** Gwinnett Area Technical School, 1990-92; studied DC Circuit Analysis, Digital Electronics, Soldering/Assembly Technology, and other areas.

EXPERIENCE

UTILITIES EQUIPMENT REPAIRER. U.S. Army, Ft. Bragg, NC (1999-present). At the world's largest U.S. military base, work with a team of people installing, repairing, and servicing a wide range of air conditioning, heating, and refrigeration equipment in commercial and industrial properties; for 1-1/2 years during a period of severe understaffing, worked alone with the sole responsibility for installation, repair, and service.
- Have 7700 hours in the Apprenticeship Program working toward Journeyman status.
- Inspect equipment to determine extent of maintenance and repairs needed.
- Troubleshoot mechanical or electrical malfunctions in systems or components.
- Repair major components by complete disassembly, determination of serviceability, replacement of defective parts, and reassembly.
- Repair and fabricate new lines by cutting and bending tubing and installing fittings by flaring or soldering; repair electrical wiring and electro-mechanical controls.
- Inspect installation and condition of equipment systems.
- Control requisitioning, storage, and inventory of shop stock, materials, special tools, and necessary publications.
- Instruct lower-grade personnel in the use of applicable special tools, test equipment, and necessary publications.
- Administer quality control and quality assurance functions; inspect equipment.
- Received two Certificates of Achievement praising my "tireless efforts" and "unselfish support" during major projects.

MATERIAL CONTROL SPECIALIST. ABC Avionics, Norcross, GA (1996-98). Maintained various government forms including the 1149, 1348, and DD250 while selecting electronic components for repair, maintaining inventory at appropriate levels, and storing equipment needed for repair in bonded stores annex.

SELECTOR/MULTI-FUNCTION PRODUCTION SPECIALIST. Telecommunications, Inc., Stone Mountain, GA (1993-95). Became skilled in Just in Time Manufacturing and in statistical process control while putting orders together for customers.
- Pulled various parts for a Manufacturing Flow Line to keep the line moving; input data.
- Received a prestigious safety award for my perfect safety record.

PERSONAL

Am safety conscious, detail oriented, and career motivated with a strong work ethic.

Date

Exact Name of Person
Title or Position
Name of Company
Address (number and street)
Address (city, state, and zip)

Dear Exact Name of Person: (or Sir or Madam if answering a blind ad)

With the enclosed resume, I would like to make you aware of my interest in the possibility of putting my strong management, production operations, and sales background to work for your company. Please treat my enquiry as highly confidential at this point. Although I can provide outstanding personal and professional references at the appropriate time, I do not wish my current employer to be aware of my interest in your company.

As you will see from my enclosed resume, I have been in the multi-purpose concrete applications business my entire working life. I began in entry-level positions with a small concrete business in northern Iowa and was promoted to Plant Manager and Sales Manager. Then I joined Smith & Son, Inc. where I tripled production and transformed that company into an attractive acquisition candidate which caught the attention of Bullworth Concrete. When Bullworth Concrete Company bought Smith & Son in 1992, I became a Division Manager and in 1994 was promoted to Regional Manager.

In my current position I manage operations at 10 divisions while supervising three Division Managers and overseeing activities of 85 people at 10 locations. I also supervise four sales and customer service professionals while preparing budgets for each of the 10 divisions.

If you can use a versatile professional with a thorough understanding of all facets of the concrete applications business, I hope you will contact me to suggest a time when we might meet. Should you have ambitious goals in either the production management or sales area, I feel certain that my extensive industry knowledge and contacts could be useful.

Sincerely,

Harvey Herron

HARVEY HERRON

1110½ Hay Street, Fayetteville, NC 28305 • preppub@aol.com • (910) 483-6611

OBJECTIVE

To benefit an organization that can use an experienced manager with exceptional organizational skills who offers a background in managing multi-plant operations and expertise in multi-purpose concrete applications.

EDUCATION

Business Administration studies, Faison Technical College, Faison, IA, 1974.
Completed numerous seminars including AGC Seminars, Capital Associated Industries Seminars; also completed extensive training related to EPA, DOT Procedures Applications, and other areas.

CERTIFICATIONS

ACI Certified; NRMCA Sales Certified

AFFILIATIONS

Member, Homebuilders Association
Former President, Iowa Concrete Association, Faison Chapter

EXPERIENCE

With Bullworth Concrete Company, have been promoted to positions of increasing responsibility by this multi-purpose concrete company while playing a key role in annual sales increases of more than 10%:
2000-present: **REGIONAL MANAGER.** Faison, IA. Was promoted to this position from Division Manager for this region with multimillion-dollar annual sales; am continuing to provide valuable leadership in producing outstanding sales and profits after helping the company achieve its record year in 2000.
- Manage operations at 10 divisions while supervising three Division Managers and overseeing activities of 85 people at 10 locations.
- Supervise four Customer Service and Sales Representatives.
- Prepare annual budgets for each of the 10 division locations.
- Am accountable for production of 250,000 yards of concrete annually.

1992-00: **DIVISION MANAGER.** Bladen, IA. While overseeing three divisions, provided supervisory oversight of 30 people while directing production, maintenance, safety, and sales activities related to the production of 55,000 cubic yards of concrete annually for such applications as bridges, waste water treatment plants, as well as commercial and industrial buildings.

Joined Bullworth Concrete Company when Bullworth bought Smith and Son, Inc., a northern Iowa company which I had transformed into an attractive acquisition candidate while excelling in the following history of promotion:
1983-92: Was **GENERAL MANAGER** at Smith and Son, Inc., during these years while tripling production from 12,000 cubic yards to 36,000 cubic yards annually; managed ten truck operations.
- Directed operation of central shop for the entire company.

PLANT MANAGER & SALES MANAGER. Granger Concrete, Walton, IA (1974-83). Started with this company as a truck driver and learned the business from the ground up; was promoted to Plant Manager and then to Sales Manager, and made major contributions to the company in both roles.
- Trained and managed two sales people.
- Sold and managed production of 36,000 cubic yards of concrete annually.
- Managed operations with 12 drivers at two sites.
- Before promotion into the management ranks, worked for the company as a Loader Operator and Mechanic in addition to Truck Driver; these early experiences gave me first-hand knowledge of how the concrete industry works on the ground floor of operations.

PERSONAL

Excellent personal and professional references. Outstanding reputation.

Exact Name of Person
Title or Position
Name of Company
Address (number and street)
Address (city, state, and zip)

**REGISTERED
HOUSING
SPECIALIST**

Dear Exact Name of Person: (or Sir or Madam if answering a blind ad)

With the enclosed resume, I would like to make you aware of my interest in the possibility of putting my sales background to work for your company.

As a Sales Representative, I have developed expert knowledge of the manufactured housing industry while excelling in all aspects of sales. I was awarded the prestigious **Top Gun** Award for Best Sales Performance, and I was inducted into the **Million Dollar Club.** I have completed numerous inhouse seminars designed to refine sales and marketing skills as well as product knowledge specific to manufactured housing, and I have become known for my highly refined skills in developing and maintaining outstanding customer relations; and live by the philosophy that a satisfied customer is worth numerous referrals and repeat business.

With an excellent personal and professional reputation, I am a trusted and respected by my colleagues, and am known for my willingness to generously share my product knowledge and sales know-how with my associates.

I believe my natural sales ability combined with my genuine enthusiasm for manufactured housing as a product has been the key to my exceptional sales achievements in this job.

If you can use a top-notch sales professional to join your organization, I hope you will contact me to suggest a time when we might discuss your needs.

Sincerely,

Joseph Walter Arnette

JOSEPH WALTER ARNETTE

1110½ Hay Street, Fayetteville, NC 28305   •   preppub@aol.com   •   (910) 483-6611

OBJECTIVE   I want to contribute to an organization that can use a dynamic sales professional with a proven track record in achieving high levels of profitability and customer satisfaction while consistently meeting or exceeding ambitious sales targets.

EDUCATION   Completed one year of General Studies, Halifax Community College, Halifax, NJ.
Have excelled in extensive sales and sales management training sponsored by Raven Distributing Company, Thomas Homes, Anheiser-Busch, and John Topper.

LICENSE   Became a **Registered Housing Specialist**, March 1999
Hold a Commercial Driver's License.

EXPERIENCE   **SALES REPRESENTATIVE.** Thomas Homes, Loring, NJ (1999-02). Have developed expert knowledge of the manufactured housing industry while excelling in all aspects of sales.
- Was awarded the prestigious **Top Gun** Award for Best Sales Performance.
- Was inducted into the **Million Dollar Club.**
- Have completed numerous inhouse seminars designed to refine sales and marketing skills as well as product knowledge specific to manufactured housing.
- Have become known for my highly refined skills in developing and maintaining outstanding customer relations; and live by the philosophy that a satisfied customer is worth numerous referrals and repeat business.
- Am trusted and respected by my colleagues, and am known for my willingness to generously share my product knowledge and sales know-how with my associates.
- Believe my natural sales ability combined with my genuine enthusiasm for manufactured housing as a product has been the key to my exceptional sales achievements in this job.
- Have learned how to balance customers' needs for quality and features with the dealer's need to maximize gross profit; am skilled at making tradeoffs that assure profitability.
- Have acquired expertise related to inventory ordering and control; am experienced in ordering specialized homes from manufacturers.

SALES REPRESENTATIVE. Raven Distributing Company, Loring, NJ (1990-98). For this consumer products giant, advanced rapidly and was promoted to Sales Representative in the company's top-volume market because of my exceptional sales achievements.
- Earned a seat in the prestigious **President's Circle** of Raven Distributing Co.
- Won numerous inhouse sales contests.
- Won two district sales contests in which "the best of the best" were competitors.
- Became adept at selling the retailer additional inventory during promotional periods because of retailers' trust and confidence in me.
- Always tried to think of the retailer's business as though it were my business, and made numerous suggestions that improved sales and profitability of my customers.
- Maintained excellent customer relationships through high frequency of personal contact.
- Prided myself on my ability to deliver on all my promises to customers, and assured the timely delivery of merchandise.

SKILLS   Offer highly refined skills and abilities in sales and sales management, inventory control, product merchandising, retail marketing, and interpersonal communication

PERSONAL   Can provide exceptionally strong personal and professional references.

Date

Exact Name of Person
Title or Position
Name of Company
Address (number and street)
Address (city, state, and ZIP)

RENTAL PROPERTY MANAGER

Dear Exact Name of Person (or Dear Sir or Madam if answering a blind ad):

I would appreciate an opportunity to talk with you soon about how I could contribute to your organization through my experience in financial management as well as through my skills in the areas of personnel and operations management along with my strong customer service orientation.

You will see from my enclosed resume that I offer an in-depth knowledge of finance and business. My most recent job was as Controller and General Manager of a real estate rental company for approximately eight years. During this time I substantially reduced the company's debt load, virtually eliminated the amount of uncollectibles, and increased occupancy rates to a consistently high 95%. Through my diplomatic but assertive managerial style, I brought this business out of debt and transformed it into a viable operation.

During a successful career in the U.S. Army, I advanced to hold increasingly more responsible managerial positions in the fields of finance, budgeting, and pay administration as well as in personnel administration. I gained skills and refined a natural aptitude for analyzing, controlling, and resolving problems while earning a reputation as a versatile and adaptable professional.

With an Associate's degree in Banking and Finance, I feel that I offer the dedication to excellence that would make me a valuable asset to an organization that can use a mature individual with the ability to get along with others in supervisory roles.

I hope you will welcome my call soon to arrange a brief meeting at your convenience to discuss your current and future needs and how I might serve them. Thank you in advance for your time.

Sincerely yours,

Lonny F. Geary

LONNY F. GEARY

1110½ Hay Street, Fayetteville, NC 28305 • preppub@aol.com (910) 483-6611

OBJECTIVE

To offer a track record of success in managerial roles with organizations requiring knowledge of finance, personnel, and administrative functions along with a reputation for analytical skills and attention to detail as well as a strong customer service orientation.

EXPERIENCE

FINANCE AND GENERAL MANAGER. Liberty Rentals, Sarasota, FL (1996-present). Brought about major improvements in several important functional areas while handling multiple roles as a financial manager, partner, and operations manager for a company with 160 rental units.
- Reduced the organization's debts more than $20,000 within less than a year through the application of my knowledge and prior experience in business management and finance.
- Almost totally eliminated uncollectibles while reducing them to under 1%.
- Prepared advertising materials which resulted in improved occupancy levels and consistently maintained 95% fill rates on leased units.
- Took charge of all aspects of finance and business administration ranging from maintaining books, to processing all accounting data, to accounts receivable and payable.
- Prepared and managed the budget and reconciled bank accounts.
- Diplomatically but assertively resolved a wide range of customer service as well as budget and fee problems.

GENERAL MANAGER. Fun Bingo and Novelty Co., Sarasota, FL (1992-95). Applied my knowledge of business and finance to build this company from a concept into a viable organization.
- Dealt with all aspects of establishing and successfully operating a small business: prepared and managed budgets, made bank deposits, and reconciled bank accounts as well as maintaining accounts receivable and payable ledgers.
- Controlled inventory from ordering supplies and merchandise to setting prices.

Highlights of earlier experience: Gained and refined knowledge of personnel management and finance/pay activities during a career with the U.S. Army, locations worldwide.
- As the Manager of a program studying the need for changes to the personnel structure of the Army, processed information and contributed input used in budget preparation.
- As a Senior Personnel Management Supervisor, directed the activities of 40 specialists engaged in processing promotions, reclassifications, transfers, and performance reports.
- As a Finance Section Manager, updated personnel's finance records and verified information before entering it into computers; maintained ledgers, cash books, and all related accounting records.
- As the Chief of Military Pay and Travel, processed pay activities for personnel in 11 states and four overseas areas.
- As Manager of a Personnel Actions Section, processed military personnel and their family members who were going overseas; provided information and briefings on customs, laws, and conditions in overseas areas.
- As a Retirement Counselor, oversaw activities in a center which processed personnel upon their separation from the military service.

EDUCATION & TRAINING

A.S. degree in **Banking** and **Finance,** Franklin Technical Community College, FL.
Completed numerous courses in finance, management, and personnel administration.

PERSONAL

Am known for my high level of initiative and dedication to seeing any job through to completion.

Date

Exact Name of Person
Title or Position
Name of Company
Address (no., street)
Address (city, state, zip)

RENTAL PROPERTY
MANAGER

Dear Exact Name of Person (or Dear Sir or Madam if answering a blind ad):

I would appreciate an opportunity to talk with you soon about how I could contribute to your organization through my skills in office management and knowledge of office administrative procedures.

As you will see from my resume, I am currently the Office Manager for a real estate agency where I advanced from Rental Property Manager. In August of last year, I took on the extra responsibilities of overseeing a secretary and a receptionist and expanded job requirements.

Prior to joining Choice Properties, I spent approximately three years in multiple roles with the Ft. Bragg school system. In addition to spending the bulk of my time in records management in the administrative offices for this system, I also filled in at the various schools as a receptionist and library clerk.

I feel that through my practical office management and technical computer operations skills, I offer a background of maturity and adaptability sure to make me a valuable asset to your organization.

I hope you will welcome my call soon to arrange a brief meeting at your convenience to discuss your current and future needs and how I might serve them. Thank you in advance for your time.

Sincerely yours,

Alma D. White

Alternate last paragraph:
I hope you will call or write soon to suggest a time convenient for us to meet and discuss your current and future needs and how I might serve them. Thank you in advance for your time.

ALMA D. WHITE

1110½ Hay Street, Fayetteville, NC 28305   •   preppub@aol.com   •   (910) 483-6611

OBJECTIVE
To apply my outstanding skills in office management and administration to an organization that can use a mature professional with a versatile background of accomplishments.

EXPERIENCE
Advanced in this progression with Choice Properties, Frylon, ME:
OFFICE MANAGER and **RENTAL PROPERTY MANAGER.** (2000-present). Was promoted to oversee two employees while handling all day-to-day functions related to managing approximately 25 rental properties.
- Applied my communication skills while working closely with appraisers to insure they received complete and accurate information.
- Entered each new listing into the MLS computer system and distributed appropriate information to each agent.
- Collected details on each home sale, entered data into computer system, and informed each agent of the sale.
- Made disbursements to agents and maintained ledgers on each property.
- Coordinated with home owners as the point of contact between renters and owners.
- Polished troubleshooting skills while "ironing out" problems and defusing irate buyers.
- Prepared records of each month's new construction closings and listings received.
- Created monthly and yearly reports for the brokers which included information from my records of each agent's production.

RENTAL PROPERTY MANAGER. (1995-00). Listed and sold residential real estate in addition to handling the rental department.
- Reached the $1.1 million mark in sales in just six months with the company!

RECEPTIONIST and **ADMINISTRATIVE ASSISTANT.** Ft. Bragg Schools, NC (1992-95). Displayed my adaptability while working in the personnel department of the administrative offices of the Ft. Bragg school system as well as in the libraries and offices of various schools in the system at the nation's largest military base.
- Maintained confidential files for approximately 520 employees.
- Assisted new employees to complete the various federal government forms required.
- Received and routed calls using a 15-line phone system.
- Provided help for parents, job applicants, salesmen, and others with business in the school's offices — both in person and on the phone.
- Compiled weekly enrollment summaries for each school as well as personnel break-downs for the entire system and monthly principal's reports.

Highlights of other experience:
- Maintained accurate and complete financial records for the PTA (Parent-Teacher Association) as Treasurer for both a junior high and an elementary school.
- Polished office management abilities as the Assistant Manager of an Equestrian Center.
- Provided students with clear, understandable information as a technical college Instructor.

EDUCATION
Studied English education with a minor in speech, University of Akron, Akron, OH.

LICENSES
Became certified as a Notary Public, May 1996.
Licensed as a Real Estate Salesman by the Fryylon (ME) Real Estate Institute, 1994.

PERSONAL
Prepared spreadsheets on the Zenith computer; am familiar with a variety of software.

Date

Exact Name of Person
Title or Position
Name of Company
Address (number and street)
Address (city, state, and zip)

Dear Sir or Madam:

Can you use an experienced sales professional with a history of success in training others and setting sales records while applying my knowledge of inventory control and record keeping in the process of establishing new accounts and building repeat business? I would especially enjoy discussing with you how I might serve your needs in the east/middle Tennessee or north Georgia areas. My extended family is located in those parts of the country, and I have many contacts and acquaintances throughout that region.

Since 1998, I have been a record-setting representative for Greystone, Inc., in Pinehurst, NC. After winning recognition as the top producer for 1998, 2000, and 2001, I have reached the $1.5 million in annual sales level for fiscal 2002. I regularly service approximately 160 accounts in an area which covers Raleigh-Cary, Pinehurst, and Southern Pines, and which extends as far west as Albemarle.

Prior experience includes dealing with both the general public and building contractors with Lowe's, selling heating and air-conditioning supplies and equipment, and managing outside sales for another refrigeration supply business. I am skilled at conducting sales meetings and coordinating awards programs.

I hope you will welcome my call soon to arrange a brief meeting at your convenience to discuss your current and future needs and how I might serve them. Thank you in advance for your time.

Sincerely yours,

Claude Ingersoll

CLAUDE INGERSOLL

1110½ Hay Street, Fayetteville, NC 28305 • preppub@aol.com • (910) 483-6611

OBJECTIVE

To contribute to an organization that is in need of an experienced sales professional who offers knowledge related to sales management, inventory control, report preparation, and training others.

EXPERIENCE

REGIONAL SALES MANAGER. Greystone, Inc., Pinehurst, NC (1998-present). Consistently among the region's top producers, achieved a sales volume of over $1.5 million for fiscal year 2002 for this home-comfort products company; train and coach two junior sales representatives.

- Was honored as the region's top sales professional in 1999, 2000, and 2001.
- Excelled in earning the respect and trust of professionals in the building and electrical industries through my skills in every phase of making contact, demonstrating products, and closing the sale.
- Demonstrated excellent planning skills by researching a company's needs and requirements prior to my initial call.
- Serviced approximately 160 accounts in an area ranging from Albemarle, to Sanford, to Cary and Raleigh, to Southern Pines and Pinehurst.
- Used my abilities as a communicator and my product knowledge to conduct sales meetings where employees learned effective techniques for selling the company's product line.
- Spend a great deal of my time calling on the end users of my company's products to ensure their satisfaction with our products.
- Became involved in the design and installation of display systems while selling to lighting showrooms, electrical wholesales, building supply stores, and plumbing wholesalers.

Highlights of prior experience in the sales field, Raleigh, NC:

Lowe's. Further developed my salesmanship abilities and knowledge of customer relations while dealing with both building contractors and the general public.
- Gained experience in stocking, inventory control, and computer operations.

Merritt-Holland. Sold heating and air conditioning equipment to customers throughout the eastern part of North Carolina.
- Was selected to oversee the details of coordinating special awards such as trips for high-volume sales personnel.
- Managed a wide range of advertising programs including newspaper, radio, and yellow pages advertising.
- Applied my organizational skills to arrange and coordinate dealer sales meetings.

Longley Supply Co.. Established a sales territory which included Lumberton, Hamlet, and Laurinburg as well as Raleigh; sold heating and air-conditioning equipment and supplies.
- Handled the details of arranging and then hosting dealer conventions.

W.L. Smith Refrigeration Supply. As the Outside Sales Manager, was in charge of pricing and inventory control for five stores.
- Conducted regular monthly inventories and rotated stock between the stores.

EDUCATION & TRAINING

Attended courses in professional sales techniques, stress management, and positive self-suggestion as well as a 10-week Dale Carnegie course in human relations.
Studied heating and air conditioning at Fayetteville Technical Community College, NC.

PERSONAL

Am a results-oriented professional. Offer a high degree of expertise in the qualities that add up to "salesmanship." Am skilled in establishing and maintaining effective relations.

CAREER CHANGE

Exact Name of Person
Title or Position
Name of Company
Address (no., street)
Address (city, state, zip)

**SALES & PRODUCT
LINE MANAGER**

Dear Exact Name of Person (or Dear Sir or Madam if answering a blind ad):

I would appreciate an opportunity to talk with you soon about how I could contribute to your organization through my proven administrative, sales, accounting management, and production control skills.

As you will see from my resume, most recently I have played a key role in the successful startup of a building supply company. Since beginning with the company from the day it started, I have been instrumental in developing a strong customer base while establishing procedures and systems which maximize profitability. I am involved in all aspects of the business, from selecting the product line, to managing accounts payable and receivable, to determining credit and collections policies. On my own initiative I taught myself Peachtree Accounting and have trained others to use it.

Prior to my current job, I served my country in the U.S. Army and managed offices and warehouses as well as people and projects. In every job I have ever held, I have used my strong analytical and problem-solving skills to figure out creative and efficient solutions for stubborn problems.

You would find me in person to be a poised communicator who offers the ability to rapidly master new jobs, advanced software, and sophisticated systems. With a reputation as a talented manager and motivator, I am looking for a company that I can stay with as well as a company in which everyone works as a team to contribute to the company's success.

I hope you will welcome my call soon when I try to arrange a brief meeting with you to discuss your needs and how I might serve them. Thank you in advance for your time.

Sincerely yours,

Ursula B. Glamour

Alternate last paragraph:
I hope you will call or write me soon to suggest a time convenient for us to meet and discuss your current and future needs and how I might best serve them. Thank you in advance for your time.

URSULA B. GLAMOUR

1110½ Hay Street, Fayetteville, NC 28305   •   preppub@aol.com   •   (910) 483-6611

OBJECTIVE

To offer my exceptionally strong skills related to operations management, production control, and office supervision to a company that can use a self starter and fast learner.

COMPUTERS

Proficient with Peachtree accounting software; familiar with Microsoft Word; and am known for my ability to rapidly master new software.

EXPERIENCE

OPERATIONS MANAGER. C & G Building Products, Inc., Emerson, WI (2000-present). Began with this company when it started and have made numerous contributions to profitability and overall efficiency.

- *Sales*: Manage front-counter sales which amount to 40% of gross sales; have been instrumental in developing a strong local customer base.
- *Accounting*: Taught myself Peachtree accounting; trained others to use it.
- *Accounts receivable/payable*: Manage accounts receivable, including daily invoicing, for 300 accounts valued at $1 million yearly; oversee payments to more than 40 vendors.
- *Financial reporting*: Work closely with the company's accountant; maintain accounting information for semi-annual and annual financial reports.
- *Credit*: Am the approving authority for credit terms and collections.
- *Purchasing*: Conceptualized and implemented a system of tracking purchasing orders; oversee computer entry of purchasing orders, receipt procedures, and inventory control/ updating procedures.
- *Product selection*: Select the company's product line; have learned several product lines in the vinyl and window industry.

ADMINISTRATOR. U.S. Army, Ft. Bragg, NC (1997-99). Used a computer extensively while analyzing intelligence information, preparing final reports, and communicating data to organizations worldwide. Processed security clearances for 6,000 people.

WAREHOUSE SUPERVISOR. U.S. Army, Ft. Bragg, NC (1995-96). Was specially selected for this job supervising eight employees while managing an ammunition warehouse with an inventory valued at more than $1 million.

- Transformed a warehouse officially described as being "in unsatisfactory condition," into "the best" in the supply chain.
- Drastically reorganized ingoing/outgoing shipment procedures.

OFFICE OPERATIONS MANAGER. U.S. Army, Korea (1993-94). On my own initiative, developed a new computer format for all forms utilized in this office which greatly decreased paperwork processing time; trained and managed an office staff of three people.

AMMUNITION COORDINATOR. U.S. Army, Ft. Knox, KY (1991-92). Was commended for "attention to detail" while coordinating ammunition deliveries and a fleet of vehicles.

EDUCATION

Bachelor of Science in Business Administration, Monathon College, Homer, WI, 2000. Was selected to attend the Primary Leadership and Development Course, and was chosen as the **"Leadership Graduate"** based on my leadership ability and goal-setting skills.
Was the first woman in the history of the Army to be named an **Honorary Member of Excellence in Armor**.

PERSONAL

Offer the ability to analyze a situation or problem and determine the best way of proceeding.

Exact Name of Person
Title or Position
Name of Company
Address (number and street)
Address (city, state, and zip)

SALES MANAGER, CONDOMINIUMS

Dear Sir or Madam:

Can you use an experienced sales professional with a history of success in training others and setting sales records?

Since 1992, I have excelled in the following "track record" of promotion within a company which markets resort condominium ("time share") properties at Planter's Plantation ($35 million annual sales). As Recruiting and Training Manager, I use a variety of tools including running ads and recruiting top industry candidates from other resorts, am in charge of hiring and training 60 sales employees yearly. On my own initiative, I have instituted a predictive index which has moved turnover from 120% to 50%. I have also made drastic changes in recruiting to eliminate the hiring of marginal employees.

I am interested in applying my strong sales skills outside the time share industry, and I am confidence I can become a valuable asset to a company that would value a hard charger who is highly skilled at closing the sale.

If you can make use of my considerable talents and experience, I hope you will contact me to discuss your needs. Thank you in advance for your time.

Sincerely yours,

Matthew T. Leisure

MATTHEW T. LEISURE

1110½ Hay Street, Fayetteville, NC 28305   •   preppub@aol.com   •   (910) 483-6611

OBJECTIVE

To benefit an organization that can use an innovative sales manager who offers a proven ability to increase bottom-line profits by applying my outstanding motivational and communication skills.

EXPERIENCE

Since 1990, have excelled in the following "track record" of promotion within a company which markets resort condominium ("time share") properties at Planter's Plantation ($35 million annual sales), Resort International, Williamsburg, VA:
RECRUITING AND TRAINING MANAGER. (May 2000-present). Using a variety of tools including running ads and recruiting top industry candidates from other resorts, am in charge of hiring and training 60 sales employees yearly.
- Instituted a predictive index which has moved turnover from 120% to 50%.
- Have made drastic changes in recruiting to eliminate the hiring of marginal employees.

SALES MANAGER. (1997-99). Managed 10 people and trained them in presenting the product and closing the sale.
- Transformed a team which had produced poor sales results and led it to be ranked consistently in the top half in sales and productivity.

IN-HOUSE SALES. (1996). Sold resort properties to previous time-share buyers.
- Ranked in top 20% of office.

FRONT-LINE SALES REPRESENTATIVE. (1992-95). Excelled in closing prospective buyers and obtaining referrals for potential resort property buyers.
- Was ranked #1 out of 60 of my colleagues in 1994!
- In 1993, was ranked #1 on the referral closing average.

Was promoted from Sales Representative to Sales Manager by Old South Food Service, Charleston, SC (1988-92).
SALES MANAGER. (1990-92). Because of my excellent sales record and management ability, was promoted to turn around this troubled office; transformed the operation into a top producer while increasing the sales team to 11 representatives.
- Increased sales figures 35% in 1992 compared to 1990.
- Became known for recruiting and training "top salesmen."
- Was an active member of the Charleston Jaycees; served as Charleston Chapter President and South Carolina District Director, 1990: was named one of the ten best chapter presidents in SC and one of the best in the nation.

SALES REPRESENTATIVE. (1988-90). Was named "Salesman of the Year" for the entire company consisting of more than 100 representatives, and put myself in the position where I acquired 95% of my sales through referrals!

Gained valuable customer-service and time-management experience working as a **SALES MANAGER/REPRESENTATIVE,** Trust Insurance Company, Charleston, SC; and **SALES ASSOCIATE,** Leland Hardware, Charleston, SC.

TRAINING

Completed three years of college course work in Business Administration, Charleston Technical Community College and Charleston State University, GA.

PERSONAL

Dynamic and highly motivated salesman known for my bold and innovative style.

Date

Mr. Michael Smith
Spangler Glass Company

Dear Mr. Smith:

With the enclosed resume, I would like to make you aware of my background as an articulate professional with exceptional communication and organizational skills who offers a track record of accomplishments in sales and customer service.

Currently in an inside sales position with Statesville Block, I work with general contractors and builders while handling sales and providing outstanding customer service. An outgoing person, I have natural sales ability which I have refined through 10 years of sales experience, and I have developed a strong rapport with residential and commercial customers. I am skilled at estimating jobs for concrete masonry and my extensive knowledge of construction and building supply allow me to work closely with general contractors and home builders, preparing cost estimates for concrete masonry units and related building supplies.

In an earlier position as a furniture sales representative for Doherty Furniture Company, I further polished my selling skills while assisting customers with the selection and purchase of home furnishings and accessories. My outstanding customer service abilities allowed me to quickly build a solid base of repeat and referral clients, and I always exceeded the sales quotas set by my supervisors.

Although I am highly regarded by my present employer, I am interested in exploring opportunities with your company. Please, however, do not contact my current employer until after we talk.

If you can use an experienced sales and customer service professional who offers exceptional communication and organizational skills, then I hope you will contact me. I can assure you in advance that I have an excellent reputation and would quickly become an asset to your organization. I can provide excellent references from all previous employers as well as from Statesville Block.

Sincerely,

Virginia Rankin

CC: Dick Cash

VIRGINIA RANKIN

1110½ Hay Street, Fayetteville, NC 28305　　•　　preppub@aol.com　　•　　(910) 483-6611

OBJECTIVE　　To benefit an organization that can use an articulate, enthusiastic sales professional with an outgoing personality as well as exceptional communication and organizational skills who offers a proven ability to establish and maintain effective working relationships.

EDUCATION　　Completed college computer courses at Mitchell Community College, Statesville, PA.

EXPERIENCE　　**INSIDE SALES REPRESENTATIVE** and **CUSTOMER SERVICE REPRESENTATIVE.** Statesville Block, Statesville, PA (2000-present). For this concrete masonry company, estimate commercial and residential jobs and provide exceptional customer service and sales support.
- Have established relationships with builders including Hartley Construction and Jones-Walker as well as other companies doing business.
- Develop rapport with clients, ascertaining their needs and estimating the cost of concrete masonry units and related building supplies.
- Work closely with general contractors, subcontractors, and home builders, utilizing my extensive knowledge of construction and building supplies to provide assistance.

FURNITURE SALES REPRESENTATIVE. Doherty Furniture Company, Statesville, PA (1999-2000). Assisted customers in the selection and purchase of home furnishings and accessories as a salesperson for this local retail furniture outlet.
- Consistently exceeded all sales quotas.
- Built a strong base of repeat and referral customers based on my natural sales ability and exceptional customer service skills.

SALES ASSISTANT & CUSTOMER SERVICE REPRESENTATIVE. Adams Products Company, Statesville, PA (1993-1999). Assisted the sales, dispatch, and production operations while performing customer service and receptionist duties for this local manufacturer and supplier of masonry products.
- Provided job estimates over the phone to business and residential customers, as well as acquiring dodge reports from the Internet and assisting with certifications.
- Created, updated, and maintained files for all new and existing accounts.
- Reviewed all invoices on outbound shipments and keyed contract hauler freight data into the computer, developing a template in Lotus 1-2-3 to record this data.
- Produced daily production reports, processed payroll, and coordinated safety committee activities for the production department.

SHIPPING AND RECEIVING CLERK. Meyer & Sons Furniture Company, Statesville, PA (1990-1992). Verified invoices against purchase orders to ensure accuracy; performed data entry of invoices and purchase orders on an IBM S/36 mainframe computer.

Highlights of earlier experience:
Demonstrated my exceptional customer service and communication skills as well as my strong attention to detail while excelling in earlier positions as a **SECRETARY** and **BOOK-KEEPER** for Christian Academy in Savannah, GA and a **PAYROLL CLERK** and **RECEPTIONIST** at J. K. White Company in Statesville, PA.

AFFILIATIONS　　Former member, American Business Women's Association, Statesville, PA.

PERSONAL　　Received the Parent in Education Award, Long Hill Elementary School, Statesville, PA.

Dear Sir or Madam:

With the enclosed resume, I would like to make you aware of my background as an articulate and dynamic sales professional.

In my most recent position as a Sales Manager, I developed "from scratch" a two-state territory with an extensive sales and distribution network by calling on distributors, architects, engineers, and builders. The company I represented was attempting to introduce a new "lightweight brick" product into the American marketplace, and it continuously felt the pressure of inadequate marketing funds. Although I was very successful in my personal sales role, the company itself was put on the auction block and sold twice, and different management teams experimented with a variety of internal restructuring. The most recent buyers downsized the sales force, and my position was eliminated as the new owners attempted to centralize the sales function and save costs. I am available for employment immediately and can provide outstanding references.

In my prior position, I worked for the same company for 14 years. I began as a Sales Representative and was promoted to Senior Territory Sales Manager. Throughout my sales career, I have increased existing accounts and developed new business while serving territories ranging from 33 counties in Virginia to a five-state area. I have earned a reputation as a congenial individual and skillful negotiator who can be counted on to find new ways to increase business, open new accounts, and produce outstanding bottom-line results.

If you can use a motivated sales professional, I hope you will contact me to suggest a time when we might meet to discuss your needs. I can provide outstanding personal and professional references at the appropriate time.

Sincerely,

Daryl McKinney

DARYL MCKINNEY

1110½ Hay Street, Fayetteville, NC 28305   •   preppub@aol.com   •   (910) 483-6611

OBJECTIVE

To benefit an organization that can use a seasoned sales professional and experienced sales manager with exceptional communication and negotiating skills.

EDUCATION

Associate of Applied Science degree in Agricultural Business Administration, Richmond Technical Community College, Richmond, VA.

Completed courses sponsored by employers related to sales/marketing, sales management, customer service, prospecting and closing the sale, and account management.

EXPERIENCE

SALES TERRITORY MANAGER. Bryson International, (formerly Delaby and Nortics Building Systems), Virginia and West Virginia territory (1998-present). Developed "from scratch" a territory where the company had no sales presence into a two-state area with numerous accounts. Built a sales and distribution network by calling on distributors, architects, engineers, and builders.

- Introduced a new product into the American marketplace: sold the concept of an autoclaved, aerated brick ("light brick") which was new to U.S. construction, although the product was established and highly regarded in Europe. Conducted seminars for architects and engineers to show the product's advanced insulating properties.
- The company experienced financial burdens as it attempted to introduce this product in the southeastern part of the U.S.. The company was sold and restructured twice as successive owners attempted to penetrate the American construction industry and gain the confidence of builders and consumers. In a massive downsizing, my job was eliminated as the company reduced its sales force.

SENIOR TERRITORY SALES MANAGER. Trulove Company, Crawford, VA (1984-1998). Began as a Sales Representative, and was promoted to increasing responsibilities based on exceptional production; serviced major building supply, hardware store, and farm supply accounts in a five states (NC, VA, WVA, MD, DE, and Washington, DC) for this manufacturer of construction mixes and commercial construction products.

- Attended major trade shows throughout the country, soliciting new business and networking with clients and distributors. Developed new business and serviced established accounts, selling dry mixes; construction mixes and coatings; and exterior wall systems.
- Dealt with buyers in a variety of environments, from small hardware stores to major chain stores, architectural firms, construction companies, and building owners.

Accomplishments:
- Sales in the region where I served as Sales Manager grew from $1.4 million to over $4 million. Produced double-digit sales increases in 10 of 14 years.
- Was named **Salesman of the Year, Northern Region** for 1996 and 1997.

SALES REPRESENTATIVE. Union Corrugating Company, Richmond, VA (1980-1984). Developed new accounts and maximized profitability of existing accounts while calling on building supply dealers, contractors, and farm supply dealers, covered a 33-county area in North Carolina.

- Serviced established clients and solicited new accounts, selling galvanized and painted steel roofing and siding. Assisted with ordering by figuring building supply costs.

Accomplishments:
- Substantially increased territory sales volume by consistently adding new accounts.
- Earned a reputation as a skillful negotiator and highly effective communicator.

PERSONAL

Outstanding personal and professional references are available upon request.

SALES REPRESENTATIVE

Dear Sir or Madam:

With the enclosed resume, I would like to make you aware of my background as an articulate and dynamic sales professional and experienced sales manager with exceptional negotiation skills as well as extensive industry contacts throughout the southeast. Although I am excelling in my current job and am held in the highest regard, I am selectively exploring other opportunities. I can provide excellent references at the appropriate time, but I would appreciate your holding my interest in your company in confidence at this time.

In my current position, I have developed a "virgin" territory, building a sales and distribution network through contacting architects, engineers, distributors and residential contractors who were unfamiliar with the companies product line. My exceptional salesmanship resulted in meeting and exceeding the company's first-year sales goals before May of that year.

Throughout my sales career, I have maximized the profitability of existing accounts and increased new business while serving account territories ranging from dozens of counties in one state to a five-state area. My natural sales ability, hard work, and loyalty have been consistently rewarded with promotions to higher levels of responsibility. I have earned a reputation as a skillful negotiator and articulate communicator who can be counted on to produce results, even when dealing with clients that other salesmen consider "difficult."

If you can use a motivated sales professional and experienced sales manager with a strong bottom-line orientation, I hope you will contact me to suggest a time when we might meet to discuss your needs. I can provide outstanding personal and professional references at the appropriate time.

Sincerely,

Doug Barfield

DOUG BARFIELD

1110½ Hay Street, Fayetteville, NC 28305　　•　　preppub@aol.com　　•　　(910) 483-6611

OBJECTIVE

To benefit an organization that can use a seasoned sales professional and experienced sales manager with exceptional communication and negotiating skills.

COMPUTERS

Working knowledge of Autocad, PowerPoint, Word, Access, and other software.

EXPERIENCE

SALES REPRESENTATIVE. Union Corrugating Company, Carson, New Mexico (2002-present). Developed new accounts and maximized profitability of existing accounts while calling on building supply dealers, contractors, and farm supply dealers, covered a 33-county area in New Mexico.

- Serviced established clients and solicited new accounts, selling galvanized and painted steel roofing and siding. Assisted with ordering by figuring building supply costs.

Accomplishments:

- Substantially increased territory sales volume by consistently adding new accounts.
- Earned a reputation as a skillful negotiator and highly effective communicator.

SALES REPRESENTATIVE. Carter, Inc., Las Vegas, Nevada (1995-02). For this janitorial supplies business, developed new accounts and achieved top-notch sales results.

- Earned this degree in my spare time while excelling in my full-time job which required extensive travel throughout Nevada and other western states.

TRAFFIC MANAGER. Cargill, Inc., Culver City, Nevada (1990-94). Issued billing orders for approximately 600 rail movements per month while also handling scheduling, routing, and rating.

- Was recruited for my job above by an organization which had admired and praised my organizational skills and management abilities.

SENIOR SALES MANAGER. Wilson Company, Las Vegas, Nevada (1984-1990). Began with this company as a Sales Representative, and was promoted to increasing responsibilities based on exceptional production; serviced major home builders, building supply, hardware store, and farm supply accounts in a five-state territory for this large manufacturer of construction mixes and commercial construction products.

- At major trade shows throughout the country, solicited new business and networked with clients and distributors. Developed new business and serviced established accounts, selling Sakrete dry mixes; Bonsal construction mixes and coatings; and Surewall exterior wall systems.
- Interacted with buyers who included small hardware stores to major chain stores, architectural firms, construction companies, and building owners.

Accomplishments:

- Sales in the region where I served as Sales Manager grew from $.8 million to over $6 million. Produced sales increases every year.
- Was named **Salesman of the Year, Northern Region** for three years in a row.

EDUCATION

Associate of Applied Science degree in Business Administration, Las Vegas Technical Community College, Las Vegas, NV, 1997.
Completed courses sponsored by employers related to sales/marketing, sales management, customer service, prospecting and closing the sale, and account management.

PERSONAL

Outstanding personal and professional references are available upon request.

Date

SENIOR PLUMBING INSPECTOR

Dear Sir or Madam:

With the enclosed resume, I would like to make you aware of my background as a Plumbing Inspector. My wife and I are in the process of relocating to your area, and I am seeking employment with an organization that can use an experienced plumbing professional.

As a Senior Plumbing Inspector with the city of Charlotte, I have reached the most advanced level of responsibility in my field which involves performing technical plumbing inspection work in order to enforce compliance with all applicable plumbing codes, regulations, and ordinances. I have worked closely with professionals including developers, superintendents, and contractors to maintain code requirements and resolve problems to include explaining and interpreting requirements and restrictions. My job included inspecting industrial, commercial, and residential buildings during various stages of construction and remodeling.

I hold numerous licenses and certifications as shown on my resume, and I have been elected to numerous leadership positions in plumbing associations.

If you can use an experienced plumbing professional with a strong bottom-line orientation, I hope you will contact me to suggest a time when we might meet to discuss your needs. I can provide outstanding personal and professional references at the appropriate time.

Sincerely,

Chad N. Longfellow

CHAD N. LONGFELLOW

1110½ Hay Street, Fayetteville, NC 28305   •   preppub@aol.com   •   (910) 483-6611

OBJECTIVE   To offer my technical experience as a senior plumbing inspector as well as my reputation as a professional who is fair and willing to listen to other points of view, is able to find solutions to problems through a common-sense approach, and is honest and reliable.

LICENSES   Am licensed by the state of North Carolina in the following areas:

General Contractor, 1995 **Electrical Contractor**, 1993 **Plumbing Contractor**, 1991

Met all qualifications and earned level III certifications in the areas of:

Fire Inspector, 1995	Building Inspector, July 1992
Mechanical Inspector, April 1992	Electrical Inspector, April 1992
Plumbing Inspector, April 1993	

AFFILIATIONS   Have served on numerous professional committees and participated in special events including the following:

- *President* of the NC Plumbing Inspectors' Association, 2000-present, and was *President-elect* for 1999, and *Vice President* for 1998.
  Member of the Board of Directors for the NC Plumbing Inspectors' Association, 1998
- *President of the NC Council of Code Officials,* 1995, and *member, Board of Directors* 1994
- *Chairman, the NC Plumbing Code Review Committee*, 1994, and *member* since 1992
- *Team Leader* for 1998 NC League of Municipalities Convention
- *NC Plumbing Curriculum Development Committee* — member of committee sponsored by the Department of Insurance, 1995-96

EDUCATION   Am taking courses in the Public Administration degree program, Staten Technical Community College, NC.

Completed the Plumbing program at Charlottesville Technical Community College, 1992.

EXPERIENCE   **SENIOR PLUMBING INSPECTOR.** The City of Charlotte, NC (1992-present). Reached the most advanced level of responsibility in my field which involves performing technical plumbing inspection work in order to enforce compliance with all applicable plumbing codes, regulations, and ordinances.

- Worked closely with professionals including developers, superintendents, and contractors to maintain code requirements and resolve problems to include explaining and interpreting requirements and restrictions.
- Inspected industrial, commercial, and residential buildings during various stages of construction and remodeling.
- Examined plans and specifications to determine compliance with existing codes.
- Inspected existing buildings and premises to locate changes in use or occupancy and compliance with codes.

Highlights of earlier experience:

GENERAL INSPECTOR: Inspected residential houses for compliance with electrical, plumbing, heating, air conditioning, and building codes for the City of Raleigh.

PLUMBING CONTRACTOR: Was co-owner of a plumbing repair company, Bailey Plumbing Company in Charlotte.

PERSONAL   Am familiar with the use of word processing systems for keeping records and preparing reports as well as with standard office equipment including typewriters and copiers.

SHOP FOREMAN   Dear Sir or Madam:

With the enclosed resume, I would like to make you aware of my background in the construction field, as well as of the skills and abilities which I could put to work for your company. I have completed the Building Standard Inspection Level I instructional course, and I am knowledgeable of performing inspections and reviewing plans for compliance with Building Codes.

As you will see from my enclosed resume, I am a licensed General Contractor and have excelled since 1999 in a position as Foreman. I supervised building tradesmen in duties related to building and installation, and I have become very experienced in reading blueprints and specifications. In prior experience as a Home Improvement Contractor, I planned and executed all facets of building construction in compliance with local building codes.

While serving my country as a Supply Specialist in the U.S. Army, I advanced ahead of my peers to leadership roles and positions of responsibility. In the logistics field, I learned valuable skills related to the procurement, supply, logistics, and distribution of all classes of supply, including construction.

Although I am highly regarded by my present employer and can provide excellent references at the appropriate time, I trust that you will keep my inquiry in strictest confidence until after we have had the chance to meet in person. I feel that my unique combination of education, skills, and experience would make me a valuable addition to your company.

I am certain that you would find me in person to be a congenial individual who offers the strong communication skills, analytical abilities, and technical knowledge that you are seeking. I hope you will give me an opportunity to meet with you in person. Thank you in advance for your time and professional courtesies.

Yours sincerely,

Gary F. Hernandez

GARY HERNANDEZ

1110½ Hay Street, Fayetteville, NC 28305   •   preppub@aol.com   •   (910) 483-6611

OBJECTIVE   To benefit an organization that can use a construction industry professional with knowledge of code enforcement along with the ability to perform field inspections on construction and renovation work in progress and enforce codes for building construction.

LICENSE   General Contractor's License, Alabama, limited, building; license # 43103.

EDUCATION   Completed **Building Standard Inspection Level I** instruction, Burnsville Technical Community College, Burnsville, AL, 2002.
- Subjects studied included: performance of field checks to construction work in various stages of construction; reviewing plans for compliance with Building Codes.
- Member, BTCC Student Advisory Committee on **Cabinetmaking, Carpentry, and Masonry**, 2002-03.

Completed **Law and Administration Course**, Craven Community College, New Bern, AL, 2002.

Extensive training related to the **supply** field sponsored by the U.S. Army.

Completed one year of college coursework, **Rutgers University,** New Brunswick, NJ, 1999-00.

EXPERIENCE   **SHOP FOREMAN.** Builders Millwork, Burnsville, AL (1999-present). For this construction industry firm, supervise two cabinetmakers/woodworkers involved in building and installing architectural millwork and cabinets.
- Supervise building tradesmen in duties related to building and installation.
- Have become very skilled at reading and interpreting blueprints and specifications.
- Frequently troubleshoot problems on site related to blueprints and specifications.
- Must remain highly knowledgeable of state building codes related to plumbing, mechanical, electrical, building, and fire codes.

SUPPLY SPECIALIST. U.S. Army, 82nd Airborne Division, Ft. Tacoma, KS (1997-99). At the largest U.S. military base, was extensively trained in the supply field while also constantly maintaining a high state of mental and physical readiness as a paratrooper.
- Was rapidly promoted ahead of my peers to mid-management.
- Provided logistical support at the Division level.
- Learned to purchase and distribute many different classes of supplies including construction materials and engineering equipment.

HOME IMPROVEMENT CONTRACTOR. Verity Construction Company, Augusta, NJ (1994-96). As a sole proprietor, planned and executed all facets of building construction in compliance with local building codes.
- Became skilled in complying with mechanical, building, plumbing, electrical, and fire codes as I frequently had to bring outdated housing "up to code."
- Gained extensive experience in conducting inspections of existing housing and determining what was needed in order to comply with state codes.
- Hired, trained, and supervised workers in all the construction trades.
- Refined my communication skills while discussing state codes and building plans with consumers and people outside the building industry.
- Performed field inspections on construction and installation work in process.

PERSONAL   Excellent references on request. Totally reliable and disciplined worker.

SURVEYOR   Dear Sir or Madam:

With the enclosed resume, I would like to make you aware of my background as a Surveyor.

In my current position as a Survey Crew Chief, I operate a Total Station. I have used a Hewlett Packard Data Collector and am proficient with leveling instruments. I have had some experience with GPS.

I began as a temporary employee placed in a job with my current employer by a temporary service. Within a few weeks I was offered full-time employment by the owner, a civil engineer. During my eight years of employment, the company has grown from a two-person operation into a company with two full crews, a CAD operator, and another manager. I have performed construction staking for subdivisions, and we are currently in the process of building a large public high school.

If you can use an experienced surveyor with a proven ability to train and develop junior surveying professionals, I hope you will contact me to suggest a time when we might meet to discuss your needs. I can provide outstanding personal and professional references at the appropriate time.

Sincerely,

Kelly Kirby

KELLY KIRBY

1110½ Hay Street, Fayetteville, NC 28305   •   preppub@aol.com   •   (910) 483-6611

OBJECTIVE

To benefit an organization that can use an experienced surveying professional with an in-depth background in employee training and supervision as well as quality assurance and inspection.

TECHNICAL EXPERTISE

Operate a Total Station. Use a Hewlett Packard Data Collector. Utilize leveling instruments. Some experience with GPS.

EXPERIENCE

SURVEY CREW CHIEF. Brown & Associates, Sacramento, CA (2000-present). Began as a temporary employee placed in a job with this privately owned company by a temporary service; within a few weeks was offered full-time employment by the owner, a civil engineer. During my eight years of employment, the company has grown from a two-person operation into a company with two full crews, a CAD operator, and another manager.

- Perform construction staking for subdivisions; we are currently in the process of building Sacramento Public High School.
- Have traveled to locations throughout CA to perform environmental surveys.
- Train junior employees; manage a crew which includes a Rodman and Instrument Operator.
- Perform reconnaissance and analysis related to potential survey projects; am continuously involved in reading and interpreting construction plans, performing deed research, and collecting data for future projects.

Prior surveying experience: Served in the U.S. Army and received numerous medals and awards in recognition of my technical surveying expertise and management skills. Held a <u>Top Secret (SBI)</u> security clearance.

1995-00: SENIOR TOPOGRAPHIC SUPERVISOR. Germany. Was the highest ranking mid-manager in a topographic engineering company. Managed 118 people and ensured flawless accountability of an inventory of equipment and supplies.

1991-95: SURVEY CONTROL SUPERVISOR. Italy. Was involved in quality assurance and technical inspection as I traveled throughout Germany to inspect survey teams.

- Validated all topographic survey requirements in Europe.
- Calculated cost estimates and provided customers with alternative plans of action.
- Wrote staff papers and authored doctrine; recommended equipment upgrades.

1982-90: SURVEY SECTION SUPERVISOR. Ft. Bragg, NC. Trained and supervised four mid-level supervisors who were responsible for 45 employees.

- Assigned survey projects to four sections; monitored progress of all jobs.
- Counseled employees and wrote evaluation reports on survey section chiefs.
- Assisted supervisors in their planning and advised them about technical options.

EDUCATION

Certification in **Autocad 15,** Wesley Technical Community College (WTCC), 1999.
Certification in **Microcomputer Repair/Solid State Electronics,** WTCC, 1993.
Completed **Advanced Course/Advanced Geodetic Survey,** U.S. Army Engineer School and Defense Mapping School, 1991.
Completed **Basic Geodetic Survey Course,** Defense Mapping School, 1985.
Completed **30 hours of General Studies courses toward Bachelor's degree,** Hawaii Pacific College and Austin Peay University.

PERSONAL

Outstanding references on request. Single, and will travel and relocate as needed.

CAREER CHANGE

Date

Exact Name of Person
Title or Position
Name of Company
Address (no., street)
Address (city, state, zip)

Dear Exact Name of Person (or Dear Sir or Madam if answering a blind ad):

I would appreciate an opportunity to talk with you soon about how I could contribute to your organization through my background related to surveying and construction as well as my knowledge of law enforcement and security.

You will see from my enclosed resume that I am presently taking college-level course work in the areas of criminal justice and corrections supervision. I have received training in counterterrorism operations and am familiar with U.S. and foreign weapons. An Expert with the rifle, I consistently scored at least 48 out of 50 at distances of 500 yards or more. With a Secret/NATO Secret security clearance, I offer experience as a Courier for classified documents and messages as well as in intelligence gathering and dissemination.

I feel that I have displayed my adaptability by excelling in such diverse fields as surveying, weapons system operations, personnel recruiting, and sales. I also have proven my leadership capabilities in combat—during the war in the Middle East I led a team of 50 people and saw all team members return from the inhospitable climate and stress of the situation.

Having received in excess of 3,000 hours of advanced training, I feel that I am a mature leader who could easily step into positions of responsibility where my dedication, integrity, and skills would be invaluable.

You may be interested to know that my relocation expenses will be paid by the military, and I would cheerfully relocate worldwide according to your needs. I can provide outstanding personal and professional references.

I hope you will welcome my call soon to arrange a brief meeting at your convenience to discuss your current and future needs and how I might serve them. Thank you in advance for your time.

Sincerely yours,

Victor H. Alley

VICTOR H. ALLEY

1110½ Hay Street, Fayetteville, NC 28305 • preppub@aol.com • (910) 483-6611

OBJECTIVE

To apply my experience to an organization that can use an excellent manager of human and material resources who offers a versatile background related to surveying and construction.

CERTIFICATION

Obtaining certification as a Certified Survey Technician, Levels I-IV; ACSM.

EXPERIENCE

OPERATIONS MANAGER. U.S. Marine Corps, Camp Lejeune, NC (2000-present). Selected to attend an advanced leadership and personnel management course, am now becoming familiar with state-of-the-art radar systems while supervising 47 employees and overseeing the operation and maintenance of a $3.5 million radar system.

PERSONNEL RECRUITER and **SALES MANAGER.** USMC, Pittsburgh, PA (1997-99). Successfully maintained high sales averages while becoming a visible presence in the community: made the most of telephone and personal contacts to set up appointments with qualified and talented young adults to sell them on the advantages of a military career.
- Displayed a talent for interviewing and for finding the most successful sales approach.

SURVEYOR and **SUPERVISOR.** USMC, Camp Lejeune, NC (1992-96). Oversaw a $2 million supply inventory and a department with an average of 45 to 60 employees as the senior enlisted member of a survey team.
- Singled out for superior performance, earned a Navy Achievement Medal and refined my knowledge and skills in a demanding position.
- Provided expert leadership for a 50-person team of specialists and brought everyone back safely from the hardship of combat during the war in the Middle East.

SURVEYOR and **OPERATIONS SUPERVISOR.** USMC, Okinawa, Japan (1989-91). In a position normally reserved for a higher ranking and more experienced individual, simultaneously oversaw training and daily operations of a 25-person survey team and also contributed to the intelligence section by disseminating information as it became known.
- Was credited with the success of a major project in which important control points in mainland Japan were recovered, resurveyed, and placed on common control.

CLASSIFIED DOCUMENTS CUSTODIAN. USMC, Camp Lejeune, NC (1987-88). Controlled and monitored 450+ classified documents, acting as a courier, supervising 12 clerks, and conducting security checks and background investigations.

ADMINISTRATION AND TRAINING SUPERVISOR. USMC, Camp Lejeune, NC (1984-86). Promoted ahead of my peers and named as Employee of the Quarter for the parent organization, gained experience in using mathematical calculations and meteorology to accurately direct the operation of weapons systems.

EDUCATION

Earned a **Certificate in Surveying, USMC Survey School,** Scranton, PA, 1996.
Completed 3,000 hours+ of advanced leadership training emphasizing surveying.

SURVEYING SKILLS

Familiar with surveying practices to include traverse, astronomic observation, triangulation, survey planning, conversion to common control, and Global Positioning System.
Familiar with the T-2, T-16E Theodolite, DI-3000, and DI4L Distomat electronic distance measuring equipment as well as the AN-USQ70 Position/Azimuth Determining System.

PERSONAL

Known for honesty and integrity. Have a common sense approach to problem solving.

SURVEYOR

Dear Sir or Madam:

With the enclosed resume, I would like to make you aware of my interest in exploring employment opportunities with your organization.

As you can see from my resume, I recently left the U.S. Army after serving with distinction for four years. I graduated from the four-month Defense Mapping School's Basic Geodetic Survey Course, and I completed subsequent training in both technical and management areas. I received numerous awards and medals for exemplary performance, and I was the recipient of the respected Commandant's Certificate upon graduation from a prestigious leadership course.

While on surveying teams, I became skilled in working in environments in which there was no room for error. I was promoted ahead of my peers to Survey Chief, and I trained, motivated, and managed other individuals as we completed airfield surveys, engineering surveys, safety surveys, and other surveying activities. I was commended on formal performance evaluations for "setting the standard for others to follow" and for providing leadership by example.

If you can use a highly motivated young professional to join your organization, I hope you will contact me to suggest the next step I should take in exploring employment opportunities with your organization. I can provide excellent references at the appropriate time.

Yours sincerely,

Matilda Coughlin

MATILDA COUGHLIN

1110½ Hay Street, Fayetteville, NC 28305   •   preppub@aol.com   •   (910) 483-6611

OBJECTIVE

To contribute to an organization that can use a skilled surveyor with experience in training and supervising others while operating computers and sophisticated automated equipment.

EDUCATION

Surveying: Received a Diploma upon completion of the four-month Defense Mapping School's Basic Geodetic Survey Course, Ft. Belvoir, VA, 1997.

Technical training: Received Certificates of Training from NBC Defense Course; Hazard Communication (HAZCOM) Train-the-Trainer Course; Environmental Management Course; Defensive Driving Course; Hazmat Awareness/Familiarization Course; Weaponeer Training Course.

Leadership training: Graduated from the U.S. Army's Primary Leadership Development Course (PLDC), Ft. Hood, TX, 2000. Was the recipient of the respected Commandant's Certificate upon graduation from the III Corps NCO Academy (a management development program), 2000.

COMPUTERS

Proficient with software including Word, Excel, and PowerPoint.

TECHNICAL KNOWLEDGE

Skilled in all surveying activities, especially obstruction shots, level lines, and the Global Positioning System (GPS); experienced in working the Automated Integrated Survey Instrument (AISI).

- Was also trained by the U.S. Army to operate the M1025 (1¼ ton truck); M998 (1¼ ton truck); 4k forklift; M931 (5-ton truck); and 60 kw generator.
- Entrusted with Secret security clearance.

HONORS

Received numerous awards, medals, and letters of commendation for exemplary performance.

EXPERIENCE

TOPOGRAPHIC SURVEY CHIEF. U.S. Army, Ft. Hood, TX (2000-present). Was promoted ahead of my peers to serve as Survey Chief for a topographic survey squad supporting the needs of one of the Army's largest military bases.

- Trained and supervised five employees. Directed topographic survey activities to measure, record, compute, and disseminate field data for geodetic survey collection.
- Acted as the team's **Quality Assurance Chief;** conducted checks to ensure field measurements met project specifications. Performed computations to verify field observations.
- Was selected to served as **Training Manager** for six months in an office environment. Was in charge of training records for 125 people. Utilized a computer daily to word process information and compose documents. Maintained extensive personnel filing system. Prepared paperwork for supply turn-in and issuing.

Highlights of special projects:

- **Airfield surveying:** Produced a map of a 9-mile nautical radius around an airfield to identify obstacles that posed potential hazards to arriving and departing aircraft.
- **Range surveying:** Managed a range control project which derived coordinates all over Ft. Hood; range control officials used the data we collected to manage range activities.
- **Engineering and safety surveys:** Prepared a safety survey for a military installation in Kansas; was the Party Chief in charge of six topographic surveyors. Also prepared safety surveys for Ft. Hood , Grey, and Butts Army Airfields, and Ft. Sill, OK.

Comments from performance evaluations: Was described in the following language: "Set high standards for performance; never takes shortcuts;" "Always does the right thing; initiates fresh ideas. Persuasive, convincing trainer."

PERSONAL

Excellent references. Reliable, dependable individual committed to my employer's success.

Date

Cone Applications, Inc.
ATTN: Bob Smith
4200 Georgetown Road, Suite 302
Fountain, CT

**VICE PRESIDENT,
CERAMICS
MANUFACTURER**

Dear Mr. Smith:

With the enclosed resume, I would like to make you aware of my considerable experience related to the construction industry and the ceramics business.

My management skills are highly refined. In my most recent position, I have worked as Vice President for a company which provides manufacturing and installation services to industrial companies such as Frigidaire and General Motors. I have interacted with major firms in the construction industry, and I have established a network of contacts which could be useful to you.

You would find me in person to be a congenial individual who prides myself on doing every job to the best of my ability. I offer a unique blend of technical knowledge, communication skills, and management experience. I would certainly enjoy an opportunity to introduce myself in person, and I hope you will contact me to arrange a brief meeting to discuss my strong qualifications for and interest in this position.

Yours sincerely,

Arthur W. Charles

ARTHUR W. CHARLES

1110½ Hay Street, Fayetteville, NC 28305   •   preppub@aol.com   •   (910) 483-6611

OBJECTIVE

To benefit an organization that can use an administrator with outstanding written and verbal communication skills who is experienced in supervising and coordinating simultaneous staff functions while troubleshooting problem areas and handling public relations.

EDUCATION

Earning **Master's of Science in Administration degree,** with a Public Administration concentration, Central Michigan University, 1996-present.

Received **Bachelor of Science in Political Science (B.S.P.) degree,** University of North Carolina at Chapel Hill, 1985; inducted into Pi Sigma Alpha National Political Science Honor Society.

EXPERIENCE

VICE PRESIDENT. Ceramic Coatings, Inc., Atlanta, GA (2000-present). For a company headquartered in Georgia which provides ceramic manufacturing and installation to large industrial companies including Frigidaire and General Motors, am developing the Georgia territory while also supervising activity on job sites in other states.

- Work with companies to develop long-term and short-range budgets.
- Review and approve contract proposals; monitor subcontractor performance.
- Supervise 10 people; play key role in formulating corporate human resources policies.
- Perform liaison and public relations with major corporations.
- Recruit, train, and manage the company's sales force.

MANAGEMENT CONSULTANT. Shadow Investigations, Inc., Bluefield, WVA (1993-00). On a five-month contract, performed research, management consulting, and security assessment for Edwards Associated Coal Company: developed cost analyses and purchased specialized equipment while designing employee training programs.

- Supervised 70 personnel at seven different locations.
- Worked directly with the company's vice president of operations while testing, purchasing, fielding, and troubleshooting a variety of equipment including night vision optics, video cameras, surveillance cameras, long- and short-range optical devices, radio communications, and riot control gear.
- Developed emergency evacuation procedures for seven mining sites.
- Formulated and implemented an equipment accountability and supply system for a $1 million inventory which reduced costs.

SYSTEMS & OPERATIONS MANAGER. U.S. Army, Ft. Bragg, NC (1988-93). Specially selected by the Commanding General for this job with the U.S. Army Special Forces Command, was in charge of reviewing and refining major classroom curricula and doctrine used by 11 different Special Forces organizations with more than 15,000 people.

- Planned and administered a multimillion-dollar budget.
- Personally authored the Special Force's Standards for Weapons Training.
- After conducting extensive cost/resource analysis and consulting with high-ranking military officials, made major improvements to Special Forces training programs; identified and corrected deficiencies in advance skills requirements in key training programs while increasing the number of graduates required for critical skill areas.
- Developed and implemented training programs nationwide.
- Earned widespread respect for my top-notch analytical and communication skills.

PERSONAL

Knowledgeable of PowerPoint, Word, Excel Lotus 1-2-3, and Office Writer. Proven ability to establish and maintain cordial relationships. Known for unquestioned integrity.

Exact Name of Person
Exact Title
Exact Name of Company
Address
City, State, Zip

**WATER PURIFICATION
SUPERVISOR**

Dear Exact Name of Person (or Dear Sir or Madam if answering a blind ad):

With the enclosed resume, I would like to make you aware of my strong technical skills and natural leadership ability as well as the background of excellence in Water Treatment and Purification Systems operation, management, and training which I could put to work for your organization.

As you will see from my resume, I am currently excelling as a Water Treatment Supervisor for the U.S. Army, where I train and direct the work of eight employees in the development of water sources and analysis of raw and treated water, as well as the operation and maintenance of water treatment equipment. In addition to overseeing the security, maintenance, and accountability of $750,000 worth of equipment, I cross-trained petroleum and ammunition supply employees to perform water treatment functions, increasing the versatility and effectiveness of these personnel. While stationed in Korea, I was the first water treatment specialist to purify saltwater using the Reverse Osmosis Water Purification Unit (ROWPU), and I trained 10 Korean personnel to operate various types of water treatment equipment.

A graduate of the Level I, II, III, & IV Wastewater Treatment Plant Operator course at Fayetteville Technical Community College, I have also completed numerous military technical and leadership training courses. These included the U.S. Army Quartermaster School Water Treatment Specialist Course, Water Treatment Specialist Basic Non-Commissioned Officers Course (BNCOC), Primary Leadership Development Course (PLDC), Jumpmaster Course, and Master Fitness Trainer Course.

Throughout my military career, I have demonstrated strong leadership and training skills, as well as the ability to quickly master new and complex technical information. My energy, drive, and enthusiasm have allowed me to motivate personnel under my supervision to achieve excellence both personally and professionally, and I have built a reputation as an articulate leader with unlimited potential for advancement.

If you can use a highly skilled professional whose leadership and technical abilities have been proven in challenging environments worldwide, I hope you will welcome my call soon when I try to arrange a brief meeting to discuss your goals and how my background might serve your needs. I can provide outstanding references at the appropriate time.

Sincerely,

Barry G. Alvarez

BARRY G. ALVAREZ

1110½ Hay Street, Fayetteville, NC 28305   •   preppub@aol.com   •   (910) 483-6611

OBJECTIVE To benefit an organization that can use an articulate young professional with exceptional technical, organizational, and leadership abilities who offers a background in water treatment operations and management, supervision and training of personnel, and fitness training.

EDUCATION Completed the **Wastewater Treatment Plant Operator Level I, II, III, & IV** courses, Mills Technical Community College, Mills, OH, 2001.
Excelled in a number of military leadership and technical skills training courses, including the Primary Leadership Development Course (PLDC), U.S. Army **Quartermaster School Water Treatment Specialist Course, Water Treatment Specialist Basic Non-Commissioned Officers Course (BNCOC)**, Army Institute for Personal Development **Water Treatment Specialist Course**, Jumpmaster Course, Pathfinder Course, Air Movement Operations Course (for Air Transport of Hazardous Materials), and Fitness Trainer Course.

TECHNICAL SKILLS *Water Treatment:* Skilled in the operation of ultraviolet filtration devices, osmosis (Erdlator) & reverse osmosis (ROWPU) purification units
Materials handling and other equipment: Qualified to operate 4, 6, and 10K forklifts, 5-ton cranes, 40-foot trailers, excavation vehicles, and Global Positioning Systems (GPS)
Computers: Familiar with many popular computer operating systems and software, including Windows, Microsoft Word, Excel, and PowerPoint; and others.

LICENSES Preparing to test for the Ohio Wastewater Treatment Plant Operator's License.

EXPERIENCE *Was selected for advanced technical training and promoted to positions of increasing responsibility while serving in the U.S. Army, 1994-present:*
2000-present: **WATER PURIFICATION SUPERVISOR.** Fort Gordon, GA and Korea. Supervise and train as many as eight personnel in development of water sources, analysis of raw and treated water, and maintenance of water treatment equipment.
- Oversee the security, maintenance, and accountability of equipment valued at more than $750,000; was cross-trained in aircraft refueling, including HAZMAT and safety issues.
- Cross-trained petroleum and ammunition supply personnel to perform the full range of water purification duties, increasing their versatility and efficiency.
- While stationed in Korea, was the first water treatment specialist to utilize the Reverse Osmosis Water Purification Unit (ROWPU) to purify sea water; trained 10 Korean personnel in the operation of various types of water purification equipment.
- Cited in official performance appraisals as "instrumental in setting up water point supply and distribution" and "[ensuring] that the water team monitored and enforced quality assurance of all water distributed" during a major exercise.

1994-99: **LOGISTICS SUPERVISOR.** Fort Gordon, GA. Provided training in ammunition storage, accountability, and safety to employees under my supervision, as well overseeing the maintenance of ammunition, vehicles, and equipment assigned to the unit.
- Was instrumental in directing and participating in vehicle and equipment maintenance that resulted in achieving a perfect score of 100% during a major inspection.

PERSONAL Received a number of prestigious awards for my exemplary performance, including an Army Commendation Medal, two Army Achievement Medals, and the Good Conduct Medal, as well as a Humanitarian Award for providing assistance to victims of Hurricane Andrew.

WELDER   Dear Sir or Madam:

With the enclosed resume, I would like to make you aware of my interest in exploring employment opportunities with your organization.

In my current position as a Welder, I perform various types of fabrication, mechanical work, and different phases of welding. The services I perform are primarily contract type work. In a previous job, I installed, renovated, repaired, and maintained a variety of piping systems in local schools and colleges. I dealt with all phases of pipe fitting and welding as I installed boilers, chillers, and HVAC units, maintaining strict adherence to all applicable state, local, and federal codes. Prior to that, as a Foreman, I worked with a wide variety of chemical piping systems, repairing and replacing motors and other equipment.

I have recently relocated to your area, and I am seeking employment of the same type I have always performed. If you can use a skilled welding professional who can provide outstanding references, I hope you will contact me. I can assure you in advance that I have an outstanding safety record and am well known for my emphasis on "safety first, last, and always."

Yours sincerely,

Franklin G. Hughes

FRANKLIN G. HUGHES

1110½ Hay Street, Fayetteville, NC 28305 • preppub@aol.com • (910) 483-6611

OBJECTIVE

To obtain a position as a welder/metal fabricator with a new or existing company that offers stability and is growing to meet the needs of the next century.

CERTIFICATIONS

Certified Pipe Welder, Stainless Steel Schedules 10-80, Carbon Steel Schedules 10-80, and Aluminum; Quality Control Management, Fort Polk, LA, November, 2001.

EXPERIENCE

OWNER and **MANAGER.** Currier Welding, Baton Rouge, LA (2001-present). Performed various types of fabrication, mechanical work, and different phases of welding; services performed were primarily contract type work.

FOREMAN. Smart Mechanical Company, High Point, LA (1999-2001). Installed, renovated, repaired, and maintained a variety of piping systems in local schools and colleges. Dealt with all phases of pipe fitting and welding. Installed boilers, chillers, and HVAC units, maintaining strict adherence to all applicable state, local, and federal codes.

FOREMAN. Horton's Piping & Welding, Bates Chemical Company, Baton Rouge Plant, Baton Rouge, LA (1998-1999). Worked with a wide variety of chemical piping systems, repairing and replacing motors, centrifuges, and piping throughout the plant, troubleshooting equipment malfunctions and other problems and performing repairs and maintenance.

FIELD INSPECTOR. Thermal Piping, Fort Polk, LA (1997-1998). Inspected and assisted in the installation and design of heated/chilled-water piping systems. Provided a variety of pipe fitting, welding, and metal fabrication services, ensuring proper installation of systems throughout 82nd Airborne Division facilities.

FIELD INSPECTOR. Pipe Underground Systems, Fort Polk, LA (1995-1997). Ensured that companies designing and installing heated/chilled-water piping systems were maintaining compliance with all applicable state, local, and federal codes, as well as monitoring their operations to provide proof that systems were properly installed. Viewed X-rays of welds to provide quality assurance. Verified that proper backfill was carried out on completed systems.

WELDER. Steinberg Crane Company, Baton Rouge, LA (1982-1995). Performed routine repairs and maintenance on cranes from 12 tons through 35 tons, as well as providing metal fabrication service to repair or replace broken or defective parts, saving the company thousands of dollars in parts costs.

WELDER. Old South Welding Service, Baton Rouge, LA (1987-1991). Worked as a partner with this welding/pipe fitting contractor; completed a number of contracts for metal fabrication and installation of piping systems on the Fort Polk military installation and throughout the surrounding counties. Worked under tight scrutiny on various government contracts, including some projects which were classified Top Secret.

PIPEFITTER. Livsey Construction, Superior Soup Plant, Maxton, LA (1985-1987). Installed new piping systems for use in the manufacture of soup products; worked primarily in stainless steel in order to comply with USDA regulations related to health and hygiene in manufacture and transport of food products.

PERSONAL

Hold Top Secret clearance. Am bondable. Excellent personal and professional references.

ABOUT THE EDITOR

Anne McKinney holds an MBA from the Harvard Business School and a BA in English from the University of North Carolina at Chapel Hill. A noted public speaker, writer, and teacher, she is the senior editor for PREP's business and career imprint, which bears her name. Early titles in the Anne McKinney Career Series (now called the Real-Resumes Series) published by PREP include: *Resumes and Cover Letters That Have Worked, Resumes and Cover Letters That Have Worked for Military Professionals, Government Job Applications and Federal Resumes, Cover Letters That Blow Doors Open,* and *Letters for Special Situations.* Her career titles and how-to resume-and-cover-letter books are based on the expertise she has acquired in 20 years of working with job hunters. Her valuable career insights have appeared in publications of the "Wall Street Journal" and other prominent newspapers and magazines.

PREP Publishing Order Form

You may purchase any of our titles from your favorite bookseller! Or send a check or money order or your credit card number for the total amount*, plus $4.00 postage and handling, to PREP, Box 66, Fayetteville, NC 28302. You may also order our titles on our website at www.prep-pub.com and feel free to e-mail us at preppub@aol.com or call 910-483-6611 with your questions or concerns.

Name: _____

Phone #:_____

Address: _____

E-mail address:

Payment Type: ☐ Check/Money Order ☐ Visa ☐ MasterCard

Credit Card Number: _____ Expiration Date: _____

Check items you are ordering:

☐ $16.95—REAL-RESUMES FOR MANUFACTURING JOBS. Anne McKinney, Editor

☐ $16.95—REAL-RESUMES FOR AVIATION & TRAVEL JOBS. Anne McKinney, Editor

☐ $16.95—REAL-RESUMES FOR POLICE, LAW ENFORCEMENT & SECURITY JOBS. Anne McKinney, Editor

☐ $16.95—REAL-RESUMES FOR SOCIAL WORK & COUNSELING JOBS. Anne McKinney, Editor

☐ $16.95—REAL-RESUMES FOR CONSTRUCTION JOBS. Anne McKinney, Editor

☐ $16.95—REAL-RESUMES FOR FINANCIAL JOBS. Anne McKinney, Editor

☐ $16.95—REAL-RESUMES FOR COMPUTER JOBS. Anne McKinney, Editor

☐ $16.95—REAL-RESUMES FOR MEDICAL JOBS. Anne McKinney, Editor

☐ $16.95—REAL-RESUMES FOR TEACHERS. Anne McKinney, Editor

☐ $16.95—REAL-RESUMES FOR CAREER CHANGERS. Anne McKinney, Editor

☐ $16.95—REAL-RESUMES FOR STUDENTS. Anne McKinney, Editor

☐ $16.95—REAL-RESUMES FOR SALES. Anne McKinney, Editor

☐ $16.95—REAL ESSAYS FOR COLLEGE AND GRAD SCHOOL. Anne McKinney, Editor

☐ $25.00—RESUMES AND COVER LETTERS THAT HAVE WORKED.

☐ $25.00—RESUMES AND COVER LETTERS THAT HAVE WORKED FOR MILITARY PROFESSIONALS.

☐ $25.00—RESUMES AND COVER LETTERS FOR MANAGERS.

☐ $25.00—GOVERNMENT JOB APPLICATIONS AND FEDERAL RESUMES: Federal Resumes, KSAs, Forms 171 and 612, and Postal Applications.

☐ $25.00—COVER LETTERS THAT BLOW DOORS OPEN.

☐ $25.00—LETTERS FOR SPECIAL SITUATIONS.

☐ $16.00—BACK IN TIME. Patty Sleem

☐ $17.00—(trade paperback) SECOND TIME AROUND. Patty Sleem

☐ $25.00—(hardcover) SECOND TIME AROUND. Patty Sleem

☐ $18.00—A GENTLE BREEZE FROM GOSSAMER WINGS. Gordon Beld

☐ $18.00—BIBLE STORIES FROM THE OLD TESTAMENT. Katherine Whaley

☐ $14.95—WHAT THE BIBLE SAYS ABOUT... *Words that can lead to success and happiness* (large print edition) Patty Sleem

☐ $10.95—KIJABE An African Historical Saga. Pally Dhillon

_____ **TOTAL ORDERED (add $4.00 for postage and handling)**

PREP offers volume discounts on large orders. Call us at (910) 483-6611 for more information.